A Christian in the Land of the Gods

A Christian
in the Land of the Gods
Journey of Faith in Japan

Joanna Reed Shelton

CASCADE *Books* · Eugene, Oregon

A CHRISTIAN IN THE LAND OF THE GODS
Journey of Faith in Japan

Cascade Books
An Imprint of Wipf and Stock Publishers
199 W. 8th Ave., Suite 3
Eugene, OR 97401

www.wipfandstock.com

ISBN 13: 978-1-4982-2491-8

Cataloguing-in-Publication Data

Shelton, Joanna Reed

    A Christian in the land of the gods: journey of faith in Japan / Joanna Reed Shelton

    xiv + 290 p. ; 23 cm. Includes bibliographical references.

    ISBN 13: 978-1-4982-2491-8

    1. Presbyterian Church—Missions—Japan. 2. Presbyterian Church (U.S.A.)—Missions—History. 3. Christianity—Japan—20th century. 4. Protestantism—Japan. I. Title.

BV2570 S434 2016

Manufactured in the U.S.A.   11/30/2015

Macrons (overstrikes) in Japanese names or places are not used, except when quoting original sources that include such symbols. Japanese names are presented family name first, followed by given name.

I have made best efforts to find copyright information whenever applicable. For some old or Japanese-language sources, this has proved difficult. In the event that any photograph, illustration, or other material referenced or contained herein does not accurately reflect copyright information, please inform Wipf and Stock Publishers, so that we may provide correct attribution in future printings. I apologize for any oversight or omission.

Apology to e-readers: In order to minimize the use of footnotes that would break up the narrative, I have used endnotes that electronic devices are not able to track. Most endnotes consist of source citations, but there also are some explanatory notes interspersed among them. I apologize for any inconvenience.

You may contact me through my website, www.joannashelton.com.

Dedicated to all those who came before.

Tom Alexander's Calling Card in Kyoto

Very truly, I tell you, unless a grain of wheat falls into the earth and dies, it remains just a single grain; but if it dies, it bears much fruit.

(John 12:24)

Contents

Preface | xi
Alexander Family | xii
List of Abbreviations | xiii

Author's Note | 1
Chapter 1: Leaving Home | 4
Chapter 2: The Early Years | 11
Chapter 3: Stranger in a Strange Land | 24
Chapter 4: The Last Samurai | 32
Chapter 5: A Time to Prepare | 48
Chapter 6: Firestorm | 60
Chapter 7: Into the Heart of Buddhism | 66
Chapter 8: A New Calling | 80
Chapter 9: An Opposition Leader Reaches Out | 92
Chapter 10: Planting Seeds | 102
Chapter 11: A New Badge of Honor | 110
Chapter 12: Home to America | 119
Chapter 13: You Can't Go Home Again | 129
Chapter 14: A Death in the Family | 138
Chapter 15: Nationalism on the Rise | 148
Chapter 16: Unsteady Ground | 161
Chapter 17: Worlds Apart | 173
Chapter 18: An Independent Spirit | 186
Chapter 19: A Happy Reunion | 199
Chapter 20: Papa Went to Heaven | 208
Chapter 21: He Gave His Life for Japan | 218

Epilogue Part I: A Living Legacy | 227
Epilogue Part II: My Own Journey of Faith | 239

Appendix I: Whatever Happened To . . . ? | 257
Appendix II: T. T. Alexander Letter Defending Uemura Masahisa | 273
Appendix III: T. T. Alexander Publications (partial list) | 277

Acknowledgements | 281
Picture Credits | 285

Selected Bibliography | 287

Preface

A Christian in the Land of the Gods is the true story of one man's journey of faith in nineteenth-century Japan, set against the backdrop of social and political turmoil in Japan and great power rivalries on the international stage. I have made every effort to portray my great-grandfather's life and experiences as accurately as possible, drawing on a wealth of information, including personal journals, letters, scholarly works, and contemporary accounts of daily life in Japan in the late 1800s. My aunt, Emma Shelton, gave me my great-grandfather's diary to read before my first trip to Japan in 1980 and filled in some of the family history that appears in the pages that follow. Visits to places of importance in my great-grandfather's life in Japan and America yielded helpful information about his work. These visits also allowed me to see firsthand the places he lived and traveled and to meet ministers and members of churches he founded in Japan.

My own extensive experience of living and traveling abroad has given me a unique perspective on my great-grandfather's life and the challenges of living in a country without knowing a soul or speaking a word of the language upon arrival. Living in Europe for six years—including two formative years in my late teens and early twenties—and traveling to thirty countries during my life and career, I have experienced the acute loneliness and sense of isolation that comes from living far from family and friends in the days before Internet, Skype, and cell phones. I also have experienced the deep satisfaction that comes from mastering foreign languages and building lifelong friendships in countries other than my own.

Finally, as I have come to know my great-grandfather through his own writings; through written accounts by his family, friends, and colleagues; and through family oral history, I have identified some obvious family traits that have passed down through the generations to me and other family members. These family characteristics have helped me paint a fuller picture of my great-grandfather, including his response to the many challenges, sorrows, and successes he experienced during his life in Japan and America.

Alexander Family

Thomas Theron Alexander
(1850–1902)
Married
Emma Edwina (Brown) Alexander
(1855–1937)

Their children:

Ella Lillian Alexander
(1878–1892)

Emma Thomasina Alexander (Young Emma)
(1880–1904)

Theron Ralph Alexander
(1882–1968)

Lois Alexander
(1884–1958)

Mary Victoria Alexander
(1887–1973)

Eva Alexander (Evie)
(1889–1980)

Lula Christine Alexander (Christine)
(1893–1975)

Abbreviations

BFM	Presbyterian Board of Foreign Missions, records located in Presbyterian Historical Society, Philadelphia
MC	Maryville College, Maryville, TN
MG	Meiji Gakuin University, Tokyo, Japan
PCUSA	Presbyterian Church in the U.S.A.
PHS	Presbyterian Historical Society, Philadelphia
TTA	Thomas Theron Alexander

Author's Note

I was barely five when my Grandmother Evie put a pair of chopsticks in my right hand, showing me how to anchor one stick with my middle and ring fingers and move the other with my thumb and index finger. I wasn't very good at using them then, but the lesson served me well many years later when I visited Japan for the first time as a young government economist deeply involved in US-Japanese relations. Of course, by the time of my visit to Japan, I had used chopsticks many times, mostly eating meals with friends at American-style Asian restaurants. But my ability to use the utensils without dropping my food or looking completely foolish had impressed my Japanese hosts and helped me feel more at ease in their culture.

Evie, daughter of a missionary, was born in 1889 and spent her formative years in Japan. When I first met her, she lived in a suburb of Washington, DC, having moved there with my grandfather, father, and aunt during the Great Depression. My family moved frequently as I was growing up, from one coast to the other and to states in between. But we managed to visit Evie and Pappy every few years. During each visit, she would tell me stories about her life in Japan.

Those stories flooded back into my mind early in my career, when I served as the Japan economist at the US Treasury Department—the first woman to do so—and struggled to learn the difficult Japanese language. Not only had Evie taught me how to use chopsticks, but she also had taught me to pronounce a few Japanese words, including the name of a well-known Japanese fairy tale, "*Shita kiri susume no doko ita*," or "The Tongue-Cut Sparrow." She gave me Japanese dolls and other toys and books she had used as a child. She told me how her Japanese nanny, kneeling on a sidewalk during a morning outing in Tokyo, had pulled urgently on her skirt, beseeching her to bow down as a royal family passed by with their elegant procession of horses, carriages, and courtiers.[1]

1

Evie also told me I had a relative buried in Japan, or was it two? I couldn't remember who it was or where this relative was buried. Details of these stories had faded into dim memory, as if not quite real. What I did know was that Evie's father, the Reverend Thomas Theron Alexander, had served twenty-five years as a Presbyterian missionary in Japan in the late nineteenth century, an era of unprecedented change for Japan. Evie's daughter, my Aunt Emma, had given me a copy of his journal to read just before my first trip to Japan in 1980. His story had fascinated me, and I'd longed to know more. I vowed during that trip that I would write about his experiences one day.

First page of Tom Alexander's journal

In 1999, after reaching top levels of government and diplomacy in the field of international economics and trade, I moved with my husband from Paris, France, to a farm in the Rocky Mountain Northwest region of Montana. One of my first thoughts upon arrival in my new home was that I finally would have time to write the story of my great-grandfather and how he helped shape a new Japan emerging from centuries of self-imposed seclusion. It took more years before I actually embarked on research and writing. When I finally did so, I found my own path changing in surprising ways.

A Christian in the Land of the Gods tells the human side of one man's—and one woman's—journey, set against the backdrop of wrenching change in Japan and great-power jockeying for territory and influence that would culminate in two world wars in the first half of the twentieth century. This story of personal sacrifice, devotion to duty, and unwavering faith sheds new light on the role that missionaries like the Reverend Thomas Theron Alexander played in Japan's transformation from a largely agrarian nation ruled by shoguns, hereditary lords, and samurai to a democracy and industrial powerhouse. The narrative also proves that one person can change lives more than he or she ever realizes.

Notes

1. In 1884, the Meiji regime adopted a new nobility system granting the titles of prince, marquis, count, viscount, and baron to hundreds of men who had served the regime in significant ways. Trinity Church in the foreign settlement of Tsukiji in Tokyo attracted Christian members of the nobility. In addition, some members of the nobility lived in large estates in the area surrounding Tsukiji. Young Evie and her nanny, Etsu-san, may have been on their way to church one day or simply out for a walk when a nobleman passed by with his family and retainers. Following ancient tradition, many Japanese people knelt down and touched their foreheads to the ground to avoid looking at aristocrats. Although this practice had formally ended by the early 1890s when this incident occurred, some Japanese, such as Etsu-san, clearly still observed it. Evie recalled that the procession stopped in front of her. The nobleman in the carriage looked directly at her and then signaled to his driver to continue. He evidently decided that the foreign girl was too young to consider her staring as a sign of disrespect.

CHAPTER 1

Leaving Home

At the gate stood her father, leaning on his crutch and weeping.

Maryville, East Tennessee, October 24, 1877. Tom Alexander hated good-byes. Parting from his family at Mount Horeb just ten days before had been hard enough. "It was, for me, a sad trial to leave my father, sister and brothers. They did not then, nor will they ever, know how hard a struggle I had."[1] But today's farewell was even worse. He stood with his bride of five months, Emma Brown Alexander, surrounded by her parents and eight siblings in front of the rough-hewn log farmhouse she had called home for most of her twenty-two years. Tom's words reflected his and Emma's angst.

> That was a sorrowful parting, especially for Emma, who had hardly been from home at all, since her childhood. She was the first among five sisters to get married and leave the old home. When we came to start, they all clung to her; with many tears and kisses reluctantly let her go. It was harder still to leave her mother, how hard no one can know except by sad experience.
>
> At the gate stood her father, leaning on his crutch and weeping. He bade us goodbye as cheerfully as he could, but said he never expected to see our faces again in this world.
>
> Were these words prophetic? Would we ever see all these friends again? We hardly dared to <u>hope</u> it. Which one would be taken first? The future seemed dark and uncertain.

---

1. Alexander, *Personal Journal.* Unless otherwise specified, all quotations attributed to Tom Alexander are from his journal spanning twenty-five years in Japan. In order to minimize use of notes, no further citations will appear for excerpts from the journal.

Brown family homestead.

Emma's father, the Reverend William Beard Brown.

Emma's mother, Mary Elizabeth Bicknell Brown.

Tom struggled with his emotions as Emma's close-knit family embraced, possibly for the last time. He was almost as heartbroken as Emma in saying goodbye, since in many ways he felt closer to her family than his own. A mixture of fear, excitement, nervousness, and hope churned inside, but he hid his anguish behind the wall of reserve he had built up since the earliest days of childhood. Years of back-breaking farm work and his up-bringing by a stern, God-fearing father and a series of loveless stepmothers had long since taught him to keep his feelings to himself.

Tom could hardly believe how much his life had changed in the past six months. He had graduated from New York City's Union Theological Seminary in early May and been licensed as a Presbyterian minister just a few weeks later. In late May, he had married the love of his life, Emma Brown, at the homestead where they now gathered with her family. In September he had been ordained as a minister[2] and in October celebrated his twenty-seventh birthday. Together with Emma, he was about to embark on a journey to the other side of the world, to a country just emerging from two and a half centuries of self-imposed seclusion. Soon Tom would take on the mantle of missionary in Japan.

What had he been thinking? Not long after accepting the posting in Japan, he had received offers from four churches in America, each one promising positions that were closer to home and more prestigious than overseas service. He could have accepted one of them, even though doing so would have meant breaking his word. Surely he would not have been the first seminarian to change his mind. But something, some indefinable force, had pulled Tom toward Japan. Maybe it was the lure of the unknown drawing him to an exotic land where he could plant his faith in unplowed territory. Maybe he sought release from the mundane world of everyday life in America or a way to distance himself from his dysfunctional childhood and ne'er-do-well father. Or maybe Tom was caught up in the missionary zeal that had swept America and propelled so many young men and women to far-flung posts in foreign lands.

Whatever the reasons, Tom relished new challenges and knew in his heart that going to Japan was the right move for him. Tom also trusted God to set him on the right path. Before deciding, he had talked the matter over with Emma, and she had agreed to join him on this bold new adventure. But now reality was hitting home. He and Emma were saying goodbye to the people they loved most.

From his vantage point on the outskirts of Maryville, Tom was treated to a panorama of town and country. This late October morning probably was like most fall days in the southern Appalachian foothills. Golden sunlight bathed fields and hillsides, still damp with morning dew. Radiant leaves of yellow, red, and orange shimmered on towering maples, elms, and oaks; some leaves lost their hold on life-giving branches and fell to earth like tiny cradles rocked by the breeze. Dried corn stalks and a rough blanket of wheat stubble stood as mute reminders of the bountiful crops harvested a few months before. The musky scent of decaying foliage contrasted with the sweet smell of hay, and the melody of mockingbirds' full-throated songs filled the air. In the clear light of early morning, Tom could pick out the Three Sisters Peaks of the Smoky Mountains to the east, their weathered crowns forming a soft purple backdrop to the lower elevation Chilhowees. The forested hillsides stretching north to south as far as Tom could see were part of the great Appalachian mountain chain dividing Tennessee from eastern coastal states.

Maryville in the 1870s

Looking west, Tom could see familiar landmarks of Maryville, a town of about twelve hundred nestled in the hills that rose from the banks of a meandering Pistol Creek. Church steeples and the town hall tower dominated the horizon, keeping silent watch over homes, barns, mills, and shops that dotted the rolling landscape. The three-story brick façade of Anderson Hall, one of Maryville College's proud new additions, stood high above a thick stand of young cedars on campus. Though hidden from view, a winding network of roadways and hidden paths connected town and campus. During their college years, Tom and Emma had spent many hours ambling side by side along those lanes, the two of them falling a little more in love with each step.

But the time had come to say goodbye. Tom pulled Emma gently from her mother's arms, choked out a few words of farewell, and guided his young wife into the two-horse carriage that would carry them to the train station about a mile away. Emma's brother, John, had loaded their trunks into the back and climbed into the driver's seat beside them. "Git up," he commanded the team, and the carriage lurched forward. Tears still flowing, Emma turned and waved to her family, not stopping until her loved ones had faded from sight.

The Industrial Revolution brought steam power to America, opening western territories to new waves of settlers and shrinking the distance between America and Asia. Tom had booked passage on the transcontinental railroad, opened to traffic just eight years before in 1869. Traveling first to Chicago, Tom and Emma's five-day trip across America took them through Iowa, Nebraska, Wyoming and Utah territories, Nevada, and on to San Francisco.

A wide expanse of territory lay between their Tennessee home and the Pacific Ocean coast of California. Tom and Emma went to sleep on open plains of grasslands and scrub brush and woke up hours later to largely the same surroundings. They passed through boomtowns that had sprung up seemingly in the middle of nowhere, settled by unemployed soldiers, miners, and other adventuresome men and women pushing west after the Civil War. Herds of sheep and cattle grazed on native grasses where millions of buffalo once had thundered. Those proud animals faced extinction from hunters hungry for their pelts and soldiers aiming to wipe out the Indians' main source of food and sustenance. Huge piles of buffalo bones and hides sat near the tracks along the way, destined for factories and tanneries back east. As their train passed into Wyoming territory, passengers likely talked about Custer's Seventh Cavalry, whose men had met their death the year before in nearby Montana territory as the Plains Indian Wars had drawn to a close.

The vastness of the Great Plains eventually gave way to the majesty of the Rocky Mountains, rising like a massive wall of forest and stone from a sea of dried grass and sagebrush. Snow-covered peaks glistened in the late autumn sunshine. The coal-fired steam engine labored up steep, winding canyon slopes and over mountain passes towering five to seven thousand feet above sea level. The fresh scent of mountain pine, spruce, and cedar competed with smoke and coal dust that seeped through partially opened windows and settled like a gritty crust on everything and everyone inside. Mountain goats, pronghorn antelope, elk, and deer, panicked by the approaching train, scrambled over rocky outposts or bounded through snowdrifts forming along the tracks.

As October drew to a close, Tom and Emma arrived in San Francisco, a rough and tumble city whose population had burgeoned after the Gold Rush of 1849 and California's entry into statehood in 1850. Although the attractions of San Francisco may have enticed them, they didn't linger long; they held tickets for *The City of Tokyo*, a steamer that would depart November 3 and carry them on a three-week journey across the Pacific. *The City of Tokyo* was the largest steamship in America and second largest in the world, with four sailing masts to complement its powerful steam engine.

The City of Tokyo

After two or three nights in the city, surely glad to sleep in a bed that wasn't rocking back and forth, Tom and Emma made their way to the wharf and settled their belongings in a small second-class cabin. Tom climbed up on deck as the steamer pulled away from its moorings and began moving slowly through the harbor. The ship picked up speed as it neared open waters.

Tom wasn't prepared for the wave of sadness and fear that washed over him as he watched the shoreline recede from view. Although Emma was with him on this journey, he felt more alone and isolated than ever before. He poured out his emotions in his journal.

> What a strange feeling is that which comes over one, as he flies away from all past associations of home and childhood! Every day and night put him hundreds of miles farther from all the scenes which have hallowed and blessed his earlier days! Stranger still is the feeling when he stands on the steamer's deck and sees the last connection between him and his native land severed; sees the shore slowly receding, and, at last, is out at sea!

Notes

2. Licensure and ordination are two separate steps in acquiring a pastoral ministry. The Presbyterian Church in Tom's time required a candidate wishing to be ordained to be examined by his Presbytery (women were not eligible for the ministry until 1956) following studies at a theological seminary. The Presbytery examined the candidate's knowledge in a range of areas, including the Bible, ecclesiastical history, theology, original languages of Scripture, and church doctrine. After licensure, the candidate was eligible for ordination after receiving a call from a ministry and going through further examination. Some branches of the Presbyterian Church today (e.g., Orthodox Presbyterian Church and Presbyterian Church in America) still observe these separate steps for ministerial candidates. Westminster Theological Seminary, "Ordination Process." Online: http://www.wts.edu/students/services/careerplacementhandbook/ordainedministry/ordinationprocess.html.

CHAPTER 2

The Early Years

For us, the course of true love did run smooth.

Mount Horeb, East Tennessee, October 8, 1850. Tom was the first of twelve children born to Elias Alexander, a stern, devout man, who dreamed of great things but was weighed down by the grim reality of subsistence farming in East Tennessee's hill country. Elias couldn't hold onto wives any better than he could hold onto money. He divorced Tom's mother, Jane Rankin Alexander, a few years after Tom's birth, leaving the shy, sensitive lad to the mercy of one stepmother after another, three in all. The second was of the storybook kind, harsh and unloving. Tom tried to shield his siblings from her unpredictable bouts of wrath, becoming a welcome island of stability in the midst of family dysfunction.[1]

The hardscrabble Alexander farm offered a bare living. Its poor, red clay soil sprouted just enough corn, hay, potatoes, and vegetables to feed the growing family, sometimes yielding enough extra to sell for some much-needed cash. A few chickens, pigs, and cows supplied eggs, meat, and milk. Situated amid East Tennessee's rolling gaps and hollows and its spring-fed ponds and lakes, Mount Horeb seemed like an ideal place for a young boy to grow up. Tom loved exploring the fields and forests surrounding his farm, playing imaginary childhood games under the canopy of shade from hickories, oaks, pines, and chestnuts. But Elias frowned on idleness and put Tom to work as soon as he was old enough to wield a pickax and guide the horse-drawn plow.

Mount Horeb Presbyterian Church

Tom loved his father and knew his father loved him, but he craved an occasional word of encouragement or praise. Instead, all he ever felt was Elias' severity and discipline. Son of a Scot, Elias was a strict Calvinist and a leading elder in Mount Horeb Presbyterian Church, located across the dusty road that passed by the farm. Perhaps mindful that the Presbyterian Church had strong roots in his ancestral home of Scotland, Elias seemed to take personal responsibility for making others live up to the most conservative interpretation of biblical teachings.[2] He imposed a daily regimen of work, study, and worship in his household and made his children's lives miserable on the Sabbath. No running, playing, whistling, or otherwise having fun on Sundays. Instead, Tom and his siblings remained cloistered inside, learning psalms and memorizing the Shorter Westminster Catechism, a tome containing more than one hundred questions and answers about God, creation, and the Scriptures. Elias always began with the first question and worked down the list.

"What is the chief end of man?" he asked. "Man's chief end is to glorify God, and to enjoy him forever," the children answered dutifully.

"What is God?" came another question. "God is a Spirit, infinite, eternal and unchangeable, in his being, wisdom, power, holiness, justice, goodness, and truth" came the well-memorized reply.

Because true believers never worked on the Sabbath, Elias made his family prepare for the holy day on Saturdays. Tom and his brothers hauled water and wood inside, while his sisters helped their mother peel potatoes and prepare meals. Elias even shaved on Saturday evenings, as did Tom and his brothers when they were old enough. The strict regimen carried over to mealtimes on Sundays. Elias ordered his children to stand at the table to eat their dinner and contemplate God's grace, lest they forget the source of their blessings.

Although Tom never rebelled against his father's rules, he learned early on to bury his emotions deep inside, hidden from the sight of others and possibly even from himself at times. He never did manage to control his occasional flashes of temper, though. Before he could stop himself, he sometimes would lash out at siblings or friends—never his parents—with sharp, biting words that he bitterly regretted afterwards. But Tom also knew how to make people laugh. He aimed his dry wit at himself as often as at his family and friends, bringing welcome relief from the day-to-day drudgery of life on the farm.

School proved to be his greatest escape. Tom relished the hours spent in the schoolhouse next to the church and the time he devoted to studying. His thirsty mind soaked up lessons taught by the local schoolmarm, and he began dreaming of life beyond the farm and the narrow confines of East Tennessee. But the Civil War cut his boyhood short, as soldiers and their battles spilled into the valleys of East Tennessee. Unlike the plantation owners of Middle and West Tennessee, who depended on slave labor to work their larger land holdings, many hill country East Tennesseans were Union sympathizers who had voted not to secede from the Union. They even had tried to break away from Tennessee when the state did secede in 1861, but Confederate troops moving into the area quickly crushed their efforts to remain with the North.

Southern armies weren't the only aggressors. Confederate and Union forces both swept through the strategically important state from the onset of hostilities in 1861, seizing horses, cattle, grain, and other necessities for armies on the move. Even churches succumbed to the divisiveness rending the nation, with Presbyterians splitting into northern and southern factions. Half of Mount Horeb's congregation threw their lot in with their southern brethren, leaving the Alexanders and other Union supporters struggling to keep worship services going during the war.[3]

The war ended in 1865, leaving death, destruction, and divided families in its wake. In 1868, Tom headed to Maryville College in a Tennessee town of the same name. The college, like most others in the region, had closed its doors for six years during and just after the war, resuming classes in 1867. Tom was shocked by what he saw. General William T. Sherman had come to

Maryville in 1863, bringing nearly 30,000 men, but little in the way of food or other provisions. His army had stayed just three days but left much havoc in its wake. Soldiers not only had wiped out Blount County's entire stock of hay and food but had also used the college dormitory and classrooms as barracks and horse stables. Confederate forces did the same when they swept into the area. Floorboards still bore the imprint of boots and steel horseshoes. Soldiers had ripped wooden banisters and door and window frames from walls and burned them as firewood.

The college seminary had been dismantled and its bricks used to build ovens for cooking. The library and its six thousand-plus books lay in ruins. In downtown Maryville, only the courthouse had survived fires set by Major General Joseph Wheeler's Confederate cavalry during its October 1863 raid on Union supply lines, and it still bore ugly scars from bullets and cannon-balls. The rest of the town lay in cinders and ash. Tom's experiences during the war and its aftermath would help him understand, in a deeply personal way, the turmoil and divisiveness plaguing Japan as it plunged headlong into the modern world just a few years later.

Working during breaks from his studies, Tom labored alongside other students to repair damaged buildings and to assist in construction of three stately buildings to be called Anderson Hall, Memorial Hall, and Baldwin Hall, while college leaders struggled to rebuild the school's curriculum and funding. The work was hard, but Tom flourished in the new environment where his intellect was free to explore classical knowledge and new ideas. Work consumed most of his time and energy, but something else— or someone, rather—also captured his attention: his future wife, Emma Edwina Brown.

Emma as teenager

We—Emma and I—first saw each other sometime in the autumn of 1868, at Maryville, East Tennessee. I cannot recall the
occasion on which we first met: the exact when and where have
alike vanished from my mind beyond recall. I only know that
early in September of the year mentioned above, I left my father's home in Jefferson County and went to Maryville in order
to enter upon my college course.

It was only three or four years after the close of the "Great
Rebellion." The roar of cannons had just died away among the
hills and the smoke of battle had barely had time to clear away
from the valleys of East Tennessee. The country had hardly
begun to recover from the dreadful ravages of the fierce and
bloody conflict. Maryville College had, with difficulty, survived
the shock which had paralyzed the whole country. However, an
earnest effort had been made to revive the institution, and the
effort had not been altogether without success.

Previous to the war, Emma's father, the Reverend W. B.
Brown, had been living in Georgia. But soon the political atmosphere became too hot for a union man to live there in peace,
so in 1864 he removed with his family to Cleveland, Tennessee,
where he remained till the close of the war. When he heard of
the effort to revive Maryville College, he determined to remove
to Maryville in order to educate his children in the same institution where he himself had been educated years before.

So early in 1867, Emma found herself in Maryville. What
was left of the college buildings after the war was over stood
on Main Street, truly in a most dismal and dilapidated condition. Its advantages, such as they were, were open to both sexes.
Emma's older sister, Ella, with one or two other young ladies,
was reciting in some of the classes. Emma was attending a girls'
school in another part of the town. She was then thirteen years
old and I was eighteen. I remember to have seen her passing the
streets on week days, and on Sundays at the church service then
held in the old college chapel—for want of a better place.

I recall now, with ease, her girlish face, form and manner:
her round cheeks, short hair and keen black eyes. How little did
she or I think in those bygone days how closely linked together
our destinies were! The college year came to a close without our
becoming acquainted, except in the most distant way. It had
been a hard year to me, and when it was past, I drew a long
sigh of relief as I thought of getting home once more. Though
anxious to get away, I decided to remain over one day longer
in order to attend the closing exercises of the Female Institute.

It was a warm evening in June (1869), and the audiences were provided with seats in the open air. I went alone and took my seat among them. I had not been seated long when I saw Emma sitting not far away, and without an escort. I inwardly resolved that it would be my duty to see that she got home safely after the exercises were over.

In due time, I presented myself. She took my arm voluntarily and with a ready consent to my request for her company. The walk (a mile or more) to her home was a pleasant one. I liked the frank and girlish creature at my side. Her pleasant face and cheery talk were refreshing after the hard experiences of the year just past—far more than she suspected at the time.

Arrived at her door, I took my leave at once and walked back to my room with a lighter step than usual. The next morning I was just about taking the train for home when someone said to me: "Emma Brown said tell you goodbye for her!"

After a summer break spent working on his father's farm, Tom returned to college and boarded with a family outside of town. He and Emma saw little of each other for a couple of years, except for an annual visit he made to her home. Tom tried to convince himself that the other young men flocking to her side did not concern him. No, Emma is only a friendly acquaintance, nothing more, he thought. Tom moved back to campus his senior year. By then, Emma was a freshman. Both sang in the church choir, and they found themselves thrown together more often than ever before. Soon, fate would draw them even closer.

During the Christmas holidays—1872—she and I, with other students were invited to a party at the house of the good lady with whom I had formerly been a boarder, two miles from town. I and another young man united in hiring a hack for ourselves and partners. In the morning of the day on which the party was to be, I sat down and began writing a note to Emma asking for her company that evening, when a young man who was present intimated that she was going with him. As he had been keeping her company, I said nothing, but just quietly erased the "Emma" and wrote "Ella" instead, sent the note and got an affirmative answer.

At the time appointed, I called for Miss Ella. She was not quite ready, and as I waited, I enquired about Emma. "Oh, she isn't going," was the reply. "Why?" "Hasn't any company." I said: "She <u>must</u> go, she can ride with us." So they both went with me. The weather was bitter cold but we enjoyed the ride as well as the party.

From that night, we thought of each other not as friends only but as something more. But in comparing notes afterwards, we agreed that we <u>always had a liking</u> for each other. A short time only passed till I was in her company again. I then made known the state of my mind. I got no immediate response, but felt sure I was treading on safe ground. That was late in the winter or early in the spring of 1873. From that time till the term closed, we were often in each other's company, and though there was no formal engagement between us, we were conscious within that our hearts were mutually pledged and so were happy.

My college course was completed May 30 (?). The trustees of the Institution, however, offered me the position of tutor for one year. I gladly accepted. Emma and I went together very much during the year that followed, and learned to know and love each other more and more.

Tom in 1874, age 24

From Maryville College, Tom ventured to New York City and Union Theological Seminary. His roommate, a college friend, was the only familiar link to home in a city that impressed Tom with its grandeur and rush of life.[4] New York City in the 1870s was America's showcase, home of high-rise buildings, factories, and financiers. The city's population had swelled to nearly one million, and its ports handled almost half of America's burgeoning overseas trade. Opera houses, theaters, and Tammany Hall, with its well-known purveyors of graft, were juxtaposed with disease-ridden neighborhoods, where a flood of foreign immigrants, freed slaves, and fortune-seekers from America's rural heartland crowded into dark, airless tenements.

A brand new Gothic-style Presbyterian church on Fifth Avenue boasted New York City's highest steeple, rising 286 feet into the sky and dwarfing neighboring buildings. With its seating capacity of two thousand, graceful vaulted ceilings stenciled with intricate designs, massive pipe organ, and dazzling stained glass windows, it was the most majestic church Tom had ever seen. America's Gilded Age was on full display in New York City, but so were many sad reminders of the Panic of 1873 that had sparked an economic depression lasting four years. Large numbers of homeless boys and girls had been forced into begging or worse. Legions of unemployed men wearing tattered clothes, many without socks or overcoats, waited forlornly in the city's long bread lines.

Union Theological Seminary's brand of teaching offered a sharp contrast to Tom's strict Calvinist upbringing and opened his eyes to a new way of viewing religion and faith. The first major seminary established in a vibrant city rather than a small secluded town, the Presbyterian-affiliated school also had broken new ground with its ecumenical approach, opening its doors to students from all Christian denominations. The seminary challenged traditional interpretations of the Bible and encouraged students to embrace emerging fields of sociology, comparative religion, and science—including Darwin's controversial theory of evolution, first published in 1859. While this open-minded approach may have prepared seminarians to confront the challenges of an increasingly secular America, it also enraged conservative theologians, who decried these teachings as a threat to the central role of religion in society.

One of Tom's professors, Henry Ward Beecher, was a noted social reformer, who supported women's suffrage and opposed slavery. His sister, Harriet Beecher Stowe, had penned America's popular novel, *Uncle Tom's Cabin*, a searing indictment of slavery that had strengthened abolitionist sentiment in northern states. As for evolution, the Reverend Beecher firmly believed that natural selection was God's way of bringing about change in species. He argued that the church, like species in nature, must adapt to modern culture if it hoped to remain relevant. But Beecher also was a man of voracious appetites, some of which landed him in trouble.

While still a first-year seminarian, Tom wrote to a friend at home that "Beecher is stretching himself now. He draws immense crowds to his church as well as to the court house. Everyone wants to hear him now while his trial is going on," referring to Beecher's trial for adultery that ended without a verdict after six days of jury deliberations.[5] Beecher eventually was exonerated by a church board. His female accuser, though, was excommunicated along with her husband, a prominent New York City newspaperman, who had dared to support his wife's assertion that Beecher had initiated the illicit relationship. Beecher's acquittal by church peers delighted his supporters, but questions about the truth lingered, particularly since another of Beecher's sisters supported his accuser's story.

Another one of Tom's professors, Dr. Charles A. Briggs, was chair of Hebrew and cognate languages at the seminary and one of the country's most respected biblical scholars. Briggs challenged traditional views of the Scriptures, including the long-cherished notion of biblical inerrancy. He was one of a growing number of "new" theologians, who viewed the Scriptures not as God's literal word but rather as man's interpretation of God's will. Conservative theologians, who believed that everything in the Bible must be taken literally, accused Briggs and other liberals of blasphemy. Briggs would be tried for heresy in the 1890s, at a time when Tom was teaching theology in Japan. Just as Briggs' liberal views invited opprobrium and attack from his colleagues, so, too, would the liberal views Tom formed at the feet of Briggs, Beecher, and other professors come back to haunt his career.

Tom thrived in the competitive, stimulating atmosphere of the seminary. He honed his rhetorical skills in weekly debates and gained real-world experience by working with the city's poor. Tom also took on outside tutoring jobs to help pay for school. Hard work, perseverance, and high standards propelled him to the top of his class, but high grades were not the only thing that distinguished him from his classmates. A lanky six-footer, Tom stood at least a head taller than most of his friends. And while he normally shunned displays of ostentatiousness, he secretly admired the fine clothing worn by many well-heeled New Yorkers and a few of his fellow seminarians. One day, taking some of his hard-earned money, Tom indulged himself in a new black wool coat and soft kid gloves, completing the outfit with a silk top hat that set off his keen, observant eyes.

Perhaps Tom justified this unaccustomed splurge by telling himself he would need good, warm clothing when he ventured forth as a new preacher. Or, just as likely, he had someone special in mind when he bought his new outfit. During his three years in seminary, he kept up a lively correspondence with Emma. He also visited her each summer in Maryville and welcomed her at least once in New York City, where she could see him in his new surroundings. "For us, the course of true love did run smooth," he wrote. But not everything was going his way.

Tom may have earned top marks in his class, but he grew more and more concerned as graduation approached. He congratulated one friend after another as they told him about positions they had accepted in different parts of the country, but their successes only reminded him of his own failure to find a place to serve. What was wrong? Why hadn't he received a call from any church? Tom knew he did not control his destiny—only God did that—but he grew more worried with each passing week. He told himself that something would turn up, that surely God had a place for him and would direct him to it at the right time. Before long, Tom's faith was rewarded as his good friend and classmate, Thomas Winn, reminded him of an option he had considered before but never seriously pursued: service in a foreign country.

Tom was not alone in contemplating a faraway venture. America in the 1870s was on the move, pushing into Indian territories in the West and caught up in yearnings for a new frontier beyond the nation's borders. Americans were driven by a strong missionary zeal stemming from their renewed belief in America's Manifest Destiny "to shine as a beacon among nations for the natural rights of man," as John L. O'Sullivan had put it in his famous—and controversial—article, "The Great Nation of Futurity," published in 1839.

Although not nearly as zealous as some of his contemporaries, Tom felt the choice of overseas missionary service was right for him. After consulting with Emma, he offered to go anywhere, and the Presbyterian Board of Foreign Missions promptly appointed him to serve in Japan. Three churches in Tennessee and one in Texas soon offered him attractive positions, each one closer to home and more prestigious than overseas service, but he turned them all down and remained faithful to his commitment to go to Japan. He served twenty-five years there and never regretted his decision.

Maryville train depot

Tom graduated from seminary in early May, 1877, and traveled to his home church at Mount Horeb, which was hosting a meeting of the Union Presbytery, the regional governing body of the Presbyterian Church. After examining in great depth and detail his knowledge of Greek, Hebrew, the Old and New Testaments, and other ecclesiastical matters, members of the Presbytery licensed him as a minister. As excited as he was by this milestone, Tom could hardly contain his excitement over his next big step.

> On the morning of the 21st, I started to Maryville to attend my own wedding. The day dragged slowly by, for I was impatient to see my dear girl. It had been eight, or nine, months since we had seen each other. As the long day drew toward its close, I drew near to Maryville—a happy man if ever there was one. . . .
>
> The train stopped at the Maryville depot, and when I got off, I found Emma's brother, John, waiting to convey me to her house. The horses, as if conscious of my feelings, made due haste and soon brought me to the door. On the verandah and in the house, a goodly company of friends had already gathered to witness the ceremony.
>
> I pushed my way through more expeditiously than politely, and was shown to Emma's room, where she, dressed as a bride, awaited me. Just as the sun was sinking in the west, we were married by the Rev. T. J. Lamar. The next day, we took a little journey to the hills in Anderson County, where we spent two, or three, of the happiest days we ever saw.

Tom in 1877

Emma's wedding picture, 1877

After their brief honeymoon in Tennessee's Welsh coal country—an odd choice for a bridal tour, Tom admitted—the young couple divided the summer between their families' homes in Mount Horeb and Maryville. Time raced by as they prepared for an autumn departure for Japan. In early October, with his call to missionary service in hand, Tom was ordained as a full-fledged minister. On October 24, 1877, Tom and Emma boarded a train bound for San Francisco and the steamer that would carry them to their new lives halfway around the world. They were the first graduates of Maryville College to serve as missionaries abroad.

Notes

1. Descriptions of Tom's father, Tom's relationship with his father, and Tom's childhood are drawn from Thomas Theron Alexander, *Personal Journal*; Emma Edwina Brown Alexander, *Recollections*; Mary Alexander, *Japan Notes*; and oral family history related to the author by Tom's granddaughter, Emma Shelton.

   Descriptions of Mount Horeb, the Alexander family farm, and Elias Alexander's role in the Mount Horeb Presbyterian Church stem from the author's visit to the site and from records of Hebron Presbyterian Church (the church's current name).

2. America's Presbyterian Church has strong roots in Scotland, where preacher John Knox (c. 1514–72) set an austere moral tone for the church and shaped its democratic form of governance. Knox is considered to be one of the founders of English Puritanism.

3. Descriptions of East Tennessee and Maryville during the Civil War are drawn from Thomas Theron Alexander, *Personal Journal*; Wilson, *Chronicles of Maryville College*, 115–17.; and information related to me by Maryville's historian, Dr. Sarah Brown McNeill. The Presbyterian Church split into northern and southern factions just before the war began in 1861, reuniting as the Presbyterian Church in the U.S.A. (PCUSA) only in 1983.

4. His roommate was Edgar A. Elmore, an 1874 graduate of Maryville College hailing from Newmarket, Tennessee, near Tom's home at Mount Horeb. They shared Room 36 of the seminary's student housing. *Catalogue of the Union Theological Seminary 1874–75*, Burke Library archives. New York: Union Theological Seminary.

5. TTA letter of March 3, 1875, to the Rev. G. S. W. Crawford at Maryville College, cited in Crawford, *Tall Tennesseans*, 83–84.

CHAPTER 3

Stranger in a Strange Land

We had not a single friend in Japan, not even an acquaintance.

November 23, 1877, approaching Yokohama, Japan. After a long, monotonous voyage on a northerly route roughly paralleling Alaska's Aleutian Island chain—shorter and faster than rounding the globe near the equator—*The City of Tokyo* neared its destination. Although the seas had been relatively calm during the crossing, the ship's endless rolling and swaying had sent Emma below deck most days. "Emma was <u>horribly</u> sick all the way, and I was sick for two, or three, days," Tom wrote. The only traffic to break the endless expanse of ocean during their three-and-a half-week journey would have been an occasional whaler or a steamer from the Pacific Mail Steamship Company plying new routes to China.

Like others before them, Tom and Emma surely rushed onto deck and joined other passengers crowding the railings as their ship neared Japan's shoreline. After weeks of endless, open seas, the sight that greeted their eyes must have mesmerized them.[1] Distant hills, barely visible at first, were thrown into sharp relief as the sun broke over the horizon and bathed the densely forested hilltops in light. Neat farm patches fanned out from small villages, whose thatched-roof homes and religious shrines looked like children's toys arrayed behind the wooden fishing boats rising and falling on the waves.

"Right glad were we when our ship—'The City of Tokiyo' [*sic*]—arrived in the Bay of Yokohama, November 23, very early in the morning." Given its massive size and the bay's shallow waters, the steamer had to drop anchor more than a mile from shore. A small flotilla of long wooden boats sculled by men in loincloths surrounded the vessel, hugging the ship like magnets. These sampans were there to carry passengers and their belongings to shore. One of them brought the Reverend John C. Ballagh, an American missionary in Yokohama, who ran a Protestant boys' school with his wife, Mary. Ballagh boarded the steamer and welcomed Tom and Emma to Japan.

Yokohama harbor

The scene was a chaotic one. As the ship's crew unloaded the heaviest cargo onto a barge, Japanese boatmen hefted large, unwieldy luggage and other packages onto their bronzed backs and clambered down into their small crafts. Passengers scrambled to grab the last of their belongings from their berths and join the exodus. The ship's stewards rushed from one group to another, lending a hand wherever it was needed and trying to maintain a semblance of order in the unloading process. Tom and Emma climbed into a small boat, eager to put their feet on solid ground again.

Tom's heart must have swelled with a mixture of excitement and apprehension as the sampan skimmed over the water, the landscape sweeping by in rhythm with each pull of the oars, his senses heightened by the newness of all he saw. Japan's iconic Mount Fuji, often shrouded by clouds, stood that day like a sentinel over the wooded hills rising gently from shore, surely a good omen for the future. Yokohama harbor, Japan's main east coast entry point for passengers and cargo, teemed with vessels of all kinds. Small sampans, fishing boats, junks, merchant steamers, local canal steamers, whalers, and naval vessels from many nations crowded into port.

The only American flags Tom and Emma likely saw flew from a small fleet of schooners, in port after a long hunt for seal and otter in Pacific Ocean waters. The acrid smell of burning coal mixed with briny sea air, as a chorus of sounds met their ears. Steam engines and boat whistles competed with the boatmen's cries of *hei hei cha, hei hei cha* that accompanied their rowing. Seagulls floating and dancing overhead mimicked the acrobatics of their cousins on the California coast Tom and Emma had so recently left behind.

As the sampan neared the waterfront, the soothing vista of gentle hills gave way to a more discordant sight. Buildings lining the harbor were a rough mixture of Japanese and European architecture, vivid proof of Yokohama's status as one of Japan's few treaty cities open to foreign residents. A vibrant port and home to mixed classes of Westerners, Japanese, and Chinese, Yokohama offered something for every taste, from the sordid to the sublime. Club houses, first class hotels, warehouses, and private dwellings competed for the limited space along the water, with the Customs House located prominently in the center. Tawdry bars, inns, and brothels on the edge of the settlement catered to whalers and other seamen, their drunken brawls often spilling into the streets. Downtrodden Japanese, drawn to the city in search of jobs, crowded into flimsy houses and roamed the avenues, crying out to each other or to dirty children in tattered clothes trailing behind, some of them the illegitimate offspring of sailors passing through town. Chinatown sheltered immigrants often scorned by Westerners and Japanese alike, their native dress, opium dens, and loud celebrations setting them apart from Yokohama's other inhabitants.

Largely to escape the unsavory aspects of the crowded city's life, Yokohama's wealthier merchants, naval officers, consular officials, and many missionaries had relocated to a section known as The Bluff, which rose nearly two hundred feet above the harbor. There, Westerners had created a home away from home, building stately villas and smaller abodes, all with gardens and some with lawn tennis courts. Shrubs and fences divided the properties, which foreigners leased from Japanese owners. Although Western powers had forced Japan to open its doors to trade, diplomacy, and foreign residents in 1858, Japanese authorities strictly limited aliens' privileges. They could not own property, were forced to live in foreign "concessions"—restricted enclaves in the handful of cities opened to foreign habitation through treaties—and needed a Foreign Ministry passport to travel outside treaty city limits. Many years would pass before Japanese authorities would allow foreigners to live and travel freely throughout the island nation.

As the sampan finally reached shore, Tom's worries pushed to the surface. "We had not a single friend in Japan, not even an acquaintance. Everything was strange, and everybody a stranger." But his inner fears were swept aside for the moment by more immediate demands. He and Emma made their way inside the stately brick Customs House overlooking the harbor, crowded with passengers, visitors, and Japanese from all walks of life. Uniformed customs officers, their white caps perched atop gleaming black hair, barked orders to underlings and passengers, demanding passports and trunks for inspection. The Reverend Ballagh helped Tom and Emma navigate the confusing process and guided Japanese porters as they loaded the couple's trunks into rickshaws waiting outside. As Tom listened to the strange-sounding words filling the air around him, he wondered if he ever would understand, much less speak, this exotic foreign language. Ballagh barely spoke Japanese, even after living in the country for sixteen years.[2] Tom surely vowed to himself to do better.

Yokohama customs house, 1890s

Tom and Emma climbed into a rickshaw, whose driver fell into line behind Ballagh's. Trunk-laden rickshaws followed, forming the tail of this small caravan. These two-wheeled carriages pulled by a man had appeared in Japan less than a decade before, at about the same time the Meiji regime had seized power from the long-ruling shogun. By 1877, they were everywhere. Some drivers wore loose, indigo-colored coats, dark-blue knee-length tights, straw sandals, and a bowl-shaped straw hat covered with cotton. Other drivers were barefoot, bare headed, and wore just a breech cloth around their middle. The gentle up-and-down motion that followed the long, swinging lope of the driver assured passengers a surprisingly smooth ride through city streets.

Tom and Emma surely reveled in the exotic sights and scents of this vibrant port. The heart of Yokohama resembled a European city. Two-story wood frame or brick buildings, many surrounded by stone walls, brick pillars, and wrought-iron gates, lined streets made of hard-packed dirt or cobblestone. New gas lights lent an air of modernity to the scene. Curbs, sidewalks, gutters, and drains—a new feature on the Japanese landscape—brought welcome relief to pedestrians when torrential downpours during Japan's rainy season turned dirt streets into mud. Signboards on the stores caught their attention: T. Batchelor, hair dresser and tobacconist; A. & W. Carrothers, tailors and outfitters; Brett & Co. dispensary; and the corner Bible House. Two-horse carriages competed with rickshaws and pedestrians for space on the avenues. Hotels, consulates, churches, bars, and residences served the needs of Yokohama's foreign population of about five thousand.

They passed through the Japanese section on the way to Ballagh's home on The Bluff above, marveling at the first view of a picture they had seen only in books. Japanese shops lined the narrow streets, their fronts open wide to passers-by. Colorful banners displaying Japanese *kanji* characters that spelled out shop names hung from wooden storefronts. Merchants inside chatted with family members, smoked small reed pipes, or served customers. Cookware, silk, ceramics, clothing, fans, toys, and wares of all kinds were displayed on low, step-like shelves placed on the floor, with most shops specializing in just one item. American-made sewing machines in use in several shops were proof of how quickly a newly opened Japan was adopting foreign technologies. Families slept in back of the shops or above, on soft bedrolls laid out on woven straw tatami mats that measured roughly 3-by-6 feet. Small wooden headrests served as pillows, and quilted comforters provided warmth. Except for shelves, an occasional chest of drawers, and folding screens used for privacy, no furniture of any kind was visible in most shops. Pungent odors from tea kettles warming on charcoal burners and from kerosene lamps and traditional oil lanterns mixed with the sweet smell of cedar lining shop walls.

Yokohama shop

Yokohama vendor and workmen

The streets were alive with people. Workmen, some of them scantily clad in loincloths despite the cool temperature, balanced tools and other implements on bamboo poles draped across their shoulders. Women in street kimonos and men in kimonos or *hakama*—long, flowing, split-skirted garments—walked in twos or threes, or clustered in small groups, sharing the latest gossip. Many wore tall wooden clogs that clattered noisily on the sidewalk, removing them when they entered shops and homes. Despite the tight confines of the shops and dwellings, shopkeepers worked hard to keep the area as clean as possible, sweeping the streets in front of their shops and even sprinkling water to help reduce dust.

Their rickshaws crossed a canal and then tackled the steep rise to The Bluff, the remarkably fit drivers barely slowing their pace. Passing elegant foreign residences, tea houses, churches, consulates, and even a hospital for foreigners, Tom and Emma came at last to the Ballaghs' home, where they would stay for two weeks until moving into their own home in Tokyo. Both of them were excited to begin work in their new mission field, although they surely knew that life in Japan wasn't always easy for foreigners—especially missionaries—in those turbulent times. Many Japanese blamed Western colonial powers for the demise of their old culture and traditions, and anti-Christian attitudes persisted despite official tolerance of the long-banned religion.[3]

If Tom had realized at that moment the heartaches, natural disasters, and setbacks he and Emma would face in the years ahead, he might have turned around and headed back to America. But giving up was not part of his inner fabric. His faith in God and strong sense of duty drove him forward, even in the face of hardship. In times of trial, he often sought wisdom and strength in Scripture. Perhaps he turned to these verses.

> Trust in the Lord with all your heart,
> And do not rely on your own insight.
> In all your ways acknowledge him,
> And he will make straight your paths.

(Prov 3:5–6)

Notes

1. Descriptions of Yokohama and the steamship's arrival in Japan are based on photographs of the 1870s and written materials in display cases in the Yokohama Archives of History viewed during my visit May 11, 2007; Benfey, *Great Wave*, 76–77; Imbrie, *Church of Christ*, 7; Morse, *Japan*, Vol. I, 1–8; and Scidmore, *Jinrikisha Days*, 1–20. A large pier, capable of berthing up to four passenger ships, was built in 1894, allowing for easier loading and unloading of passengers and cargo.

2. J. C. Hepburn to J. C. Lowrie, BFM, March 12, 1877. PCUSA, "Correspondence."
"Ballagh will never get the language. Indeed I believe he has given up trying to learn
it. He teaches altogether in English and that is no doubt the main attraction of the
school."

3. Thomas, *Protestant Beginnings*, 161.

CHAPTER 4

The Last Samurai

"Rich country, strong military" became their rallying cry.

November-December 1877, Yokohama. During their two weeks in Yoko-hama, Tom and Emma made themselves at home with the Reverend John Craig Ballagh and his wife, Mary, and tried to adjust to the still-strange sights and sounds of the city. They joined the Ballaghs in services at Kai-gan Church, Japan's first Protestant house of worship founded by Ballagh's brother, James, in 1872. Tom also accompanied his host to the boys' school run by the missionary couple, meeting young Japanese students eager to learn English, science, math, and other subjects taught in Western schools. Bible studies also were a staple of the daily lessons. Tom's exposure to meth-ods used in Japan's sole Protestant school proved useful when he joined the faculty just a year or so later as a teacher and director of English language studies. Emma also gained valuable insights from Mary and other mission-aries for her future work teaching young girls and women in Tokyo.

Emma took time on December 4 to write to the secretary of the Board of Foreign Missions in New York City, sharing first impressions of their new home.

> We are <u>agreeably</u> impressed with Japan. The missionaries have given us a most hearty welcome and have made us quite at home. They all seem to be earnest, godly men and women. . . . We are stopping with Mr. John Ballagh. Dr. Hepburn and Mrs. Hepburn give us good, wholesome advice which we are very glad to receive and profit by. I have been to Tokio [sic] today to see about furnishing the house in which we are to live. It is much nicer than we expected and I need not say that we are highly pleased with it. The situation is beautiful. . . .

You may know perhaps that the mission here has decided that teaching shall be my work, at the first anyway. I think I told you while in New York that I was fond of teaching so far as I had tried it. I am glad it is to be my work for some time to come. I have visited some of the mission schools and intend visiting more with my ears and eyes open, to catch suggestions in regard to the best methods of conducting them. I intend writing you with some of my first impressions concerning Mr. and Mrs. Ballagh's school (with their permission). Mrs. Hepburn thought I ought to do it while everything seems fresh to me. But my head is full of chairs, tables and other articles of house furniture, so that to write now is all but impossible.

Yours very truly,

Mrs. T. Alexander

Religious studies and academics were not the only matters occupying Tom and Emma's time and attention in November 1877, though. Japan was reeling from a civil war that had ended in dramatic fashion just two months before their arrival. In September, Emperor Meiji's new conscript army had defeated the country's most famous samurai warrior and former imperial advisor, Saigo Takamori, who had led an armed insurrection against the Tokyo regime. At the outset of hostilities in February, few people would have believed that Japan's army of draftees from all walks of life could defeat nearly thirty thousand ex-samurai warriors, disgruntled imperial soldiers, and young cadets from military academies in Saigo's home region of Satsuma on Japan's southern island of Kyushu.[1]

The fact that commoners had prevailed in the bloody uprising proved that Japan's traditional protectors, armed at the end with old-fashioned swords after ammunition for their cannons and rifles had run out, were no match for the latest Western armaments and military know-how. The new regime's controversial decision to import Western arms and advisors to bolster Japan's outmoded defenses had been validated. Equally validated by the imperial army's victory was the notion that Japan was a unified nation under the Meiji regime's control and not a loose collection of semi-independent domains ruled by hereditary lords. A September 1 editorial from the English-language *Tokio Times* had extolled the regime's victory.[2] Ballagh may have saved it for Tom to read.

The idea of national integrity has been stated and established. Widespread throughout the empire it is accepted and appreciated, as never before, that this is one country;—not a bundle of semi-sovereign and jealous powers, but a nation. In this respect the moral of the strife coincides strikingly with the lesson of the civil war in America. There, as here, one of the vital issues was the question of the relation of the state to the central authority, and the result in both cases has vindicated the claims of the latter to be the superior and final arbiter. That this, an "inevitable crisis," here as in America, has been fairly met and satisfactorily adjusted is matter for congratulations.

Although the war had been fought on territory far from Yokohama, the sight of war-weary soldiers trudging through the streets on their way back to barracks in Tokyo and other cities offered tangible evidence of the toll the conflict had taken on families and the nation. Seeing these seasoned fighters surely rekindled old memories Tom would just as soon forget— memories of death and destruction in Civil War Tennessee that had robbed him of his youth and exposed the cruel, dark side of humanity.

The reasons for Japan's 1877 civil war mirrored those that had fueled America's conflict just over a decade before. As the Meiji regime had centralized control over Japan's semi-autonomous domains, leaders in the south and southwest especially had balked at Tokyo's increasingly tight hold on power and at imperial advisors' increasingly corrupt, self-serving rule. Many rebels also resented the growing adoption of Western culture and technologies, which threatened Japanese customs and practices. Proud samurai warrior-statesmen rebelled at an imperial edict stripping them of their privileges, including generous government stipends and the right to wear swords symbolizing their elite status. Moreover, the regime's push for a more egalitarian Japan, in which merit more than heritage determined a person's chances for success, had spelled the end of the samurais' highly treasured role as the nation's administrators and defenders. These and other changes imposed by the imperial regime since sweeping into power in 1868 had upended many of the values and traditions Saigo and his conservative supporters held dear.

But Saigo's challenge to the emperor's regime had failed miserably, and now he was dead. Or was he? By the end of September, just a few hundred men had remained on Saigo's side, trapped by the emperor's forces in the hills of the southern Satsuma region where the insurrection had begun. Refusing to surrender, Saigo eluded his pursuers and retreated to a cave with a few loyal retainers. As imperial troops closed in for the kill, Saigo deprived them of the biggest prize of all—his life. He managed to escape from the cave to a nearby escarpment. There, according to popular lore, Saigo took his own life in honorable, samurai fashion—by gutting himself with a dagger, while an aide lopped off his head with one well-aimed blow from a sword. Rumors persisted for years afterward, though, that Saigo had escaped death and would return to lead the battle again. But the rumor mongers were wrong. Even though Saigo's head had disappeared, at least initially—probably spirited away by aides to keep it out of imperial army hands—it eventually was reunited with the tall man whose body lay prone on the hilltop where he had died. There was no doubt that the body was that of the last samurai.

As a keen student of history, Tom undoubtedly knew that Saigo had not been alone in resisting the dramatic changes sweeping Japan. Unresolved tensions between conservatives wanting to restore Japan's ancient values, and realists and reformers pressing to adopt Western ways had festered for decades, as Western colonial powers had pushed ever more strongly into Asian territories in the nineteenth century. The restoration of young Emperor Meiji as Japan's sole ruler in 1868 had initially represented a victory for conservatives, for whom the emperor symbolized a virtuous past characterized by high moral and ethical standards. As the new regime had settled in, however, imperial advisors soon realized that in order to bolster Japan's defenses, Japan would have to adopt Western technologies and know-how, despite the threat this move posed to tradition. Saigo's defeat meant that Japan's path of Westernization would continue, but his defeat did not spell the end of conservative, nationalist voices opposing the radical changes taking place in the name of the emperor.

The roots of Japan's discord at the time of Tom's arrival were deeply entwined with the country's history and its ambivalent, sometimes hostile, attitude toward Western influences, including Christianity. That history went back to a period long before America had been founded.

Ever since 1603, when a warlord named Tokugawa Ieyasu had gained power after defeating other warlords in battle, Japan had been ruled by a powerful shogun based in Edo (later called Tokyo). As he consolidated control over Japan's roughly 270 hereditary lords and their domains, the first Tokugawa shogun and his heirs had imposed a sort of hostage system, under which the families of all the country's lords were required to live in

Edo year-round, with the lords themselves ordered to live in the capital every other year. Japan's leaders also imposed strict controls over trade with foreign nations, depriving independent-minded lords, especially those in the south, closest to China and Korea, of an important source of money, technology, weapons, and foreign know-how.[3]

During the Tokugawa shoguns' long reign, Japan's emperor remained the nominal head of the country. Widely believed to be a descendant of the sun goddess Amaterasu Omikami—mythical founder of Japan—the emperor was revered by Japanese as the earthly embodiment of the divine spirit. The shogun ruled in the name of the emperor, supposedly with the emperor's blessing. Reality was a bit different, however. As the Tokugawa regime tightened its control over Japan, it also confined the emperor and his entourage increasingly tightly within the imperial capital of Kyoto.

By controlling court rankings, coveted appointments to leadership posts, and other levers of power, successive Tokugawa shoguns gradually shifted authority from the imperial court to themselves, leaving the emperor and his court relatively powerless. By 1680, the highest ranks of nobility and the most desirable appointments—many of them hereditary—were awarded only to those lords closely affiliated with the Tokugawa family or to lords who had supported Tokugawa Ieyasu in his 1603 battle for dominance over Japan. This division of lords and their domains into "inside," or favored, and "outside," or disfavored, lords resulted in resentment and jealousies kept alive by disgruntled "outsiders" throughout the generations. Saigo had come from Satsuma, one of the "outside" domains of southern Japan.

Over time, a symbiotic relationship developed between the Edo-based shogun and Japan's semi-autonomous domains. Because the shogun and his close allies directly controlled only about one-quarter of the nation's territory, the shogun relied on domain authorities in the rest of the country to carry out national edicts and to help suppress internal unrest or foreign incursions. A nearly 250-year period of peace ensued, bringing a welcome change from pre-Tokugawa era skirmishes between ambitious warlords.

Larger domains, including some of those located in Japan's south and southwest, functioned almost like independent states, with large tax bases and powerful armies. Lords dutifully pledged their loyalty to the shogun, as expected and required; but the shogun's regime took additional measures to protect its hold on power. A national household registration system and a strong network of "inspectors," or spies, helped the regime monitor local officials' performance and detect any signs of political unrest or violations of the law. Signboards placed in well-traveled locations, such as bridges and intersections, informed the public of the shogun's orders and directions. A consistent target of signboard warnings was the "evil sect" of Christianity.

"Bakufu" refers to the shogun's government.

Christianity had come to Japan in 1549, when Francis Xavier, a Span-
iard working for the Portuguese, planted the first Jesuit mission on Japan's
southern island of Kyushu. Missionaries came on the heels of traders, as
Portuguese, Spanish, Dutch, and English merchants plied Asian sea routes
carved out previously by Chinese, Korean, and Japanese traders. Within a
few decades of the missionaries' arrival, nearly 2 percent of Japanese were
Catholic, including a number of powerful southern warlords, their samurai
retainers, and thousands of commoners. Although Christian missionaries
and their knowledge of Western ways at first were welcomed by successive
shoguns, rulers in Edo grew increasingly concerned about the spread of
this foreign religion. Fearful that the religious and political conflict then

rending Europe might be played out on Japan's shores, the shogun ordered all missionaries to leave Japan in 1587. Japan was the "land of the gods," the shogun's edict noted, and Christianity was an undesirable doctrine that had no place in the country. The shogun allowed profitable trade ties with Western nations to continue, however, but under tight control.

While some missionaries left, most did not, and they continued their efforts to convert Japanese to their faith. Edo's rulers grew increasingly worried that the religion threatened their control over the Japanese people, especially in the strategically important area around Nagasaki, the main port for Japan's authorized trade with other nations. If there were a crisis, would a Catholic warlord and his Catholic samurai and peasant fighters give their loyalty to Japan's earthly rulers or to a sovereign Christian God and the pope in faraway Rome? Unwilling to take this risk, the shogun cracked down harder and even ordered twenty-six Franciscan missionaries to be crucified in 1597. Missionaries' bodies left to rot on their crosses sent an unmistakable message to Japanese believers about the fate that awaited them if they persisted in their belief in the subversive religion. On more than one occasion that same year and later, groups of converts had their ears cut off before being paraded through streets as a warning to others not to listen to Christian teachings. These ill-fated believers then were staked to crosses and left to die.[4]

After the Tokugawa shoguns gained power and tightened their hold on Japan, persecution against Christianity intensified. In 1614, the shogun again ordered Christian missionaries to leave and took firm measures to stamp out the religion. Government officials demolished hundreds of churches, burning altars, wooden crucifixes, and anything else that could be torched. Southern Christian lords, whose loyalty to the shogun was suspect, joined in the search for Christians in their domains. They killed or tortured hundreds of thousands of believers in an effort to force them to deny their faith and to trample on a cross or a bronze image of Madonna and child. In 1638, tens of thousands of Christians and other impoverished individuals rebelled against this fierce persecution and their intolerable living conditions, ultimately seeking shelter in a castle near Nagasaki. Forces loyal to the shogun mercilessly slaughtered them all, aided by Dutch warships firing upon the castle from Nagasaki harbor in an effort to prove Dutch disinterest in Christianity and gain the trust of Edo officials.

On other occasions, men, women, and even children in the Nagasaki area, where Christianity flourished, were crucified or thrown into scalding volcanic waters. Or they were staked far from shore with hands tied behind their backs, dying a slow, painful death as the rising tide filled their lungs with water. Equally gruesome, authorities sometimes bound unrepentant

Christians' hands and feet and suspended them upside down, making tiny incisions in the victims' necks and puncturing the main arteries. Pitiful moans and screams filled the air as blood drained slowly out of their bodies. The fate of these believers must have reminded survivors of the biblical verse, "Then they will hand you over to be tortured and will put you to death, and you will be hated by all nations because of my name" (Matt 24:9).[5]

In addition to ousting Catholic missionaries (for there were no Protestant missionaries in Japan at the time), the shogun and his regime tightened controls on trade and contacts with Western nations. By 1639, only officially authorized ships could venture overseas, and any Japanese daring to travel abroad faced the death penalty upon return. Japanese individuals risked dire punishment for themselves and their entire family by having any contact with foreigners, with generous rewards offered to anyone who turned in offenders. Because many missionaries hailed from Spain and Portugal, the shogun exiled all Spanish and Portuguese merchants and their families as risks to the ban on Christianity. (These merchants also brought unwelcome competition in Japan's trade with Western nations.) To reinforce the message, Japanese rulers beheaded forty-eight Portuguese in 1640, noting in an edict: "So long as the sun warms the earth, any Christian bold enough to come to Japan . . . even if he be the god of the Christians, shall pay for it with his head."[6]

But not all foreigners were exiled, nor did Japan close itself to all countries. Japan maintained strong trade ties and political and cultural exchanges with China, Korea, and other Asian nations. Chinese merchants continued to live in Nagasaki, albeit in a restricted enclave. And because Japan's rulers valued the country's lucrative trade with Portugal, Spain, and other Western nations, they continued working through Dutch traders, as English merchants gradually gave up the increasingly unprofitable commerce with Japan. The Dutch, whose ships already carried the largest share of the world's cargo, thus secured a long-sought monopoly on trade with Japan. Dutch merchants gained permission to live in Japan, but authorities confined them to the small man-made island of Deshima in Nagasaki harbor.

Dutch traders lived little better than prisoners. A strong iron fence topped by spikes prevented them from leaving by sea, and a stone bridge linking the island to the mainland was guarded by armed men to make sure the Dutch did not depart without authorization, which was rarely granted. Nagasaki's police entered at will and came often to harass the merchants and keep a close eye on their every move. Most of the Japanese clerks working with the merchants were government spies, making sure that no praying, hymn singing, or other signs of Christianity occurred in the presence of Japanese workers. Any Japanese traders or translators interacting with the

Dutch had to trample on a cross to prove their hatred of the barbarians' religion. Although the annual delivery of goods by Dutch ships gradually dwindled in importance, since Japan could obtain the same goods at home or from other sources, Edo officials seemed to value the intelligence about Western developments that came from reports each Dutch sea captain was required to present upon his arrival.

By the early 1800s, much had changed during two centuries of peace in Tokugawa Japan.[7] Samurai were no longer the fit, highly trained warriors of the past, ready to repel invaders or suppress domestic dissent. Some had been lucky enough to secure prestigious jobs in Edo or in domain administrations and thus maintain incomes and lifestyles befitting of their elite status. But other members of this largely nonproductive upper class lived lives of leisure or debauchery, while still others struggled to meet high household expenses and support their large cadres of retainers. Wealthy merchants and farmers, although officially ranked lower than samurai, grew more willing to challenge authority by protesting high taxes or other onerous demands imposed upon them by local or central administrations, actions that would have prompted severe crackdowns in early Tokugawa years. Independent-minded lords in southern Japan increasingly ignored Edo's trade restrictions and strengthened their domains' commercial ties with China and other countries. Some, such as Saigo's Satsuma lord, even began importing Western weapons and know-how. And the Tokugawa regime in Edo, weakened by corruption and incompetence, proved increasingly unable to cope with mounting financial problems and periodic crop failures that led to famine and violent peasant uprisings.

Vast changes had occurred on the international scene as well by the early 1800s. The United States had secured its freedom from England; Europe's internal wars had largely subsided; and Western ships were beginning to enter Japanese ports seeking to establish trade relations. In response to these unwanted incursions, Japanese authorities tightened their already restrictive policies, ordering in 1825 that any unauthorized foreign ship approaching Japan's shores should be fired upon by cannons lining most harbors. The official decree added, "Should any foreigners land, they must be arrested or killed, and if the ship approaches the shore it must be destroyed."[8] American newspapers began receiving reports of Japanese jailors mistreating shipwrecked sailors, including accounts of sailors being confined within small cages and sometimes starved. In 1850, the US Senate launched an investigation into these reports, as well as prospects for trade with Japan.

By the mid-1800s, America was flexing its economic muscles. A highly lucrative whaling industry, growing commerce with China, and a gold boom in California spurred business interest in expanding trade with Japan and establishing Asian refueling stations for whalers and merchant ships. Growing political pressure to open Japan to trade, to protect shipwrecked American sailors, and to share American science, democracy, and Christianity with this secluded Asian nation added to the impulse to challenge Japan's prohibition on dealings with the West.

The Tokugawa regime had rebuffed periodic efforts by Russian, British, and American representatives to establish trade relations, but the picture changed in 1853. On July 2 of that year, American Commodore Matthew Perry's four dark-hulled warships belching black coal smoke— aptly called "Black Ships" by the Japanese—powered into Edo Bay. Perry's command of the largest and most heavily armed ships the Japanese had ever seen signaled a new approach to dealing with what American leaders saw as Japanese intransigence. Perry would not be rebuffed, nor would he depart Japan for good until his message from President Millard Fillmore had been responded to by the emperor himself. Leaving a letter from the president with Japanese officials to give them time to reply, Perry sailed to China, returning in February 1854 with seven warships and insisting upon satisfaction for American demands. On March 31, 1854, Japanese authorities and Perry, as America's representative, signed a treaty that, among other provisions, opened two ports to American ships for coal and other supplies, assured the protection of shipwrecked American seamen, and authorized the United States to send an official envoy to reside in Japan in 1856. Perry had achieved his and the president's objectives.

The treaty added to pressures already weighing on the Tokugawa regime. Then, when America's first envoy, Townsend Harris, arrived in 1856, his demands to establish trade and diplomatic ties added fuel to the fire. Japan's rulers, both in Edo and in its domains, knew that China had succumbed to British forces in an 1842 conflict over opium trade; and that some of China's ports had been opened to English and other Western traders under treaties strongly favoring Western powers. Japanese officials who had dealt with Perry had witnessed firsthand the superior strength of America's fleet and knew their own defenses were inadequate to protect Japan against a determined military onslaught, if one were to come. They also knew that whatever agreement they reached with America inevitably would be extended to other Western powers. In the face of these uncomfortable realities, pragmatic voices called for signing a treaty opening Japan to trade and diplomatic relations with America and, ultimately, other Western nations. Conservatives, though, argued against meeting America's demands. They pushed instead for repelling Westerners and moving aggressively to strengthen Japan's military to allow Japan to keep these foreigners at bay.

As deliberations dragged on, the unexpected death in 1858 of the ruling shogun, who left no heir, sparked political infighting over his successor that further complicated Japan's response to American pressure. China's defeat that same year in a second opium war, which opened even more Chinese territory to Western merchants and diplomats and saddled China with a large indemnity to be paid to England and France, added urgency to Japan's predicament. In the end, bowing to what seemed to be the best of a range of bad options, Japan's leaders acceded to Harris' demands and, on July 29, 1858, signed a Treaty of Amity and Commerce, opening the country's doors to American trade and diplomacy. Six "treaty ports" were to be opened to American traders and diplomats, including the important commercial city of Osaka and Japan's capital, Edo.[9] Opium imports were prohibited. And Americans in Japan were to "be allowed the free exercise of their religion, and for this purpose shall have the right to erect suitable places of worship." Other provisions addressed import tariffs, assistance to ships and their crews, and a host of additional topics. England, France, Holland, and Russia entered into similar treaties with Japan in rapid succession.

The shock waves stemming from the regime's decision to open Japan to Western trade, residents, and diplomacy compounded the turmoil already churning Japan's political waters. But the provisions that would spark the biggest backlash in future years were those that robbed Japan of full sovereignty in two areas that most countries guard jealously: foreign trade and legal authority over foreigners living in Japan. Japan's treaty partners dictated the tariff, or tax, on imports into Japan, setting it at a low level, so their own exports would be able to compete easily against Japanese products. They also prohibited Japan from changing the tariff rate without their approval. This clause not only deprived Japan of an important source of revenue—most governments in the nineteenth century raised the bulk of their funds through import tariffs—but it also put Japan's main commercial policy tool directly into the hands of its competitors. And by retaining legal jurisdiction over their citizens committing crimes in Japan, Western nations seemed to send a message of outright contempt for Japan's unfamiliar judicial system. The Japanese people chafed under these humiliating provisions, which not only undermined the country's sovereignty, but also its pride.

The unequal treaties and rapid influx of Western merchants, diplomats, clerics, and fortune-seekers into Japan's treaty ports did not, by themselves, cause the downfall of the Tokugawa shogun's regime. But they hastened its collapse. By opening Japan's doors to Western trade and diplomacy, the shogun's regime had failed to meet one of its key responsibilities—that of protecting the nation from encroachment by foreign barbarians. That failure seriously undermined the regime's legitimacy, especially in light of the fact that the emperor, in whose name the shogun supposedly ruled, had opposed the treaties. A violent power struggle erupted over the best path forward for Japan—whether to reform the country along Western models or reject all Western influences. Conservative "outside" lords from Japan's south and southwest capitalized on what they saw as an opportunity to change the power structure in a way that might favor their domains and also restore Japan's past values and traditions.

"Revere the emperor, expel the barbarians," the shogun's opponents cried as they battled for control of Japan. Only the divine emperor, they argued, could save Japan from foreigners who were polluting the "land of the gods." After a series of hard-fought military battles, rebel forces ultimately toppled the shogun and restored the emperor to the pinnacle of power as Japan's sole sovereign. In 1868, in a highly symbolic move, sixteen-year-old Emperor Meiji—whose name, adopted posthumously, meant "Enlightened Rule"—relocated his official residence from Kyoto to Japan's traditional seat of power in Edo, which was renamed Tokyo, or "Eastern Capital." The young emperor and his cadre of advisors, initially including Saigo Takamori, moved quickly to tighten their hold over the nation.[10]

The challenge of ruling is always more difficult than the challenge of formulating slogans and organizing opposition to unpopular leaders, as Japan's new imperial advisors undoubtedly discovered once in power. Faced with the task of fending off more powerful Western forces, they soon realized that Japan would have to upgrade its own military capabilities, as well as unify the country to meet the growing threat posed by Western expansion into Asian territories. Acting in the name of the emperor, as leaders had done for centuries with limited input from the emperor, they launched an ambitious campaign to Westernize Japan and seek knowledge throughout the world. If Japan's leaders couldn't keep barbarians from their shores, at least they could try to match them on the same field of play.

"Rich country, strong military" became their rallying cry. In the early years of the Meiji era, the regime funneled an astounding one-third of the Imperial budget to the Ministry of Education to bring foreign advisers to Japan and send Japanese abroad for study.[11] They imported advanced Western armaments and naval vessels, along with European military experts to teach modern strategy and tactics. American and European educators, scientists, and merchants helped build strong schools and universities and establish new industries.

Under pressure from Western powers and as part of a general move towards leniency, the regime lifted the death penalty against Christians in 1869—substituting whipping instead—and removed public signboards against the religion in 1873. Although Christianity remained officially banned, Japan's leaders tolerated foreign missionaries as an inexpensive source of Western learning and languages, which they viewed as an essential element of Western power, along with military strength.[12] These radical changes not only transformed Japan, but they also sowed bitter seeds of discontent that did not end with the beheading of Japan's most famous samurai warrior—Saigo Takamori—in September 1877.

While at the Ballaghs', Tom surely saw English-language newspapers available in Yokohama. On November 24, 1877, the day after his arrival, *The Japan Weekly Mail* reprinted an editorial that had appeared in the Japanese language *Hochi Shimbun* on November 20.[13] The editorial made it clear that Japan's unequal treaties with Western nations chafed on a proud people:

> There are two articles in the existing treaties with foreign powers which curtail the free exercise of the rights of Japan as an independent nation in her intercourse with foreign powers. . . . The right of exercising jurisdiction over foreigners resident among us is a matter which is in the hands of the Ministers of the various foreign countries. This is greatly to be regretted, for it shows a contempt for the rights of eastern nations. . . .
>
> Much as we dislike the extra-territorial clause, it does not compare in importance with the question of the levying of duties on exports and imports. The proper development of the arts, manufactures, productions and national resources of our country depends much on the way in which the levying of duties is managed. . . . The duties form, moreover, a portion of the revenue, and thus we consider that on our possessing or not possessing the power of exercising full control over the tariff question, depends the future condition of our manufactures.
>
> The public generally only express displeasure at our not possessing [jurisdiction over foreigners], but to us the tariff question seems of paramount importance. . . .

After two weeks of waiting, Tom and Emma finally received inland passports authorizing them to travel to Tokyo, where they would begin their new calling as missionaries in service to Christ. Knowing what he did of

Japan's history and its recent civil war, Tom must have realized that he and Emma were venturing into challenging terrain, in which Christianity was hated or viewed with deep suspicion by many Japanese, and converts often were considered traitors to their emperor and nation. Although the religion was making some inroads into Japanese society, many men and women brave enough to defy official edicts and peer pressure and convert to Christianity—especially those in rural areas or cities not yet opened to foreigners—faced lives of persecution, social isolation, and sometimes even physical attack. Adding to the challenges Tom knew lay ahead was the fact that he and Emma had no family or friends to support them. More than ever before, Tom would have to rely on himself, on Emma, and on his faith to sustain him.

Yokohama railway station 1890s

On December 12, 1877, Tom and Emma boarded a train—Japan's first, which had begun operating in 1872—and traveled eighteen miles north to Tokyo. Not long afterward, Tom reflected on the unforgettable journey of the past few months and on their arrival in Japan's capital.

> There our life began in the world. Emma was homesick a great deal, still we were very happy indeed. My <u>wife</u> was more dear to me than my "sweetheart" had been. Thus at last the year of 1877 came to an end. For us, it had been an eventful one. In it, I had completed my student life, was licensed and ordained to preach the Gospel, and in it we were married; took our final leave of home, crossed the continent of America and the Pacific; landed in Japan and settled down in a home of our own.

Life looked good for Tom just then, but it wouldn't be long before his out-look would change.

Notes

1. See Ravina, *Last Samurai*, for an excellent treatment of the politics and personalities involved in Japan's War of the Southwest, or Satsuma Rebellion. My description is taken largely from this source.

2. Yokohama Archives. *Tokio Times*, September 1, 1877, Vol. II, No. 9, 116.

3. See Jansen, *Modern Japan*, "The Tokugawa State," 32–62, for an in-depth description of Tokugawa era Japan and the persecution of Christians. The description in this chapter is drawn largely from this source.

4. John Reddie Black, *Far East: A Monthly Illustrated Journal*, Vol. 7, No. I, July 31st, 1875, 24.

5. See Endo, *Silence*, for examples of torture. Other methods recounted to me by Japanese ministers.

6. Walworth, *Black Ships*, 5. See also 5–17 for descriptions of Dutch living conditions, Japan's ban on foreign ships, and America's response to mistreatment of US sailors.

7. See Jansen, *Modern Japan*, "The Opening to the World," 257–93, and "The Tokugawa Fall," 294–332. Much of the information presented in this section is from this comprehensive source.

8. Shunzo Sakamaki, *Japan and the United States: 1790–1853* (Tokyo: 1939), 184, cited in Walworth, *Black Ships*, 6.

9. Treaty of Amity and Commerce between the United States and Japan, concluded at Yedo [Tokyo], July 29, 1858. The full text of the treaty appears in Cosenza, *Townsend Harris*. Article VIII at 582–83 reads:

   Art. VIII. Americans in Japan shall be allowed the free exercise of their religion, and for this purpose shall have the right to erect suitable places of worship. No injury shall be done to such buildings, nor any insult be offered to the religious worship of the Americans. American citizens shall not injure any Japanese temple or *mia*, or offer any insult or injury to Japanese religious ceremonies, or to the objects of their worship.

   The Americans and Japanese shall not do anything that may be calculated to excite religious animosity. The Government of Japan has already abolished the practice of trampling on religious emblems.

10. See Burkman, "Urakami Incidents," 167; Ravina, *Last Samurai*, 110–11; and Jansen, *Modern Japan*, "The Meiji Revolution," 333–70.

    In Japanese tradition, eras are named after the reigning emperor. The period 1868 to 1912—from the first full year of Emperor Meiji's rule until his death—is known as the "Meiji Era," or "enlightened rule," and was so named in 1868. The emperor himself was not called Meiji until after his death. His first name, given by his father shortly after his birth, was Sachinomiya. In 1860, at the age of ten, a ceremony proclaiming Sachinomiya as crown prince took place, and his father selected the name Mutsuhito as his adult name, the name by which he signed documents throughout his reign.

The "Restoration" of Emperor Meiji as Japan's sovereign ruler, replacing centuries of rule by shoguns in the emperor's name, represented an effort to restore traditional values to a country beset by troubles from within and without. Only after a few years in power did the new regime embark on radical reforms, including adoption of Western technology and learning, aimed at strengthening Japan to meet the perceived challenge to its security posed by Western colonial powers.

The Meiji regime included imperial advisors of great talent and ambition. Although the young emperor did not play a strong role in decision-making in the regime's early years, he did weigh in on a number of important matters and began to play a stronger role in governance as he matured. See Keene, *Emperor of Japan*, esp. *xiii*, 14, 52, and 295–96.

11. Benfey, *Great Wave*, 57.

12. Keene, *Emperor of Japan*, 182; and International Christian University, *Chronology*, 48.

13. *Japan Weekly Mail*, 1,060–61, Yokohama Archives.

CHAPTER 5

A Time to Prepare

The Japanese language did not have a word for "sin."

Tsukiji Foreign Concession, Tokyo. In 1877, Tom and Emma began their new life in Tokyo's foreign settlement, or "concession," of Tsukiji, a low-lying expanse of land on the capital's eastern edge. Although America's treaty with Japan had stipulated that "From the 1st of January, 1862, Americans shall be allowed to reside in the City of Yedo [Tokyo]," the first trading settlement had not been established until 1869. As in other "treaty cities," Japan's leaders had set aside an area designated exclusively for foreign residents to live and work. The tract of reclaimed land once shared by high-ranking lords, lowly fishermen, and a garbage dump was surrounded by water— the Sumida River on one side and several among Tokyo's large network of canals on the others.[1]

Lords' mansions and fishermen's huts had been torn down to make room for Tokyo's new inhabitants, and by 1877, the mix of American and European architecture offered unmistakable signs of new players on the scene. Western-style homes, churches, diplomatic offices, and the eye-catching Seiyoken hotel were interspersed with schools, small parks, and young trees that softened the urban landscape. High stone retaining walls protected the reclaimed marshland from the slow, steady march of the Sumida, whose waters had borne silent witness to centuries of human drama played out along its shores. Gracefully arched bridges spanning the canals offered egress to the rest of the city.

On December 12, the newlyweds moved into a mission-owned home, Number 6B, which was much nicer than Emma had expected. She had every reason to like the house, which put her Tennessee log homestead to shame. Two chimneys spoke of warming fireplaces inside, which offered cozy gathering spots for long evenings at home and helped ward off Tokyo's cold, damp weather. Large square tiles arranged in a diamond-like pattern covered the home's outer walls, and a steep, undulating tile roof protected it against Tokyo's frequent rains—and fires. A two-story veranda fronted the house, each level boasting six white pillars connected by graceful arches. From an open-air porch on top, Tom and Emma enjoyed a panoramic view.

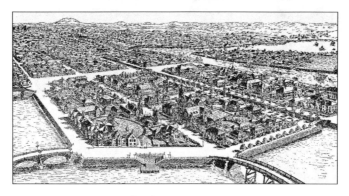

Tsukiji foreign concession

Tsukiji home, No. 6B far left

Looking east, they could see junks, merchant vessels, sailboats, and gondola-like boats on the Sumida, the city's principal eastern waterway that flowed south into nearby Tokyo Bay. Cherry trees lining the river drew large crowds in the spring to view flowers and drink cherry blossom tea in restaurants and tea houses on the riverbanks. The highlight of every summer was the river opening ceremony and fireworks display in July. Lantern-bedecked boats plied the waterway, offering thousands of patrons music, drink, and sometimes even companions from one of the geisha houses located in a "pleasure" district upstream along the river.

Tsukiji home and Union Church

Looking west and southwest, Tom and Emma enjoyed spectacular views of forested hills and mountains, including the Hakone Range, summer home of many missionaries escaping the capital's sweltering summer heat and disease. Sunsets of crimson, gold, and purple painted a splendid backdrop to the ever-changing hues of Mount Fuji, its frequently snow-capped peak visible for miles in every direction.

Next door to their home was Union Church, the main Protestant house of worship in the concession for foreigners; another church served Japanese Christians, who managed their affairs largely on their own with the assistance of a missionary. On the corner was Edo Hotel, a home away from home for many foreign visitors. Just beyond the hotel, a canal and its bridge offered a range of unforgettable experiences for children in the concession. At high tide, the water "was about a foot below the open square sewer hole out of which great rats came to be chased by us," one boy later recalled. "In typhoons we would sail our rowboat up and down the canal. The Japanese boys would gather on this bridge and spit at us. We would beach the boat and chase them with oars as weapons, thus cementing our mutual love. Stones were often thrown also. In this canal we would find bodies of suicides, their long sleeves filled with stones to ensure a quick death."[2]

Tokyo's centuries-old canals offered an easy means of transportation in the crowded city, but they had a less savory side, too. Rats, mosquitoes, and fleas thrived in the slow-moving waters, spawning malaria and occasional outbreaks of typhus. Canals were not the only potential source of disease, though. Farmers used human waste to fertilize rice, vegetables, and other foodstuffs, contributing to the spread of cholera, typhoid fever, dysentery, and intestinal worms that afflicted Japanese and foreigners without discrimination. Ladling waste from city residents' toilets through small out-side openings, farmers hauled it home in oxcarts or in buckets that they car-ried by hand or balanced on each side of a pole across their shoulders. The putrid smells from these "night soil" collections repulsed the city's newcom-ers, but old-timers had largely grown used to them. The Meiji government tried hard to control some infectious diseases, largely eliminating smallpox through a nationwide vaccination program launched in 1870, even as other diseases continued to ravage the population.

Tom and Emma gradually adapted to life in the foreign settlement, surrounded as they were by fellow sojourners from Europe and America. Watchmen no longer guarded gated entrances, demanding visitors' official permits to enter as they had in the first two or three years of Tsukiji's life as a foreign compound. Japanese guards still patrolled inside at all hours, though. As they made their rounds, some of them carried large wooden staffs topped with bells, which jingled in rhythm with the beat as their own-ers struck them on the pavement. Other guards carried two sticks of wood, which they clapped together in rhythmic fashion, signaling to all within hearing that they were on the job.

Tasked with warning residents of thieves or fire, the patrolmen also were in a position to monitor the flow of people into and out of the settle-ment and thereby serve as subtle reminders to inhabitants and visitors alike that eyes were watching their movements. Although the Meiji regime in 1873 had removed public signboards warning Japanese against the "evil sect" of Christianity, missionaries who had been targets of government surveil-lance in the 1860s and early 1870s may have wondered whether guards were posted for their protection or to keep tabs on their evangelical activities.[3]

"After we were settled, our first care was to learn the language. We had no other work, save that on Sabbath mornings, I taught a class of young men, who came to me and wished to study the Bible," Tom noted in his journal. "The language was difficult, and we found it sufficient to occupy all our time." Tom and Emma met daily with personal tutors, drawn from the high-ly educated samurai class. Unlike earlier missionaries, who had struggled to learn the language without any written materials, the couple benefited from a Japanese-English dictionary written by their colleague, Dr. James C. Hepburn, the first Presbyterian missionary and physician in Japan.[4] They also studied various books from the Bible translated by Hepburn and other Protestant missionaries.

Learning the notoriously difficult language was slow at first and often frustrating, but little by little, Tom and Emma made noticeable progress and could communicate reasonably well with their Japanese students, colleagues, household staff, and shopkeepers. Tom read passages aloud in Japanese each day and practiced writing some of the thousands of Chinese-origin *kanji* characters that made up the written language, forging a daily habit he kept up during his twenty-five years in Japan. Emma focused more on learning useful phrases for everyday use and for her work teaching English, music, sewing, and household skills to Japanese girls and young women.

Tom soon did have responsibilities beyond those of learning the language and teaching Bible studies. In January 1878, just weeks after his arrival in Tokyo, Tom assumed the role of secretary for the Presbyterian Mission in Japan. He kept minutes of meetings and handled necessary but often tedious administrative work, including communications with the Board of Foreign Missions in New York City. At some point, he began teaching English at *Tokyo Ichi Eiwa* School, Tokyo's first English-language school. And his colleagues assigned him to join John Ballagh in the "general care" of the boys' school in Yokohama, with "both gentlemen to devote their missions to instruction. Mr. Ballagh, however, to assume for his special department the accounts, buildings, Japanese and Chinese teachers and general discipline of the school; and Mr. Alexander to assume for his special department the general direction of studies pursued in the English department," Tom reported to the board in January 1878 in his capacity as secretary.

As Japan's only Protestant boys' school, the academy's location in the old port town of Yokohama eighteen miles south of Tokyo became less and less desirable, as interest in Christianity grew in the capital. Not only did many students have to travel from Tokyo for their studies, but the heart of the mission's work was in Tokyo, not Yokohama. Tom and his fellow missionaries lobbied the board for permission to move the school to Tokyo to meet growing demand in Japan's largest city. Writing on behalf of the mission on January 28, 1878, Tom argued:

> Young men frequently come to the Mission wanting to be taught and inquiring for a school. One of the Christian professors at the Imperial University said a few days ago that he thought we should have two hundred students almost as soon as the school could be started. His estimate may be too large, but there is abundant evidence of the need for a good school. It seems almost certain that in a very few years . . . all Christian teachers will be shut out from the University. It will then assume an

openly infidel character, and such the need for a school with a strong Christian character.

Imperial University in Tokyo, established in 1877 as Japan's first national institution of higher learning, aimed at creating a highly educated class of young men who could take leadership positions in a new Japan seeking to absorb Western learning and know-how. All incoming students were required to read and speak English. Upon graduation, they could move directly into desirable government positions without taking the competitive exam required of other job seekers.

Like most new educational institutions at the time, Imperial University relied heavily on foreign advisors and professors to help shape its programs and teach the latest in science, medicine, and other disciplines. And, like other institutions, Imperial University sought to develop its own corps of Japanese administrators and instructors, who eventually could take the place of foreigners in these specialized fields. As Tom suggested in his letter, Christian teachers faced a particularly large hurdle in seeking longer-term employment at Japan's prestigious university. The bias they faced probably reflected the continuing ambivalence, or even outright hostility, which some Japanese felt toward their new foreign residents, especially those representing an "evil" religion that had been banned for two and a half centuries.[5]

At the same time, some Japanese, especially the wealthier and better educated urban dwellers, sought out Protestant missionaries for help in carving out new lives in a rapidly changing country. Japan's traditions, institutions, and rigid social order had been upended by reforms imposed on the nation as the Meiji regime consolidated its hold on power. Former samurai, once Japan's respected warrior-statesmen, had been stripped of their treasured hereditary status, leading some of them—particularly those without connections offering prospects of employment with the new government—to seek leadership positions in the church or other institutions. Protestant values of humility, hard work, self-discipline, and education appealed to members of this old ruling elite, whose own code of ethics shared many of these same attributes.

Many Japanese also viewed Christianity, along with Western leadership in science, technology, and military strength, as a key to Western prowess. Moreover, missionary schools offered almost the only education readily available to girls and women in the early years of the Meiji regime. In that environment, it wasn't surprising that missionary schools offering training in English and other foreign languages, literature, science, and other disciplines became a powerful magnet for sons and daughters of elite samurai families, as well as for children and adults from the rapidly expanding merchant class.

Despite widespread acceptance of missionary schools in treaty cities, Christianity still carried a terrible stigma in many segments of Japanese society, especially in conservative Buddhist circles, rural areas, and cities not yet open to foreigners. Even in Tokyo and other treaty cities where the religion was more readily accepted, foreign missionaries and Japanese Christians experienced episodes of subtle or overt bias and discrimination. Although the Meiji regime had lifted the prohibition against Christianity in 1873, the fact was that Christianity had been outlawed and punishable by death—not only for believers, but for their families as well—ever since the shogun's edict banning it and expelling Jesuit missionaries in 1614. Public sign boards had been posted throughout the empire since 1664, warning people against the evil sect and offering rewards for turning in Christians and other criminals.[6]

A change in the law could not guarantee a change in long-held attitudes. Prejudices can linger, often for years or even decades. Sometimes they never fully disappear. Japan's treaties with Western powers had guaranteed freedom of religion for Americans and Europeans living in Japan, thereby exposing limited numbers of Japanese in treaty ports to Christianity after the return of missionaries in 1859. And although the Meiji regime tolerated Christianity after 1873, Japanese Christians often faced discrimination in educational and job opportunities, and families and friends frequently shunned them. Moreover, local officials sometimes disobeyed edicts from Tokyo by refusing to allow Christians to hold meetings or by ordering educators and employees to avoid contact with converts.

Some of their fellow countrymen even scorned Christians as being unpatriotic and not completely Japanese. This attitude may have stemmed from centuries of official policy proclaiming that Christianity brought disorder to Japanese society and corrupted goodness, or perhaps from Meiji officials' more recent efforts to promote the native Shinto religion and loyalty to the emperor as a Shinto god. Even though a number of prominent leaders had adopted the Christian faith by 1877, popular antipathy made the decision to enter a life of Christ a difficult and heart-wrenching one, particularly in rural areas and towns far from Tokyo and other treaty cities. Only the most dedicated souls braved such isolation in Japan's group-oriented society, which valued conformity over individualism.

Tom and his colleagues knew that many students tolerated the missionaries' religious studies only because they wanted to acquire English language skills and Western learning and that they likely would leave the foreign faith behind as soon as they had gotten what they wanted from the schools. The early missionaries' limited success in converting students and other individuals to their religion was reflected in the fact that the Presbyterian mission counted fewer than 650 Japanese as members in 1877. Other sects did not do much better.

Hostile attitudes among some Japanese, widespread belief in Buddhism and Shintoism, and overall indifference to religion, especially in cities, were not the only challenges missionaries faced in seeking to plant their faith. The Japanese language did not have a word for "sin," forcing Tom and other early missionaries to improvise by using the concept of "crime against God." Finding meeting places to carry their message outside the foreign settlement also could be hard in the days before churches were built, so missionaries often held Bible studies and conducted preaching sessions in the homes of willing converts in various quarters of the city.

Missionaries also rented theaters and other public meeting halls for preaching. Christian workers posted placards in hotels, barber shops, bath houses, and other public places, inviting people to meetings by posing questions designed to appeal to nearly everyone's curiosity. One such poster read in part:

> How did you come into this world? Why were you born into it? When you die, where are you going? All who want to know, come to the meetings. We will tell you very simply. Young and old, men and women, come and welcome. We will show you how to serve God, and how to serve man.[7]

Although a few of the people who came to the meetings knew virtually nothing about Christianity, most knew at least a little bit about the religion, whether accurate or not. Some of the more educated attendees were quite knowledgeable, thanks to the spread of foreign literature and English-language newspapers.

Although a growing number of Japanese individuals could read English by the late 1870s and thus could use English-language materials, missionaries struggled to find enough Japanese-language Christian literature to allow them to reach beyond the highly educated class of men and women. A few books translated from English by the first Protestant missionaries in Japan, including *The True Doctrine Made Plain or Easy* and The Gospel according to Luke, offered useful tracts for study. Chinese-language books, used centuries before to introduce Christianity to Japan, still offered a window into Christian teachings for people who could not read English well, since Japan's written *kanji* characters were of Chinese origin. And a Japanese-language Christian journal, *Weekly Miscellany* (*Shichi Ichi Zappo*, later *Fukuin Shimpo*) had first appeared in December 1875 to spread the

Christian message among wider groups of people. These meager resources spurred missionaries on in their efforts to translate more books of the Old and New Testaments into Japanese.[8]

Despite the challenges of missionary work, learning the language, and adjusting to life in a new culture and as a young married couple, Tom and Emma found many aspects of their surroundings quite appealing. Like most Americans at that time, Tom and Emma had not known much about the culture or character of the Japanese people before they departed America. They were pleased to discover that young men and women coming to the mission for study and training were highly inquisitive and eager to learn. Students hailing from the old samurai class took great pride in a heritage that had stressed education, loyalty, integrity, and bravery. Even those students and acquaintances from more humble origins were almost uniformly polite, frugal, and attentive to their studies—although missionaries sometimes had to discipline rambunctious young men unaccustomed to sitting still in a classroom for hours on end.

Many small gifts and other gestures of kindness from students and members of the small Japanese Christian community conveyed to Tom and Emma a spirit of genuine respect and generosity. And the fact that most Japanese homes had no locks or bolts offered proof of the honesty of a population in a city of roughly one million. Japan surely was a country of contrasts. Although amply aware of the challenges facing him and his fellow Christians, Tom wrote to the mission board in New York in March 1878, just a few months after their arrival, that "Mrs. A and I are well pleased with our situation and are as well satisfied as could be expected." Indeed, Tom never wrote an unkind word about his Japanese brethren or his adopted home during the twenty-five years he served there. In his letter, though, he added a disquieting note:

> There was a very destructive fire last night in this city which threatened to give us some trouble for a little while, but the wind carried it in another direction. It burned over a great deal of ground and in a very thickly settled portion of the city. Many hundreds of people are, I suppose, homeless on account of it. We are very thankful that we escaped.[9]

Tom soon would learn that fire was a regular feature of life in Tokyo.

Life was not all work and study for Tom and Emma. Whenever they could, they took rickshaw or carriage rides through Tokyo, stopping occasionally to walk in the city's bustling neighborhoods. The crowds and noise in some places contrasted sharply with the quieter confines of the Tsukiji foreign district. Pedestrians' wooden clogs echoed with a deafening roar on hard-packed or cobblestone roads and newly constructed sidewalks, sometimes sounding like a small army of steel-shod horses crossing a wooden bridge. Smells wafting from shops and vendors selling noodles, tofu, and Japanese-style pancakes filled the air, along with the pungent scent of burning char-coal, lamp oil, and small bamboo pipes puffed on by knots of men gathered in small groups or in shops. The gleeful laughter of children chasing balls or pulling kites filled narrow side streets lined by tightly packed wooden houses and small shops. Other sights were more poignant. Numerous blind people, victims of smallpox and other highly contagious diseases, wandered the streets, emitting a high, shrill whistle as they walked to advertise mas-sage skills learned in special schools for the blind.

As Tom and Emma moved through the city, small crowds of curious onlookers often stared at their unfamiliar pale faces, round eyes, and other Western features. Emma surely was more uncomfortable than Tom with this unaccustomed attention, which persisted despite the emperor's order that his subjects not stare at foreigners. And although Tokyo was a large, crowded city, there were plenty of open green spaces, thanks to still-unde-veloped estates previously owned by high-ranking lords in the days when the shogun had required them and their families to live in Tokyo. A big attraction for all Tokyo residents was the emperor's palace, located on high ground in the center of the city and surrounded by massive stone walls and wide moats. Like many others who gazed at those walls, Tom and Emma undoubtedly tried to imagine how the nation's revered leader lived.

The face of Tokyo was changing as Western technologies and styles wove themselves deeper and deeper into the fabric of the city. Telegraph lines and gas lights had appeared, and imposing brick buildings rose on university campuses, in the commercial Ginza area, and in the government district near the imperial palace. Tailored suits and bowler hats mixed with kimonos on the sidewalks, and horse-drawn buses, their drivers clad in vel-vet livery and jaunty hats, vied with two-wheeled rickshaws for passengers and space on crowded city streets.

These surface changes were not the most far-reaching ones, though. Western legal and educational systems replaced Japan's home-grown ver-sions. Modern factories, shipyards, and railroads fueled the nation's grow-ing industrial capacity. And authorities built up the nation's army and navy, relying on European military advisers and importing Western armaments and vessels. Many Japanese leaders believed that the more they could model Japan in the West's image, the more likely Western powers would be to renegotiate the unequal treaties of the 1850s that all Japanese resented so deeply. A strong military and vibrant economy also would allow Japan to protect itself from Western colonial powers. For many Japanese, though, these changes were too much to accept. The push for Westernization and industrial development sowed the seeds of political unrest as it swept away the livelihoods and traditions of samurai warriors, craftsmen, farmers, and small merchants. Popular anger at foreigners and Japan's new leaders would fester and grow with time.

Notes

1. Descriptions of Tsukiji and of the view from the second-story porch of Tom and Emma's house are drawn from Carrothers, *Sunrise Kingdom*, 54; Keene, *Emperor*, 164; Whitney, *Clara's Diary*, 31; and photographs and illustrations in MG Archives.

2. Charles Imbrie, "Into the Sunset."

3. Sources mentioning government spies monitoring missionary activities include Burkman, "Urakami Incidents,"153; and Cary, *History of Christianity*, 154.

4. The Hepburn method is still used for Romanizing Japanese words.

5. By 1881, Imperial University was dismissing its foreign professors and replacing them with Japanese. G. W. Knox to BFM, August 17, 1881. PC, "Correspondence."
   The independent spirit of Japan's new leaders was widely recognized by missionaries and other foreign observers. J. C. Hepburn wrote in 1877, "Judging from the independent character of this people and nation I am fully of the opinion that whatever we do for them must be done at once or as soon as possible. They are thoroughly of the opinion that they can manage for themselves, and very jealous of foreign help and foreign influence. This seems to be a national characteristic and is evidenced in political and civil matters, as well as religious. There is a great deal of national pride evident in them. The fact of their employing so many foreigners in every department of government matters is only from a desire to bring themselves abreast with western nations. The moment they can feel they can do without them, they will resolve to get rid of them." Hepburn to BFM, March 12, 1877, PCUSA, "Correspondence."
   Even in recent years, some foreign instructors at Japanese colleges and universities have believed they faced barriers to long-term employment. See article by James McCrostie and John Spiri, *Japan Times*, December 30, 2008. Online: http://www.japantimes.co.jp/community/2008/12/30/issues/foreign-university-faculty-face-annual-round-of-musical-jobs/#.UvlCTJWYaM8.

6. Information about anti-foreign and anti-Christian attitudes, including social exclusion and sometimes violent persecution of converts, is found in numerous sources. See, for example, Scheiner, *Christian Converts and Social Protest in Meiji Japan*,

57–59 and 120 for instances of strenuous family objections to converts in the late 1870s. Whitney, *Clara's Diary*, recounts stories of persecution, including stoning, of Christians in the southern region of Kumamoto in 1876 (261); and of speeches in Tokyo in 1877 against foreigners, their morals, and religion (124). Carrothers, *Sunrise Kingdom*, 268, notes that Buddhist priests were the main opponents of Christianity. See also Cary, *History of Christianity*, 92, on persecution by and opposition from family members, friends, neighbors, and Buddhist priests in the 1870s.

Various sources recounting the history of Christianity in Japan during the Meiji era contain stories of Japanese Christians facing accusations of being traitors. See, for example, Nakazawa, *Winn*, 23–24: "[In Kanazawa,] the people's attitude toward Christianity was that it was an evil religion, and they severely hated and rejected it. Moreover, those who believed in Christianity were regarded as unpatriotic people and traitors to the nation." Burkman in "Urakami Incidents," 178–79, notes that in 1872, a member of the Iwakura Mission to the West—Shimaji Mokurai—petitioned the government to discontinue teachings under the officially sanctioned Three Principles of Instruction, including the notion that failure to revere the *kami*—or gods, including the emperor—did not imply failure to love one's country. Some Japanese Christians of the twenty-first century also suspect that their fellow countrymen may not always view them as completely loyal Japanese citizens, a view expressed to me in a moment of candor by a Japanese minister during one of my visits.

7. Imbrie, *Church of Christ in Japan*, 113–14.

8. Information about early Christian publications appears in Thomas Theron Alexander, "The Preparation and Spread of Christian Literature," 439–40 and 447. Alexander also references a letter from J. C. Hepburn concerning his efforts to publish the first Japanese language Protestant work, *The True Doctrine Made Plain, or Easy*. In a letter published in *The Spirit of Missions* in February 1864, Hepburn wrote: "I have to be very secret in getting the blocks cut. No doubt, if the officers of the Government knew it, they would soon put a stop to it." The Gospel according to Luke was translated by J. C. Hepburn and S. R. Brown in 1875. See International Christian University, *Comparative Chronology*, 52.

9. Letter to Lowrie, BFM, March 18, 1878. PCUSA, "Correspondence."

CHAPTER 6

Firestorm

Then it was, that, for the first time, I wished I had never seen Japan.

Tsukiji Foreign Concession, Tokyo. Little by little, things that at first had seemed so strange to Tom and Emma took on a mantle of familiarity: the practice of bowing slightly whenever they met a Japanese acquaintance or entered a room with Japanese present; the morning greeting of *ohayo-gozaimasu* and other pleasantries which now rolled off their tongues more easily; or removing their shoes when entering Japanese homes, taking care to point toes toward the wall to make it easy to step back into them when departing. They appreciated the many small gestures of kindness from Japanese they met—small gifts or kind offers of assistance in navigating unfamiliar customs or daily tasks.

Emma also was pleased to discover she could get virtually all the ingredients she needed to make their favorite meals: fine flour imported from England and California; coffee, tea, milk, and sugar; fruits and vegetables of every kind brought to the house by merchants balancing large baskets on either side of a pole draped across their shoulders; and inexpensive potatoes, onions, and corn. She worked patiently with her cook, teaching her how to transform raw ingredients into dishes that tasted just the way she and Tom liked them.

"The months passed quietly away and there was but little to break the monotony, or to disturb the peace and joy of our lives," Tom wrote in 1878 after about a year in Tokyo, adding:

> But this state of things could not <u>long</u> endure, Oh no! For very early on the morning of October 18th, our little girl, Ella Lillian, was born, and there was an end of our long honeymoon. Thenceforth, we took on the dignity of a family. Ella was small in stature, but otherwise seemed to be grown up already. She had, from the first, we have always thought, a grown-up look

and manner. She seemed to have come into the world with the solemn conviction that "where there's a will, there's a way," and faithfully has she endeavored to live up to her convictions even in the most trivial matters, as well as in the more weighty ones.

If only the peace and joy could continue as it had before. As delighted as the new parents were by the arrival of their baby girl, Tom was even more worried about Emma's physical and emotional health after Ella's birth. "Emma did not become herself again. I noticed with grief that her face looked older, her step was not so elastic as before, and she was often in pain. Still, she was able to be up, and to look after the baby girl, [who] was the light and joy of our home."

Emma's pain may have reflected undiagnosed complications from a difficult labor and childbirth. But she also may have suffered from post-partum depression, not then identified, which afflicts new mothers with feelings of sadness, fatigue, worthlessness, and anxiety. Just twenty-three and living far from family and lifelong friends, Emma had none of the support systems common to young mothers at the time—no mother, sisters, or close friends to lend a hand during the baby's birth and infancy. Tom was deeply engrossed in his work and studies and soon would be on the road, leaving Emma to fend for herself with just one or two Japanese household staff and occasionally other missionary wives, who were busy with their own families and duties. Emma's initial excitement at serving the Lord in an exotic foreign mission must have given way quickly to the realities of life far from home, with all its day-to-day concerns and drudgery.

Emma's mind may have wandered back to days past, to a time when she had been young and innocently coquettish. "I developed into womanhood very fast so that at twelve years I was mistaken for sixteen by the boys—and had attentions from them that did me harm I think. I had numerous 'affairs' with boys till in my senior year [of college] when I became engaged to Tom Alexander."[1]

Emma had been in the first class of women to graduate from Maryville College and, while still a student, had been elected president of the prestigious Adelphic Union Literary Society. The townspeople of Maryville considered her a heroine for venturing so far from home to spread her faith in a foreign land. But her carefree adolescence and the admiration of her hometown did little to help her now as she struggled to adapt to a new culture and to the challenges of motherhood. Perhaps Emma tried to console herself with the biblical admonition: "Do not worry about tomorrow, for tomorrow will bring worries of its own"(Matt 6:34). Sadly, tomorrow did bring worries of its own, as Tom wrote in 1879:

We were sitting in our room early one morning in March, when the American mail was brought in. Emma opened her letter and reading it burst into tears. I took it from her hand and read: "Your father passed away this morning." (Feb. 26). His words had come true. We were to see his face no more on earth. He had laid aside his crutch and, with it, his suffering too, and gone to his reward in glory.

The old ties were being broken and new ones were taking their place; no, not taking their place either. Nothing can quite replace the affections and associations of childhood and early life. When these are taken away, a void always remains, and nothing can quite fill it up. Though new ties may be formed which render life equally happy, still the happiness is of a different kind. The halo with which childish fancy clothes this life, if once dispelled, can never be restored.

Emma's heartache over losing her father surely magnified her feelings of homesickness and isolation. Then, several months later, she suffered another blow, of which Tom wrote, "About the middle of July [1879], Emma, in coming downstairs with Ella in her arms, fell and sprained her ankle. Though Ella escaped entirely unhurt, Emma suffered severely, and in the evening, I carried her upstairs where she remained for several weeks. Before she was able to come down, I went, in company with Rev. O. M. Green, to Ikao and Kusatsu to spend a month."

Ikao and Kusatsu were two remote towns nestled high in scenic mountains northwest of Tokyo, both famous for their health-giving hot springs and breathtaking views. His trip to the interior was part of missionaries' efforts to reach beyond Japan's urban areas and spread the gospel to people who had not yet heard the good news of the Bible. This month-long separation was the first of many to come, and Tom and Emma both found it hard to bear. When he returned to Tokyo, Tom found Emma almost completely healed but still walking gingerly. She was delighted to have her husband home again, and he was equally happy to be back with his little family.

Daily life for Tom and Emma resumed its normal rhythm after his return. A comfortable routine of language study, teaching, reading by the fireplace, and occasional strolls along the banks of the Sumida with baby Ella filled the days and nights. Informal dinners and outings with friends broke the monotony and helped the young couple cope with the homesickness that inevitably plagues sojourners far from home. Tom kept up his duties as mission secretary and, being increasingly comfortable speaking Japanese, peppered his Japanese students and colleagues with questions about Japan's history and culture. He also learned as much as he could about Buddhism and Shintoism, not only because he was interested, but also because he felt that understanding Japan's main religions and beliefs would help him as he worked to convert Japanese men and women to Christianity. By December 1879, Emma's health had recovered nicely, and she was expecting their second child within a few weeks.

Then disaster struck. On the day after Christmas, Tom and Emma were relaxing inside when they heard the unmistakable sound of metal fire bells mounted on posts throughout the foreign concession clanging loudly, signaling one of the worst dangers that could strike Tokyo's tightly packed homes and shops. Tom must have known they were in serious trouble. Acres of the city burned each year in fires sparked by oil lamps or charcoal fires and fueled by wooden structures that burned like dried kindling. Even though Tsukiji's Western-style homes and buildings were more solid than their Japanese counterparts, they could not always withstand flames driven by high winds that so often accompany massive fires. Tom described the "great fire" in his journal and in a letter to the foreign mission board.[2]

> It did not last more than eight or ten hours, but the wind was blowing fearfully hard, so that the pace was rapid beyond anything I ever saw of the kind. The fire broke out some two miles north of Tsukiji [in Tokyo's Nihon Bashi district], coming directly towards us. It reached Tsukiji in an incredibly short time.
>
> It burned several houses and threatened to burn all. I was in great distress, for Emma was unable to walk any distance, so delicate was her health. I could not leave the house to take her to a place of safety and so knew not what to do. By and by, Miss [Kate] Youngman, whose house had been burnt, came and offered her assistance. She took Emma and the baby off to a safe place, and left me to look after the house.

The heat and noise were intense. Mothers and Japanese nannies pulled toddlers by their hands and cradled babies to their breasts as they fled the nightmarish scene. Horses' nostrils flared as their handlers struggled to control the frightened beasts. The roar of flames and crash of timbers mixed with men's shouts and women's cries of fear. Luck, more than the skill of amateur firefighters armed with little more than shovels, pick-axes, and buckets, saved Tom and Emma's house from the raging flames. The tile roof and walls probably made the difference. Not everyone was so lucky, though.

The Mission buildings <u>all escaped</u> (that is, our Mission buildings) though we had a hard fight—and everyone has lost <u>something</u> in one way or another. The new house which the mission had rented for Miss Youngman was entirely burned up. She lost more than half her clothing, furniture, etc. Some of the lumber intended for the boys' school house was burnt. I don't know how great the loss will be when counted up, not <u>very large</u>, I hope.

The M.E. [Methodist] Church Mission lost all their buildings that stood in Tsukiji, as follows: one church, one dwelling, and two large buildings belonging to the Ladies' Board and used for Girls' School. Their loss is great.

It is said on good authority that from eight to ten thousand Japanese homes were burned, and not less than 25,000 to 30,000 people turned into the streets. Of course, suffering has been great, seeing that it is winter.

After the fire was over, I went and found my wife and child and brought them home. Emma was worn out with pain and anxiety and Ella tired and fretful—the house and furniture in the utmost confusion. I, too, was worried and felt very badly. Emma and the baby were soon in bed, and I sat down by the fire alone, to collect my thoughts and rest.

I was thankful that our house had been left us while such multitudes had been turned out of house and home by the ruthless flames. But then it was that, for the first time, I wished I had never seen Japan.

With Emma and Ella safely in bed upstairs, Tom stared vacantly at the fire, surely marveling over the simple fact that the flames they relied on for warmth and cooking could turn so deadly at a moment's notice. Worse, he was now responsible for two lives other than his own, with another baby on the way. He wasn't sure what God had in mind for him, but as bad as things seemed just then, Tom must have consoled himself with the belief that God had had a purpose in guiding him to Japan. He resolved, not for the first time, to put his faith and trust in God, knowing that God would not give him or Emma any trial that they were not strong enough to bear. Perhaps he drew strength from the words of Psalm 55:22: "Cast thy burden upon the Lord, and he shall sustain thee. . . ."

Within a few days, Tom and his little family had largely recovered from their ordeal, and he felt a renewed sense of hope for the future. But, as he soon would find out, natural disasters were not the biggest challenge he would face as he worked to plant his faith on foreign ground.

Notes

1. Emma Edwina Brown Alexander, *Recollections*, 9–10.

2. Letter to BFM, January 2, 1880. PCUSA, "Correspondence." The fire's description is based on an eyewitness account of another fire in Tsukiji in 1872. Carrothers, *Sunrise Kingdom*, 156.

CHAPTER 7

Into the Heart of Buddhism

Foreigners, especially those preaching an alien, subversive religion, were distinctly unwelcome.

As much as Tom appreciated his work in Tokyo, he longed for a posting in the field, the "real" Japan, where few missionaries had gone. His good friend and classmate from Union Theological Seminary, Thomas Winn, was laboring in Kanazawa on Japan's west coast, teaching English and other subjects in a government school and leading some of the students in Bible study. Tom envied Winn his independence and his work bringing the gospel to Japanese in far reaches of the country.

Despite his yearning for new adventures, Tom buckled down to his duties in Tokyo and satisfied himself with occasional trips into the hinterlands. On January 18, 1880, just three weeks after the Christmas fire that had sent him and Emma fleeing from home, their second daughter was born. They named her Emma, after her mother. Once again, though, mother Emma's health suffered greatly after childbirth, and she remained weak and feeble for more than a year. But her ailments did not stop Tom from pursuing his calling with the same fervor and single-mindedness he brought to most new challenges. As soon as he could leave Emma and the children "with impunity," he traveled to Shimonoseki and other towns on Japan's southwestern coast to oversee work being done by several Japanese preachers.

The Straits of Shimonoseki were strikingly beautiful, with forested hills rising abruptly from azure waters. They also were famous as the site of a fierce naval battle during the campaign by xenophobic nationalists to oust foreign barbarians from Japan. In 1863, the local lord had ordered cannons to fire on foreign ships passing through the straits. His unilateral action had challenged the shogun's regime in Edo as much as it had Japan's foreign treaty partners. Western powers had responded quickly to the lord's aggression. A combined squadron of ships from Britain, France, the United States, and Holland attacked Shimonoseki and destroyed the gun batteries. Although the battle against foreigners had been lost long before Tom arrived, many locals still hated and even feared the unwelcome aliens.

Leaving home on April 21, 1880, Tom traveled to Yokohama, boarding a steamer that arrived in Shimonoseki four days later at precisely 2:00 a.m. He remained there for about two weeks, preaching and teaching Bible studies, and then journeyed to Yanagawa on Japan's southernmost island of Kyushu to organize a church. Joined in his visit to Yanagawa by the Reverend Aoyama Shozaburo, Tom baptized seven adults and four or five children. He credited a local Christian and political leader active in the nascent freedom and people's rights movement in Japan, Mr. Shina, with laying foundations for the church there. Tom listened soberly as church members told him how they dodged rocks occasionally thrown through windows of homes used for worship meetings.[1]

After a few days in Yanagawa, he returned to Shimonoseki, where he stayed until the end of May, using the town as a base for short trips to outlying towns and villages. Shimonoseki impressed Tom in many ways, as did the work being done by his Japanese colleagues, the Reverends Aoyama and Hattori Ayao, who had been laboring in the region about a year. Given the town's strategic location, Tom considered making it the base of his mission work in the region. He reported to the church's foreign mission board in America about the work underway and the challenges his Japanese brethren had faced.

> Shimonoseki is fringed along the shore of the Inland Sea [Sea of Japan] for four or five miles and contains twenty-five or thirty thousand inhabitants. The houses are good and the people, for the most part, well to do, many of them rich. The situation of the town, besides being exceedingly beautiful and picturesque, is very important. It is potentially the metropolis of a large tract of country, and there is a strong probability that it will soon be made an open port [for foreign residents]. The lack of a good harbor is the only drawback.
>
> The native brethren, the Reverends Mr. Hattori and Mr. Aoyama, as they began their labors, at first met with great opposition, not from government or any of its officials, but from the Buddhist priests. They were charged with all sorts of bad motives, and were unsparingly and unceasingly demeaned as wicked and designing men, and were threatened with violence in the streets. At first, a few came to hear them, then virtually

none. In addition to this, they found it difficult to rent houses to live in and thought they would have to leave altogether.

Still, they prayed and labored on, and in the course of time, matters began to assume a more helpful aspect. They began to be treated with more respect, audiences grew larger, and then there was a small company of men who came regularly to their meetings.

Tom baptized two of the regulars, one "a man of some education, which, together with his wealth, makes him a man of influence. The other one is a poor man, but he gave good evidence of his having become heir to an inheritance incomparable, undefiled and which fadeth not away," Tom wrote, quoting Scripture to describe the man's newfound Christian faith.

During his trip, Tom witnessed firsthand the mysterious ways in which God sometimes worked to bring new converts into the fold. With so many towns facing the open seas, the area between Shimonoseki and Yanagawa bred skilled fishermen. The mariners were as good as any in the empire, hauling in fish of all kinds, including the poisonous but highly prized blowfish that ballooned into giant orbs when threatened. But even the best sailors could not always withstand the fierce storms that sometimes blew in from the west, the wind forming giant, frothy waves that rolled, curled, and broke violently, trapping anything and anyone in their path.

Two fishermen who had heard Tom preach at some point during his sojourn sought him out and captivated him with their story. One day when they were fishing far from shore, a sudden storm had moved in, driven by high winds that quickly capsized their small fishing boat. They had clung in desperation to the wreckage as it was battered by rain and dashed by high waves, praying to their own gods for rescue. No help arrived. Then one of them proposed that they pray to Alexander-san's god. Both men vowed that if they survived, they would convert to Christianity. Tom baptized them before he left for Tokyo.

Tom was overjoyed by the results of his visit and by the growing interest in Christianity in the region. The Japanese preachers' work had been "signally blessed," he wrote to the home mission board. Not only had new churches been established, but Christians in Shimonoseki had agreed to contribute money toward the upkeep of preaching places. A new Bible store, the area's first, also had opened. Tom knew, though, that establishing a firm hold in the country would take more than prayers and devotion. He appealed to the home mission board for more money and missionaries. "Now is the time for the Church to lay deep and well her foundations in this country," he wrote, adding that despite some positive developments and a growing acceptance of Christianity, the full story still was one of "trial and difficulty on the one hand, and joy and blessing on the other; in short, the story of missionary work."[2]

With his work in the region completed for the time being, Tom headed back to Tokyo. His homecoming on May 27 after a five-week absence delighted Emma and the girls, as it always did when he returned from his journeys.

> Found Emma and the children overjoyed at my return, but not more happy than I myself. Our babies continued to grow nicely and to enjoy good health, for which we were very thankful. The younger one was, from the first, very much like her mother both in looks and disposition, while the other one was like me. In June, we moved out of No. 6, our first home, to No. 9B, where we continued for the remainder of the year.

A new year dawned in 1881 and, with it, new possibilities. But Emma's health continued to trouble her and worry Tom, as he noted in his journal. "Early in this year, Emma had a severe spell of sickness which kept her very feeble in health for two months or more." Sadly, Emma was no longer the frank and girlish creature whose pleasant face and cheery talk had captured a young man's heart during his college days. Tom loved her deeply, as Emma surely knew. Emma also understood her husband had to go where duty called, but life in Japan surely was not unfolding in ways she had expected. When she had pulled herself away from her family's bosom a little more than three years before, her anguish had been tempered by hopeful anticipation—she, Emma Brown Alexander, was traveling with her new husband to plant their faith in a barely plowed field halfway around the world. Now here she was, a sickly, twenty-five-year-old mother of two, who sometimes felt like someone twice her age.

Emma's fortitude was tested once again by the prospect of another separation from Tom. "About the end of February," Tom wrote,

> I got a letter from my friend and former [seminary] classmate, Rev. Thomas C. Winn, who had been laboring in Kanazawa (Japan) for a year or two, asking me to come and take his place for six weeks, so that he might come to Tokiyo [sic] and Yokohama on a visit. I finally decided to comply with this request, both because I needed the change myself and because I wanted

to accommodate my friend. It was, however, through Emma's influence that I decided to go, for she, always unselfish, urged me to go for my own health.

Emma urged him to go for his own health? Tom had never been robust, and a mysterious lung disease had afflicted him during his seminary studies in New York City, damaging his lungs and leaving him short of breath upon the slightest exertion. But his inner drive and mental fortitude had propelled him forward and helped him overcome any physical limitations he may have suffered. Maybe it was Tom's mental health, more than his physical well-being, that led Emma to urge him to go despite her own ailments. She knew Tom chafed under the tedium of day-to-day administrative work and thrived on new challenges. She also knew how much he longed to serve in Japan's interior. Whatever the reasons that allowed Tom to rationalize his departure, his journey to Japan's west coast would be something he would long remember. The trip would have taxed the resilience of even the hardiest traveler.

Leaving home on March 16, Tom journeyed south to Kobe by rickshaw, train, and steamer; then to Japan's old imperial capital of Kyoto; and on to a small town, Tsuruga, on Japan's west coast. From there, he faced the daunting prospect of a one-hundred-mile overland journey across towering mountain ranges dubbed the Japan Alps by foreigners familiar with the Swiss version. Northwest winds skimming across the Sea of Japan brought heavy precipitation to the area each winter, with some of the highest snowfall in the world accumulating on the range's north side. Although the Tokugawa shoguns had developed an extensive road system throughout much of Japan to speed travel and communication, this mountainous region was one of the country's most isolated areas, with roads that often were barely passable.

The roads were in "dreadful condition" as Tom began his overland trek, probably by rickshaw at the outset. Sometimes the driver would carry Tom across swollen creeks and rivers on his back and then return to pull his vehicle across the raging waters. Eventually, the rickshaw could not navigate the heavily rutted roads and steep grades of the rugged peaks, forcing Tom to proceed on foot over the roughest terrain. In some ways, he was more comfortable with this mode of transport, although by now he had grown accustomed to having a fellow human being play the role of beast of burden. In addition, walking helped him save scarce funds for more productive use in building up churches. Tom passed inns along the way but found he was not welcome in all of them, especially in this remote region where most people had never seen a foreigner. On more than one occasion during his travels, he sought shelter at unused Buddhist temples, sharing space with rats and other vermin, or asked local police for help in finding a place to sleep. He always tried to carry something to eat along the way, too, in case local tea houses or food vendors refused to serve him. Fortunately, that rarely happened in more heavily traveled areas.[3]

Tom tackled the steep climb up the mountainside the same way he tackled most of his challenges, by putting one foot in front of the other and persevering until he finally reached the top of Kinobe Pass. Winter had dumped nearly 5 feet of snow, now frozen on top from the relentless winds and frigid nights that had congealed thin layers of snow into a solid sheet of ice. Tom picked his way carefully across the hard, glistening surface, surely praying he would not fall through and find himself trapped inside the icy dome.

The breathtaking views must have helped Tom forget his fears, at least momentarily. Jagged peaks all around were clothed in a mantle of white, with hints of alpine greenery peeking through here and there. A lush blanket of evergreens, needles frosted with snow, covered the mountainsides from lower elevations on down to valley floors, where thatched-roof homes clustered close together in small villages. Tom's breaths came quick and shallow, as his weakened lungs struggled to suck enough oxygen out of the thin mountain air to fuel his burning leg muscles. Before long, he began his descent, undoubtedly relieved to be on the home stretch. After ten days of travel, Tom arrived in Kanazawa, bone tired but ready to take up his duties of teaching school, preaching on the Sabbath, and performing the work of bringing non-believers into the faith.

Kanazawa's setting made it seem an ideal place for anyone to live. Bordered on one side by the Sea of Japan and on the other by the Japan Alps, the city was famous for its arts and culture. Especially prized throughout Japan was the high-quality, paper-thin gold leaf used to decorate Buddhist temples, royal pavilions, and fine lacquer-ware. As Japan's fourth-largest city in one of the richest domains during the shoguns' rule, Kanazawa still was home to wealthy merchants and powerful old samurai families, whose massive estates encircled the turreted castle in the city's center. The castle's garden, opened to the public in 1875, offered strollers an enchanting retreat filled with trees, ponds, waterfalls, and flowers of all kinds.

In the sixteenth century, Kanazawa also had been home to Japan's only independent Buddhist state, when the Ikko-ikki, or "Single-Minded," sect established a Peasant's Kingdom in the naturally fortified location. Although civil authorities had long been in firm control of the city and surrounding region, a conservative brand of Buddhism still held strong sway over tradition-bound locals. Foreigners, especially those preaching an alien, subversive religion, were distinctly unwelcome. Thomas Winn had not minced words when describing his early days there:

> When I arrived in Kanazawa [in October 1879], I was teaching at the school and policemen guarded my house night and day, and whenever I went out, they accompanied me. I thought there was no need, but the government officials thought that it was necessary. One year before we came to Kanazawa, Japan's foreign minister was criticized for introducing too much western civilization, and was assassinated by Ichiro Shimada, originally from Kanazawa.
>
> Needless to say, at that time, foreigners and Japanese who favored and introduced western goods were severely despised. If we had known in advance how we would be treated and thought of by people in Kanazawa, we would have considered not coming to this area at all.[4]

Winn, like other missionaries serving in remote, rural locations experienced firsthand the anger and resentment harbored by people whose lives had been upended by changes forced on the country by the Meiji regime. He found himself in the middle of a tug of war between conservative forces, fueled in part by Buddhist priests, longing for a return to a more traditional Japan; and progressive forces supporting the regime's efforts to adopt Western ways. The Tokyo mission had agreed to send Winn to Kanazawa in 1879 to replace a young man, Willis Whitney, who had taught English and science for one year at a government-sponsored boys' school in Kanazawa. The school was so prestigious that the emperor himself had visited during Whitney's short tenure; and the regional governor, appointed by the emperor, had praised Whitney's work. But Whitney also had written home about Kanazawa inhabitants' strong dislike of foreigners. As a result, Whitney's family, who lived in the Tsukiji foreign settlement and was well-known to Tom and other missionaries, had occasionally feared for his safety. Evidently in response to an incident in early 1879 that had badly shaken Whitney, a local newspaper, the *Kanazawa Shimbun*, had extolled his character and praised his work at the school. Despite these public and private expressions of support, young Whitney had resigned his position before his contract expired and returned to Tokyo, appealing to Tom's fellow missionaries to send his replacement.

The Tokyo mission's seasoned missionaries with experience in Japan's treaty cities had expressed doubts about sending Winn to Kanazawa.

Although public signboards against Christianity had been removed throughout the empire in 1873, some missionaries doubted that any Christian
would be allowed to evangelize in the deeply conservative region. Others
even feared that missionary work might cause riots there. A highly regarded
Japanese Christian originally from Kanazawa also cautioned Winn against
taking the post. "If you are going to Kanazawa to spread Christianity, it is a
waste of your effort," Imamura Kenkichi told Winn as the missionary was
on his way to the city. "The other day I went back to Kanazawa and distributed [Christian] tracts to all my relatives. Then a policeman came over and
forbade me from continuing. Moreover, I could not even stay in Kanazawa."

But the mission also knew that Kanazawa offered distinct possibilities for spreading the gospel. Although not a missionary, Willis Whitney
had taught Bible classes to some young men in the school, and they wished
to continue their study. School authorities had readily agreed that Winn
could teach Christianity. Moreover, as Tom noted in the mission's minutes,
". . . Kanazawa is a good large city, situated on the opposite side of this Isle
and rather north of Tokio [sic], a little west. It is a much larger city than
Shimonoseki. We hope for great good from this movement" of sending missionaries to the city. In order to give Winn more time to engage directly in
Christian work, fellow missionary Mrs. M. T. True had agreed to accompany him to assist in teaching at the school. Despite the challenges they
knew they faced, Winn and True both viewed this opportunity as "a call of
God to go," Tom reported.[5]

Kanazawa was in many ways a microcosm of Japan, subject to the same
conflicting forces tearing at the fabric of Japanese society during a period of
rapid change. Some locals hated foreigners and their Japanese supporters in
equal measure for destroying a well-ordered society with clear rules, strong
moral values, and a strict class hierarchy that everyone had recognized and
respected, whether or not everyone always lived up to these ideals. Other
locals believed that Westerners were determined to block Japan's progress.
A conservative political group, the Eishinsha, was formed in the city in early
1880. In a pamphlet published in April of that year, the group singled out
Westerners as the enemy of a strong, prosperous Japan. "Look at those in-
satiable jackals, the blue-eyed, red-haired dogs polishing their sharp teeth
and stretching their hideous lips. Have they not always desired to seize and
gobble up weak and small nations?" In a clear challenge to the Meiji regime's
policy of Westernization, the pamphlet added, "Small and weak countries,
even if they cultivate wisdom and store up their strengths, cannot escape the
plunder and invasion of big countries."[6]

Christians were especially suspect in the eyes of some inhabitants of Japan's farther reaches like Kanazawa. In contrast to Japan's major cities, where

people were largely indifferent to Christianity and other religions, many rural dwellers and residents of more remote towns and cities harbored strong prejudices against the Western religion. Some of this hostility undoubtedly stemmed from centuries of official edicts warning people to stay away from the evil sect or risk death. Anti-Christian propaganda during the shoguns' long reign had included rumors of priests eating children and other humans and of Christian nations' efforts to subjugate Japan. Westerners traveling throughout Japan's countryside even in the late 1870s sometimes experienced the legacy of these teachings, as small children ran away in fright when spoken to or approached. The fact that warning signboards had disappeared and Christianity was no longer punishable by death had not removed the belief by some Japanese in inaccessible parts of the country that the religion still posed an indefinable danger to them and their families.[7]

Animosity toward Christianity also arose from the perceived conflict between it and Japan's native Shinto religion. Shinto, or "Way of the Gods," taught that ancestors, spirit figures, natural objects, and mythological forces all were gods containing a spiritual essence. The emperor ranked as the highest Shinto authority. According to widely accepted lore, he was the direct descendant of the sun goddess, Amaterasu Omikami, who had established Japan's imperial line. The emperor thus represented heaven on earth. Shortly after taking power, as the Meiji regime strived to unify Japan and centralize control in Tokyo, it had tried to promote Shintoism to reinforce popular reverence for the emperor. That effort had left little room for Christianity. As one Meiji official said in 1868, "To permit the instruction of the people in Christianity would mean the introduction of a second son of God, and it would never do to have two in the same country."[8] Although the regime had soon backed off its aggressive push for Shintoism, many Japanese nonetheless revered the emperor as a divine being in the "land of the gods." The most ardent believers viewed Japanese Christians as traitorous, even un-Japanese.

Shintoism, prejudice, and fear were not the only obstacles. Kanazawa's status as a center of conservative Buddhism posed an equally great challenge to Christian missionaries in the city and surrounding area. Buddhist priests throughout Japan were among the most strident opponents of Christianity. Unused Buddhist temples that offered shelter to Tom, Winn, and other travelers were a tangible sign of the decline in official support for the religion since the Meiji restoration. Once closely aligned with the ruling Tokugawa shoguns, Buddhism and Buddhist priests had lost some of their earlier prestige, along with crucial financial and political support, as the Meiji regime had embraced Shintoism and sought to distance itself from a doctrine closely associated with the shoguns.

Anti-Christian pamphlets and writings, many authored by Buddhist priests, had circulated in the empire beginning in 1868 and increased in number in the early 1870s. In the early 1880s, missionary journals reported on Buddhist attacks on Christianity and its followers. The anti-Christian campaign included not only public writings and lectures, but reportedly also bribes and threats made to Christian converts to return to their Buddhist roots. Some Buddhist priests encouraged neighbors to shun Christians and boycott their businesses. They accused Japanese Christians of disloyalty and of undermining the nation. Priests also sometimes sought to block mass Christian meetings in theaters.

Anti-foreign and anti-Christian animosity occasionally boiled over into violence. One prominent Christian in Kanazawa saw his home and furniture set ablaze by radicals opposed to his hosting Christian teaching sessions there. Other converts' businesses withered and died as previously loyal customers shunned them. Winn also was assaulted. Rowdy groups poured mud over his head after one preaching session and threw him into a river on another occasion. More than once, xenophobic locals urged on by Buddhist priests forced their way into Christian meeting rooms where Winn was preaching, squeezing the people inside into a tighter and tighter space while fiercely stamping their wooden sandals and scarring the soft floorboards. Winn found it harder and harder to convince anyone to rent out space for his preaching sessions.

Those incidents were not the worst he suffered, though. During one public preaching session in Takaoka, a town near Kanazawa, people in the crowd began to throw rocks at him. He continued preaching despite the danger. Then voices began to cry out, "Heretic," "Traitor," "Barbarian," "Christian Monk," adding that they were going to rid the area of Christians. Winn described in his diary what happened next.

> When the scheduled program ended, I thought it was dangerous to walk along the street, and got ready to go out with another [Japanese] preacher. The mob, carrying bamboo spears, broke the sliding door of the entrance, and peeped inside. I prayed for the grace of God, and though it took a little while to put on shoes, I decided to go into the midst of [the] mob. Now I ordinarily would not be able to do such a thing, but at that time I did.
>
> The mob just watched our behaviour, but just for a moment. An angry drunkard shouted, "Kill him, Kill him," and chased after me, showering me with pebbles. I turned to the mob and said "Watch out!" Then it became silent for a while. When I started walking, the mob was fiercely charging at us, but when I got into a dark alley I ran for my life, and somehow

things in back of me had become quiet. When I turned back the mob was fighting among themselves, so, greatly relieved, I was able to return to the inn.[9]

Winn later met a self-described hoodlum and former Sumo wrestler in Takaoka who had converted to Christianity. He told Winn that he had been part of the mob that had attacked him. When the wrestler had realized the mob intended to trap Winn and throw him in the river, he had turned and fought against them, probably saving Winn's life in the process. Another Japanese preacher had not been so lucky on a different occasion. Two thugs attacked him with wooden swords as he was walking by Prefectural Hall in Kanazawa after meeting with a local Christian. Slashing wildly at his head until he collapsed, they kicked him repeatedly in the groin as he lay on the ground moaning in pain. The young man, who had hoped to become an ordained minister, lingered near death for months until finally succumbing to his injuries.

Given such strong prejudice against Christianity, Tom must have been astonished that any locals in Kanazawa would risk life and livelihood by converting to Christianity, but they did. The very turmoil that had upset the world they knew had spurred their interest. Some former samurai, who had lost government stipends and high social status, viewed Christianity as a new pathway to prestige and influence in a Japan that was opening to the world. Some merchants also were drawn to the missionaries' teachings. Farmers struggling to make ends meet may have taken heart from the Christian message that "whoever plows should plow in hope and whoever threshes should thresh in hope of a share in the crop" (1 Cor 9:10) or perhaps from Jesus' promise, "Blessed are the poor in spirit, for theirs is the kingdom of heaven" (Matt 5:3). Other locals may have sought out Christianity in response to the Meiji regime's entreaties to seek wisdom and knowledge throughout the world. Still others may simply have been curious.

Whatever the reasons, the contradictory impulses of conservatism on the one hand and an embrace of change on the other played out in full force during Winn's first months in Kanazawa. Large audiences had attended his early preaching sessions, which he and his small band of supporters advertised—after receiving police permission—by posting signs inviting people to come hear the Christian message. Within a few months of his arrival, three assembly halls in various parts of the city were needed to accommodate the crowds, and new believers had emerged little by little. Soon they began to petition the Tokyo mission for establishment of a new church.

After Tom arrived for his six-week stint in Kanazawa, Winn sought much-needed rest in Tokyo and Yokohama. Tom picked up Winn's work in the region, leading Bible studies, preaching the gospel, and guiding local Christians on the steps necessary to form a church. Tom reported no physical attacks during his time there, but he must have experienced some of the locals' hostility in the form of cold stares or worse. True to his stoic nature, though, he never complained about personal slights or setbacks he experienced in his work or travels in Kanazawa or elsewhere. For despite anti-foreign and anti-Christian attitudes that pervaded parts of Japanese society, Tom found much to admire about the country and its people.

And while he certainly could not excuse the violence and persecution directed at Japanese Christians or his fellow missionaries, Tom must have understood the pain and anguish suffered by those who were lashing out at a convenient target for their anger. Having lived through America's Civil War, he had seen families divided and a nation torn asunder by forces that had swept people up into a maelstrom of emotion and righteous indignation, with each side convinced God was on its side. The scars from America's Civil War had not healed more than a decade after its end, and so Tom could not have been surprised that many Japanese still were reeling from the collapse of their old way of life. He also surely took to heart Jesus' admonition: "Love your enemies and pray for those who persecute you . . . for he makes his sun rise on the evil and on the good, and sends rain on the righteous and on the unrighteous" (Matt 5:44–45).

Despite their many challenges, Tom took heart from progress he and his fellow Christian workers were making in Kanazawa. After Winn returned, Tom joined him and two Japanese ministers in a ceremony on May 1, 1881, establishing the Kanazawa Japan Christian Church with more than twenty converts.[10] Tom left for Tokyo the next day, arriving eight days later. Absent from Tokyo more than seven weeks, he made it home in time to celebrate his and Emma's fourth anniversary on May 21. Tom's experiences in Kanazawa had opened his eyes to the formidable obstacles facing the church in Japan. Far from discouraging him from wanting to serve in a mission field outside the capital, though, his experiences had only whetted his appetite.

Tom's time would come soon enough.

Notes

1. Various contemporary accounts report strong animosity toward foreigners (especially Westerners) in Shimonoseki and Kanazawa. One noted American scientist and visitor, Edward S. Morse, wrote ca. 1880 in *Japan*, Vol. II, 179–80: "I was told that the people [of Shimonoseki] were very unfriendly to foreigners, and no wonder when one recalls the cruel bombardment years ago by the warships of four Christian nations. . . . I walked through the main streets of the town and peered into every shop. I could readily see that a foreigner was *persona non grata*. I was not treated rudely, but was simply ignored. The children ran from me as if I were the Devil, and one sweet little boy, whom I could not resist patting, held his breath as if it required the greatest courage to endure the caresses of the hated foreigner."

Mounting opposition to the perceived absolutism, favoritism, and corruption of top imperial advisors led to the growth of a popular movement for representative government and individual liberty and equality—concepts inspired in part by Western political thinkers, such as John Stuart Mill. From the first organized effort in 1874, the movement gained traction in the late 1870s, particularly after Saigo Takamori's defeat by imperial troops in the Satsuma Rebellion of 1877. By 1880, the movement had united a widely diverse group of individuals across the country, and numerous local political associations flooded the government with petitions for reform.

Mr. Shina (first name unknown) was an active member of this movement in Yanagawa, according to research in 2014 by the Reverend Inaba Hajime, pastor of Yanagawa Church. Shina's exposure to the egalitarian nature of Christian teachings and the democratic aspects of Presbyterian tenets may have influenced his political views. For information on the freedom and people's rights movement, see Vlastos, "Opposition Movements," 238–61, and Cody, "Itagaki Taisuke," 102–54. Itagaki Taisuke of the Tosa region would become the most prominent leader of this movement.

2. "The Japanese preachers' work": Letter to Lowrie, BFM, June 3, 1880. "'Now is the time'": Letter to Lowrie, January 19, 1881. PCUSA, "Correspondence."

3. The difficulties of finding inns in the inaccessible region where Tom traveled on this trip are described in "The Life of Mrs. Winn," cited in Nakazawa, *Winn*, 18–19. Her group's experiences took place less than two years before Tom traveled to Kanazawa. In addition, one Japanese Christian wrote about a mission trip with Rev. Winn on August 8, 1881, just a few months after Tom's journey to Kanazawa: "In early modern Japan there were no inns which would accept foreign missionaries and we thus asked a policeman to find us a place to stay." Nakazawa, *Winn*, 29. In his journal, Tom describes staying in vacant Buddhist temples on occasion.

4. Nakazawa, *Winn*, 22. The powerful Meiji politician and minister Okubo Toshimichi was assassinated May 14, 1878, by a group of men led by Shimada, a former samurai. The assassins turned themselves in and were executed later that year.

5. Information about Whitney's experiences in Kanazawa is drawn from Whitney, *Clara's Diary*, 196, 206, 217, 221, 226, and 261. He is identified as Winn's predecessor and as having resigned before his contract had expired in Nakazawa, *Winn*, 16. For "If you are going to Kanazawa," see Nakazawa, *Winn*, 17. Tokyo Mission minutes of September 10 and September 20, 1879, record the decision to send Winn

to Kanazawa to replace "a Christian gentleman . . . [who] resigned his position." The school in question is the Ishikawa Prefectural Teacher's School. PCUSA, "Correspondence." With his mother's and his sister Clara's help, "Willie" Whitney eventually found work in Tokyo as a translator with the US legation, America's official representation in Japan. Whitney, *Clara's Diary*, 240 and 320.

6. Baxter, *Meiji Unification*, 214–15.

7. For examples of anti-foreign and anti-Christian attitudes and propaganda in rural areas and Shimonoseki, see Bird, *Unbeaten Tracks*, 203–5; Thomas, *Protestant Beginnings*, 47, and Morse, *Japan*, Vol. II, 180.

8. Cited in Burkman, "Urakami Incidents," 180.

9. Nakazawa, *Winn*, 36. Incidents described here occurred between 1879 and 1883. The young Japanese preacher killed in August 1883 was Kato Toshiyuki, 37.

10. The ministers were Aoyama Shozaburo of Akamagaseki (as Shimonoseki once was known), who often accompanied Tom on his travels in central and southern Japan, and Aoki Nakahide, head pastor of Tokyo's Rogetsu-cho Church. Nakazawa, *Winn*, 28–29.

CHAPTER 8

A New Calling

*We felt almost as sad on leaving Tokiyo as on leaving our homes
in America.*

Life in Tokyo resumed its normal rhythms after Tom's return from
Kanazawa. Work consumed more and more of his time, but he relished
coming home on those evenings without committee meetings or Bible studies to join Emma and the girls. He delighted Ella and young Emma with the
stories he read to them before bed. Among their favorites were Japanese
fairy tales, translated into English by the Reverend Hepburn and other
missionaries and bound into small, crepe paper books with pretty pastel
illustrations from colored woodcuts. *The Tongue-Cut Sparrow, The Old Man
Who Made the Dead Trees Blossom*, and other tales taught the girls useful
lessons about the value of kindness and honesty.[1] After the girls were tucked
in, Tom often worked in his study or joined Emma by the fire, where they
shared quiet hours reading, relaxing, and catching up on each other's day.

News on the mission front was largely positive, at least in Tokyo. After many months of lobbying by Tom and his colleagues, the home mission
board had authorized moving the Protestant boys' school from Yokohama to
the larger, more influential capital city. Opened on April 26, 1880, with twenty students, the number quickly grew to fifty-five, "with our refusal to take
any more after the first part of June," Tom's coworker, John Ballagh, reported
to the board. "We hope to open the 15th of September with a greater increase
in number. We have accommodations for over seventy boarders. About
three fourths of the attendants are boarders. . . . We have given it "Tsukiji
Dai Gakku" [college or university] for a name. The natives were unanimous
in the choice of this from several suggested. It aims high, which we think
will not be amiss. The course stops at present only one year short of the great
Imperial College, which year may be added if we see fit in course of time."
The missionaries' hopes were fulfilled. By October, more than one hundred

students had enrolled, and the students' fees fully covered the school's expenses. Within a year, the mission had added another year of study.

Tom with Ella and Emma, ca. 1882

The school's full enrollment and financial success bolstered Tom's hopes that it would become a viable Christian alternative to the government-supported Imperial College, considered the most prestigious in the country. "We are glad to have it in a city where its influence will be more widely felt than in Yokohama," Tom wrote. "The short time we have had it in Tokiyo has been more successful than we had expected."[2] As Tom had predicted a few years earlier, Imperial College had begun ousting foreign professors and replacing them with Japanese instructors, as the popular sentiment, "Japan for the Japanese," began to influence government policies and actions. Many Japanese had grown increasingly resentful of their dependence on foreigners for advice and expertise and were pressing the government and private entities alike to oust the foreigners in favor of increasingly able Japanese experts.

A new girls' school, eventually named Joshi Gakuin, also was an immediate success. Opened July 20, 1881, in the heart of Tokyo, the first classes began on August 10. Mrs. M. T. True, who had accompanied Tom's fellow missionary, T. C. Winn, to Kanazawa, had returned to Tokyo and turned her energies to establishing a school that missionaries hoped would provide as solid an academic preparation for girls in Japan as Mount Holyoke did in

America. The eighty-four students in its inaugural class included "daughters of families of good rank," True reported. The Tokyo Governor's wife personally delivered their niece to school on her first day. Also attending were two daughters of the Kyoto Governor and the daughter of another region's governor. In addition to these young women from high-ranking families were students from poor families, who received financial support from the mission.

The girls' school was not immune from concerns about foreigners being forced out. True noted that mission workers at the school had a five-year permit from the government, "but even if they end up not being able to stay that long, the able native teachers should be able to carry on the work well." Despite these concerns, the schools' success and the growing acceptance of Christianity, at least in Tokyo and other cities with better educated populations, gave Tom every reason to feel optimistic about the future.

Summers brought welcome relief from routine, and this year was no different. Tom, Emma, and the girls spent the month of August 1881 in the seaside village of Tomioka near Yokohama, giving them a refreshing change of scenery and uninterrupted family time together. Warm sunshine, waves breaking gently onto shore, salty sea mist, and spare living quarters in an old Buddhist temple relaxed their minds and bodies in equal measure.

Then the opportunity Tom had waited for finally arrived. The missionaries' work in Japan's southern and central regions had progressed so well that they decided they needed a new mission station in the field. After weighing various locations, they chose Osaka, a thriving commercial center of about thirty-seven thousand located on Japan's southern coast, not far from the old imperial capital of Kyoto. As the largest city in central-southern Japan and a center of culture and trade, Osaka made sense as a home base for expanding the missionaries' reach into that region. The question then became, who would head up the new station?

The prospect of moving to Osaka and opening a new mission station appealed to Tom, but he hesitated to step forward. He handled most of the boys' school's administrative work, directed its English-language studies, and taught several classes. Who would take on these duties if he left? The more he thought about it, though, the more the move made good sense. He already bore responsibility for mission efforts in Shimonoseki and Kanazawa, and the rapidly expanding work in those regions needed more attention and care than could be provided from Tokyo. Thomas Winn also hoped for reinforcement for his labors in the Kanazawa area. In addition to these very practical reasons, a move to Osaka also resonated with Tom's strong sense of duty. As he explained to a colleague, "[A]bove all things, I think a missionary ought to be free from anything like a set of cast-iron rules—that is to say, he ought not to be a fixture, <u>bound</u> to any one place or to any one line of work, but he ought to be willing to go anywhere and to do anything that by the grace of God he can do."[3]

After weighing the pros and cons with Emma, Tom volunteered to go, and his colleagues readily supported his decision. He worked with another missionary to write a constitution outlining the relationship between the new mission station and the old one in Tokyo and establishing principles for its operation. Then, in early 1882, Tom and Emma, now three months pregnant with their third child, began the laborious task of preparing to move.

> Emma's health was still delicate and I feared somewhat the effects of the worry which would necessarily attend the breaking of our house and moving to a new place. Moreover, it seemed difficult to get anyone to take my place as teacher in the boys' school. But at long last everything was arranged and we decided to take passage on board the "*Genkai Maru*" to Kōbe on the first day of March.
>
> No one, who has never gone through the experience, knows what an amount of bother there is in getting ready to move from one place to another. I attended to the packing of all our furniture, Emma helping as much as she could, and more than I thought she ought. I took our goods through the custom house at Tokiyo, then through the custom house at Yokohama and finally got them on board the steamer on which we were to sail.
>
> Before we broke up housekeeping, however, all our Mission came one evening bringing with them a sumptuous repast and gave us a farewell party. This little act touched our hearts, for it showed that we held a place in the affections of all our fellow workers. . . .
>
> We were very sorry to leave Tokiyo. It had been our first home, and we had formed many ties of friendship among the people there. It is strange how quickly this poor human nature of ours becomes attached to places. We felt almost as sad on leaving Tokiyo as on leaving our homes in America.

Tom and Emma lived in Osaka's foreign concession, which was bordered by the Yodo River and one of the city's many canals. Their home at No. 14 Kawaguchi had been built by Japanese carpenters trained in the art of Western craftsmanship. A solid brick wall topped by decorative red clay tile fronted the property. Its entrance was flanked by two granite posts that held a tall, double-door gate, whose topline curved upward into a *fleur-de-lis*. A profusion of trees and tall shrubs obscured the view of the house from the street, and a 7-foot-high bamboo fence offered privacy on the other three sides. Inside the wall, a huge ironwood tree shaded the front garden and a two-seater swing placed there for carefree moments of quiet contemplation or easy conversation.

Osaka home, No. 14 Kawaguchi

On steamy summer days, when the family traded the stifling indoor atmosphere for the fresher air of the gazebo outside, the unmistakable scent of sage arose from herbs planted at the base of a palm tree in a rock garden nearby. A big honey locust tree, whose delicate pink and white flowers and slender, ocher seedpods marked the changing seasons, grew in the small backyard near the family well. A two-story servant quarters located next to the coal shed in back was occupied by the family's nanny, O-Chise-san, whom the family addressed with the honorific "o" and "san" to show their respect.

The house's interior was huge by Japanese standards, although not by American ones. The ground floor boasted a living room and separate dining room, formal parlor and adjoining guest room, kitchen, and family toilet just off the back porch. A large, airy study completed the floor plan. The center of home life for Emma and the children was the living room, where a fireplace offered welcome warmth on the damp, cold days of fall, winter, and early spring. The children passed many hours there doing schoolwork, memorizing gospel passages, and, when they were old enough, deciphering notes from various piano pieces as they plunked the keys of the small upright. Emma oversaw the children's play and homework, while sewing, reading, and composing frequent letters to her family in America. Every morning, after Tom had led the family in worship, they all gathered around the piano and sang hymns chosen for that day.

Tom and Emma eventually renovated the Georgian-style house, adding a second story for reasons of space and health. When they had moved in, the home's three bedrooms had been located on the ground floor in back. Not only were they dark, but they also were surrounded on three sides by neighbors' stables and outhouses. Moving them to a new second floor allowed more air and light to enter and also removed their inhabitants from the unhealthy, sometimes foul smelling atmosphere of the ground floor. Tom and Emma also added a second-floor master bedroom for themselves, with windows on three sides offering splendid views and, on nice spring days, cool breezes from the bay.

As they settled into their new home, Emma began the work of running the household and teaching O-Chise-san the particular likes and dislikes of the Alexander family. And just six months after moving in, on September 21, 1882, Emma gave birth to their third child. Theron Ralph Alexander was, according to Tom, "a strong, healthy child who seemed to think that the 'chief end of man' was to eat and sleep." O-Chise-san doted on Theron and treated him with a deference that Japanese reserved for the heir of the family. As the only boy in the family, young Theron relished this special attention from his nanny and older sisters, but as he grew, Tom was concerned he might become spoiled. He kept the lad mindful of his manners and of his responsibilities as the young man of the household. Tom, more than Emma, also disciplined their other, strong-willed children. Even though he loved to delight them with jokes and stories, his steely eyes would bore right through them if they acted up, and they would hop to obey.

Between committee work, Bible studies, and other church activities, Tom had more than his share of evening meetings. Even when he was home, he spent many hours in his study, which adjoined the living room and shared its two-sided fireplace. He loved family life, but his heavy workload and contemplative nature often drew him into the quiet seclusion of his own room. Two big windows in front and one in back gave him enough natural light during the day to read, compose sermons, and write in his journal. Oil lamps and candles lit up the darker evening hours. Despite the warmth of the fireplace, Tom often donned a thick wool sweater to ward off the penetrating cold of Osaka's damp winters. The children usually asked his permission before interrupting him, but sometimes they burst into his study to ask him questions or tell him something exciting. Their antics helped keep Tom from being too weighed down by his cares, including the sense of loneliness he sometimes felt as the only missionary from his church serving the area's small community of believers.

Emma with Theron, early 1883

Young Emma (2), Theron, Ella (4), early 1883

Tom's first big challenge was to hire enough missionaries to handle the growing workload in the central, southern, and western regions of the empire. Since more than half of all missionaries by this time were women, it was not surprising that Tom sought female missionaries to serve alongside the men. He asked the foreign mission board in New York City for $4000 to build a girls' school and hire four female teachers from America. He was pleased when the board agreed to provide the money and staff he requested but bristled at efforts to saddle him with several more teachers from an unrelated organization with no additional funds to pay them.

Convinced that the board's proposal would complicate his management of the mission station and overstretch his meager budget, Tom argued strenuously against sending the additional personnel. Tom undoubtedly also wanted to establish his own firm authority over the mission station from the outset. He didn't mince words in objecting to the board's suggestion, concluding a letter tersely but clearly: "And so far as I am concerned myself, I can never willingly assent to such an arrangement, but if forced into it would make the best of a bad bargain by having as little to do with it as possible."[4] The board ended up sending just the four teachers Tom had requested.

In addition to hiring novice teachers and a few other young missionaries, Tom welcomed the addition of more experienced workers. One of them was a world-famous scientist, Dr. John Thomas Gulick. A fellow graduate of Tom's alma mater, Union Theological Seminary, Gulick had opened a mission station in China before transferring to Japan. Like many missionaries, he combined theological training with expertise in another field. Gulick was a noted naturalist and widely published scholar, whose work on natural selection had earned him the reputation as ranking second only to Charles Darwin in the emerging field of evolution. His studies, conducted mostly in Japan and Hawaii, advanced biologists' understanding of how species evolve in isolated island environments. The great Darwin himself encouraged Gulick in his research.

Young Theron Alexander, a sensitive boy with large brown eyes and a head of golden curls, loved to shadow Dr. Gulick on his local scientific forays. The slight man and the small boy, each with a butterfly net and cyanide jar in hand, were a familiar sight in the foreign concession: Dr. Gulick clad in a swallow-tail coat with two buttons at the back; Theron in a sailor blouse, blue cotton shorts, and black shoes and stockings following close behind. Theron later took his collection of butterflies, moths, snakes, and toads home with him to America. He may have dreamed of becoming a scientist like his much-admired friend, but ultimately, Theron followed in his father's footsteps and became a Presbyterian minister.

Although young Theron knew Dr. Gulick only as the man who liked insects, snails, and other creatures that crept, crawled, and flitted, Gulick's work had a profound impact on Tom and his views on evolution. Already open-minded on the subject, Tom saw how comfortably his missionary colleague blended his devout Christian beliefs with his scientific discoveries. Gulick saw no conflict between religion and science when it came to God's plan for the world. If Tom ever had harbored doubts about his view that evolution is God's way of bringing about change in species, Gulick's views on the matter surely put those doubts to rest.

As head of the mission station, Tom began a life of travel to far-flung areas by steamer, boat, rickshaw, and foot. Before each trip, he applied for an inland passport from Tokyo's foreign ministry authorizing him to journey outside Osaka, where he and his family had official permission to live. The Meiji regime still refused to allow foreigners to live and travel where they chose, in retaliation against Western powers' repeated refusals to renegotiate the unequal treaties forced on Japan in the late 1850s. Despite years of diplomatic effort, Japan still had not achieved its highest foreign policy goal. Government officials and the Japanese public deeply resented the West's refusal to treat Japan as an equal by restoring its sovereignty over foreign trade and home justice. Growing popular and official anger over the continuing affront to national pride eventually would erupt in a fierce backlash against foreigners.

Tom ventured into the old imperial capital of Kyoto, bringing his mission's work for the first time to this conservative city, where Buddhism and tradition had deep roots. He also journeyed to towns and villages located hundreds of miles southwest of Osaka, including Shimonoseki, Nagasaki, Toyora, Yanagawa, Hiroshima, Yamaguchi, Kagoshima, and others. He was the only foreign missionary to attend every meeting of the Chinzei Presbytery, the regional church governing body for southern Japan, traveling great distances each spring and fall to join the gatherings.[5] His trips often took him away for weeks at a time and frequently left him so exhausted he could barely make it home. When he did come home, though, nothing revived his spirits as much as seeing Ella, young Emma, and Theron bounding into the road to greet him, grabbing his hands and clinging to his pant legs, asking if he had brought them any toys or souvenirs from his trip.

Because the mission focused more on evangelistic work than education, progress was slow at first. Except for the girls' school in Osaka, the mission had no English-language studies to attract students who could be introduced to the gospel as part of their coursework. And despite a growing acceptance of Christianity among better educated urban dwellers and the Meiji regime's tolerance of the religion, Tom and his fellow missionaries still encountered Japanese, especially in rural areas, small towns, and cities far from Tokyo, who persecuted Christians and the foreigners who preached the long-outlawed religion. Xenophobic locals frequently targeted one of Tom's coworkers, a Japanese minister working in Hiroshima in the early 1880s. Hooligans often threw rocks into his lecture hall, leading him to keep all doors and windows shut tight during preaching sessions, even on hot summer days. Christian workers in Nagasaki, Kyoto, and other cities recounted similar experiences. In the south, a zealous group of locals formed a society, the Kui Kai, for the express purpose of blocking the spread of Christianity. Even in Osaka, Tom periodically moved the preaching hall from one place to another to avoid harassment.

Little by little, though, the Christian message spread as popular interest in Western ways grew. In Hiroshima, several believers were joined by four newly baptized imperial soldiers from the local garrison in petitioning the Osaka mission for establishment of a church. Tom took part in a church founding ceremony on November 28, 1883—opening the gathering with prayer, giving a lecture to the congregation, and serving communion. Two Japanese colleagues joined Tom in the worship service, offering their own prayers, baptizing new converts, and preaching the sermon. They welcomed thirteen men, five women, and one child into the fold that day. And they kept the doors of the worship hall wide open.[6]

Public preaching meetings also began to attract large crowds of people, often numbering in the hundreds, who listened quietly and respectfully for two to three hours at a time. Tom sometimes found his energy and time stretched thin by the demands placed upon him and his fellow preachers of the gospel. In April 1885, he traveled with another missionary to Yanagawa on Japan's southern-most island of Kyushu, arriving late one evening in a cold, drenching downpour.

> We were tired and hungry and therefore put up at a hotel immediately in order to get a good night's rest before making known our arrival to the Christians who were expecting us. We succeeded in getting that night's rest undisturbed.
>
> Early next morning we made known our arrival and there was not much more rest for us after that. We found the work going on rapidly and we could not meet the demands upon our time and strength. The second day after our arrival we went in response to an urgent appeal to a village 5 or 6 miles from

Yanagawa and held a preaching service. The meeting was well attended, many of the town officials and chief men of the place being present.

On Sabbath we had preaching in the morning followed by the celebration of the Lord's Supper. Twenty-five persons were baptized. In the evening we had preaching for unbelievers, to which a goodly number came—among them a [Buddhist] priest or two and other intelligent men.

Working alongside other mission workers, including a growing number of Japanese Christians, Tom eventually established churches in many of the towns he visited. He took part in countless baptisms, church founding ceremonies, and ordinations of lay officers, in addition to preaching and leading Bible studies. He also conducted some of the first Christian funeral services in the south—a practice long prohibited due either to official or Buddhist opposition. Despite the challenges he and his fellow Christian workers faced, Tom felt highly encouraged by the signs of progress he witnessed during his travels.

Tom's travels exposed him to a side of Japan that foreigners and city residents rarely saw. The Meiji Government's push for modernization had brought gas lights, railways, brick buildings, and stone bridges to Tokyo and other big cities, but those amenities had not made it into Japan's rural areas. Even as Japan's overall wealth rose, peasants and villagers in the provinces remained mired in poverty, and the income gap between the urban elite and rural lower classes grew wider than it had been even during the shogun's rule. As the high cost of the government's spending spree started to spark inflation, Japan's tough-minded finance minister, Matsukata Masayoshi, clamped down with an austerity program that raised taxes and sent prices tumbling, including for Japan's main food crop, rice. An economic depression struck in 1882 and lasted four long years.

Uprisings in 1884 and 1885 by peasants seeking relief from high taxes, high debt, and countless bankruptcies were suppressed by government troops. Bad weather that winter added to farmers' misery, as crop failures led to widespread famine and starvation throughout much of the countryside. Suicides rose sharply, and reports of infanticide were common among poor families unable to feed growing families. Girls, sometimes as young as five or six, often were sent to work in silk and cotton factories or to officially sanctioned brothels in Tokyo and other cities, where they were held in virtual slavery.

Peasants were not the only ones feeling the pinch. Japan's local rulers, especially those in the independent-minded regions of the south and southwest, grew increasingly resentful of Tokyo's tightening grip on power. During his travels, Tom had heard growing calls for a constitution and a democratically elected parliament to guarantee people's rights and limit Tokyo's increasingly authoritarian rule. A prominent southwestern leader and former samurai named Itagaki Taisuke had even formed one of Japan's first political parties, the Liberal Party, or Jiyuto, to push for stronger civil rights and Asia's first constitution. Before long, Tom and his fellow missionaries would find themselves drawn into the fray.

Notes

1. The books noted here are among those given to me by my Grandmother Evie. The Japanese Fairy Tale Series was published by Takejiro Hasegawa, beginning in 1885. Even though it was not precisely these books that Tom read in this scene occurring in 1881, the fact is that Tom read to his children and that these books were valued possessions of the Alexander children.

2. Ballagh to Lowrie, BFM, August 17, 1880; Alexander to Lowrie, October 15, 1880; True to Lowrie, October 10, 1881. PCUSA, "Correspondence." Joshi Gakuin was formed in September 1889 by combining Shinsakae Jogakko and Sakurai Jogakko. International Christian University, *Chronology*, 76.

3. To Lowrie, BFM, March 30, 1882. PCUSA, "Correspondence."

4. To Lowrie, BFM, January 22, 1883. PCUSA, "Correspondence."

5. *Acts of the Chinzei [Kyushu] Presbytery*. Tom made these tiring trips to Kyushu as late as April 1893, after which he relocated to Tokyo.

6. The minister targeted was Takagi Kumajiro. Kujinosuke, "Recollections." The ministers taking part in the church founding ceremony in 1883 were Hattori Shozo and Takagi Kumajiro, minister of the church. Hiroshima Church, *History*.

   For experiences of missionaries in Kyoto and other cities, see for example, Cary, *History of Christianity*, 235–37. One anti-Christian tract distributed in Kyoto in 1884 was addressed to "Four American Barbarians," all missionaries, and signed by "Patriots in the peaceful city, believers in Shinto." It read in part: "I speak to you who have come with words which are sweet in the mouth but a sword in the heart, bad priests; American barbarians; four robbers. You have come from a far country with the evil religion of Christ. . . . We do not want to defile the sacred soil of Japan with your blood; for this reason, we will wait two weeks, and you must leave Kyoto and go to your country, if not the little robbers of Doshisha [Christian] school and all believers of this way in the city will be killed." See also Thomas, *Protestant Beginnings*, 161–62, for a discussion of anti-Christian sentiments that persisted even at a time of the religion's growth in the period 1883–89.

CHAPTER 9

An Opposition Leader Reaches Out

Mr. Itagaki had promised to lend his influence in favor of the [Christian] movement.

The Alexander family continued to grow with the addition of a third daughter and fourth child, born September 10, 1884. She was an easy, cheerful baby with black hair and dark grey eyes, but finding a name for her proved to be harder than Tom or Emma had imagined.

> Emma and I decided to give the baby a name not worn by any of our kindred. We, however, came near having to repent of our rash decision, for no sooner would one of us suggest a name than the other would mention some unfortunate relative who had borne the same name.
>
> Some of our friends thought to come to our assistance; but after suggesting various odd names and finding that some of our kindred could boast of having the same, they gave it up in disgust, leaving us to our own resources again.
>
> After a long time, we finally decided to call the baby for [a friend's] grandmother, Lois. This was Emma's suggestion and for once I failed to bring forward the memory of any relative who had borne that name.

Emma's health was better than it had been, and soon she was up and going about the house again. The nanny, O-Chise-san, seemed to take each new ward of hers in stride, making sure that each child was fed and dressed for the day's activities, even as she carried the baby around the house in a wrap on her back. Because O-Chise-san kept up near-constant chatter in her native Japanese tongue, the children soon gained a natural fluency in the language that Tom and Emma were working so hard to master.

As soon as Emma had regained her strength—and just weeks after Lois' birth—Tom left for a three-week tour of churches in Shimonoseki, Toyora, and Yanagawa in the company of fellow missionary C. M. Fisher. While they found the condition of some of the churches a bit disappointing, they took heart from the good work taking place in Yanagawa, where they baptized thirteen converts. They also took heart from the widespread acceptance of Christianity evident in the fall of 1884.

> We were glad to see signs of interest in Christianity manifested by the people everywhere we went, and our meetings at various places for preaching were very frequent and very well attended. I found the tour much more enjoyable than any of my former ones, for two reasons—one of which was the fact that I was able to speak more freely in the native tongue and so could preach more easily and satisfactorily than ever before. The other reason was that I had, in Mr. F., a most agreeable and helpful traveling companion. All my previous tours had been made alone.

In addition to progress in the southern reaches of his mission territory, Tom reported "greater prosperity" in the mission's work in Osaka. "In September, we were very fortunate in being reinforced by Mr. Yoshioka [Koki] from To-kiyo, who came down and gave his time and strength solely to preaching the Gospel and trying to build up a church. During the year [1884], I baptized in the city nineteen persons, and our prospects grew brighter and brighter."

Tom with Rev. Tada Hiroshi and family in Osaka, ca. 1884.
Tada would become the first pastor of Kochi Church in Tosa.

Tom's kindness, modesty, and strong work ethic appealed to the Japanese he met during his travels, as did the sincere interest he took in their lives. They learned to appreciate him more and more as someone who not only understood their culture, but also as someone who did not look down on them, as so many Westerners did. When Tom visited the church in Ozu on Shikoku Island's west coast, he was the first Westerner Aoyama Hikotoro had ever seen. Aoyama, who became very active in the church, later described Tom as a "rare, gentle, and sincere person; a gentleman who loved his studies. I've never seen him get angry or talk in a loud voice. Always smiling, he made me feel as if he was my kind father. I've never seen such a refined personality as Dr. Alexander, even among all missionaries and my fellow Christians. I would like to call him god-like or Christ-like. Dr. Alexander is responsible for making me as I am."[1] Tom, ever humble, would have been embarrassed by his friend's words, but Aoyama's view was shared by many of his Japanese brethren.

Tom undoubtedly surprised his Japanese acquaintances by sitting down to talk with Buddhist priests, who sometimes came to his preaching sessions. Although a confirmed Christian, Tom saw much to admire in Buddhist teachings. He also knew that to be an effective evangelist of the Christian faith, he should understand the tenets of one of Japan's leading religions. Tom upset his fellow missionaries more than once by saying that a good Buddhist stood as good a chance of getting into heaven as a good Christian. But his colleagues' disapproval didn't bother him. Tom was used to saying what was on his mind, whether other people liked it or not.

Tom's strong independent streak didn't always help him with his missionary colleagues, but it did help him understand that same impulse in the Japanese Christian community. Japanese Christians, especially the proud descendants of samurai warriors who formed the backbone of the early church, wanted to break away from missionary control and take the reins of their own churches. Tom understood and supported their aspirations. If Christianity ever was to grow and flourish in Japan, the Japanese themselves, not foreign missionaries, would have to build its foundations. Tom did all he could in private to support Japanese preachers in their work, but in public, he often stood on the sidelines and let them take center stage. Many years later, the Reverend Arima S., whom Tom had guided into the ministry, spoke about Tom's humility and his deference to Japanese colleagues. Speaking of one preaching session in Osaka, Arima recalled, "Dr. Alexander said, 'The people will gather to see a foreigner, so I am the sign-board to draw them to hear you preach the gospel.' And such a man," he continued, "called himself a sign-board for such as me!"[2]

Japan's political climate grew more and more unsettled as the regime in Tokyo centralized power and clamped down on free speech. Acting in the emperor's name, officials censored and even closed newspapers, shutting off an important outlet for pro-democracy activists. Government troops broke up rallies by opposition groups calling for greater civil rights and democratic elections. In the eyes of those Japanese intellectuals and political leaders who had supported Emperor Meiji in his battle to overthrow the despotic shogun, the new regime's moves were taking the country backwards. What had happened to the Charter Oath, they wondered, the set of principles the emperor had sworn to uphold when he had assumed power in 1868? The oath had promised deliberative national assemblies and open public debate on matters of state. Surely the pledges made so recently were not being thrown out so quickly and easily. Activists familiar with Western constitutions and political systems took the lead in pressing for greater freedom and popular rights.

Perhaps realizing they could not stop the tide of popular opinion or perhaps to avoid a repeat of Japan's violent Satsuma Rebellion which had led to Saigo Takamori's death, the emperor's advisors wrote a decree, approved and issued by the emperor in 1881, promising the adoption of a constitution by 1889 and the convening of a national assembly the following year. The big question was, what kind of constitution would it be, and who would write it? The emperor's counselors argued that the people were the servants of the emperor and that all the land in Japan also belonged to him. According to this reasoning, only the emperor could say what the constitution should contain, and these aides were more than happy to take the lead in drafting it.

Japan's democracy activists disagreed, and the most prominent among them, Itagaki Taisuke, stepped forward to press for a more open process. Itagaki was well-positioned to lead. He had helped overthrow the shogun in 1868 and had served as senior advisor to the new emperor until resigning in 1873. Unlike his former colleague and samurai-turned-rebel, Saigo Takamori, who had led thousands of men to their deaths in the failed Satsuma Rebellion, Itagaki wished to pursue change in peaceful ways. He believed the best way to do that was through the force of ideas. "Saigo fights the government with arms, but we will fight it with people's rights," Itagaki proclaimed.

Itagaki and his followers argued for a system of shared power, with authority divided between the emperor and the people. A constitution would enshrine the emperor as the head of the nation like the king or queen of England but also would put more control into the hands of an elected national assembly. By sharing power, Itagaki reasoned, the emperor actually would be in a stronger position, because people would not likely rebel against a leader who respected their rights.

Itagaki's revolutionary ideas ran into stiff opposition, not only from the regime in Tokyo, but also from many of the emperor's loyal subjects. They saw Itagaki's proposals as an affront to the emperor's divine status. They also believed that democracy would upset Japan's much-heralded social order, which already had passed through tremendous turmoil following the overthrow of the shogun. An enraged, knife-wielding school teacher shouting "Traitor!" tried to kill Itagaki in 1882. Itagaki recovered from the stab wounds, and his cry of "Itagaki may die, but liberty never," supposedly uttered when the would-be assassin attacked, had made him a near-martyr in many people's eyes.[3]

"In the autumn of this year [1884]," Tom wrote, "another interesting movement began in which I was more or less concerned. Mr. Itagaki, then leader of the 'Jiyūtō,' or Liberal Party, in Japan, had for a long time been somewhat interested in Christianity. In fact, he had been taught considerably by one of our native pastors in Tokyo, and although he did not see his way clear to be baptized and enter the church himself, he was very anxious to have the Gospel preached in his native province, Tosa."[4] In September, Itagaki had asked Tom's Osaka station to send missionaries to Tosa, where the mission did not yet have work. Because Tom's station couldn't supply enough mission workers, he turned to his Tokyo colleagues for help in meeting this request from one of Japan's most important political leaders.

As much as Tom and his colleagues might have hoped that Itagaki's motives were purely religious—that he wanted to bring Christianity to his people in order to assure their eternal salvation through Jesus Christ—they knew better. As early as 1882, Itagaki had publicly denounced Japan's native Shinto religion, along with the widespread but non-native Confucianism and Buddhism. Because they variously stressed ancestor worship, deference to authority, and acceptance of the world as it is, those doctrines hindered national progress and Japan's efforts to gain Western acceptance as an equal, Itagaki argued. He publicly supported Christianity, even at a time when the religion was considered by many of his compatriots to be un-Japanese and subversive of imperial sovereignty.

Itagaki's sentiments in favor of Christianity were strengthened by his eight-month study tour of Europe in 1882–83. Traveling through a number of Asian countries on his way to Europe, Itagaki witnessed firsthand how supposedly civilized Europeans who otherwise advocated liberty and equality often treated Asians as little more than slaves, in his view. While in Europe, Itagaki spent months in France, as well as England and Belgium, meeting with top leaders and intellectuals to learn more about democratic parliamentary systems in countries headed by monarchs. He read and brought back to Japan for translation a number of books by German, French, and English writers and political philosophers. During his sojourn, he also encountered a wide range of Europeans of all classes.

Itagaki's European trip made him even more acutely aware of European distain for Asians or ignorance about their countries. He observed that middle class Europeans frequently viewed all Asians as "Chinese" and simply weren't aware of Japan as a separate and distinct country, despite Japan's remarkable advances in culture, technology, and military strength. Itagaki concluded, rightly or wrongly, that Europeans' view of their own racial superiority was not the most important factor allowing them to justify their prejudice toward Asians. More significant, in his view, were religious differences between Europeans and Asians. Because Christianity was widespread in all "civilized" countries, Europeans generally regarded Japanese as heathens unworthy of respect.

Itagaki returned from Europe even more convinced that Japan needed to improve its system of government and bolster its military capabilities if it ever hoped to win European respect and support for treaty revision. Itagaki also believed that determined efforts must be made to improve people's social and economic conditions, both to ensure popular support for the emperor and to build a sense of national unity in the face of foreign threats. Most fundamental in his view, though, was the need to build a true Japanese spirit, if Japan were to compete successfully with the civilizations of Europe and America. Religion certainly was one piece of the overall picture.

Itagaki must have given a great deal of thought as to which missionaries to approach in his quest to educate himself and the people of Tosa in Christian teachings. He certainly was aware that many former samurai and educated urban residents had joined the Union Church of Christ, made up of Presbyterian and other Reformed churches, leaving Catholicism as a religion more popular in rural areas. In addition, Catholicism at the time may have borne a greater stigma than the more recently arrived Protestant sects as the religion that Japan's first shoguns had outlawed in the early 1600s. But it was the democratic aspects of Tom's Presbyterian faith that especially appealed to Itagaki.[5]

Itagaki Taisuke as a young party leader

In 1877, four Protestant missions in the Reformed tradition—the Presbyterian Church in the U.S.A. (North), the Reformed Church of America (Dutch), the Reformed Church in the United States (German), and the United Presbyterian Church of Scotland—had joined forces as the Union Church of Christ (renamed the Church of Christ in Japan, or Kyodan, in 1890). Mission leaders felt that a united approach to their work would avoid splintering an already small body of Japanese believers. In 1884, missionaries had organized a United Evangelistic Committee to further strengthen coordination among the partner churches. Although individual churches had retained their identity within this union, they agreed to operate under the Presbyterian Church's constitution.[6]

The Presbyterian constitution divided church governance between pastors and lay officers, who were elected by church members and worked side by side to guide the church and strengthen the congregation in its faith and spiritual life. In addition, each church member was valued for the contribution he or she could make, regardless of wealth or social standing.

Undoubtedly also helping the missionaries' cause with Itagaki and his supporters was their vocal public support for treaty revision. In 1884, the Conference of Missionaries in Japan voted unanimously for revision of the unequal treaties, especially the clause that denied Japan control over import tariffs and over foreigners committing crimes in Japan. "We trust that the Christian nations will act in a Christian way in removing the obnoxious clause from their treaties with this empire," their official statement read.[7] Like Itagaki's pragmatic support of Christianity, however, the missionaries' support of treaty revision probably was not done for purely unselfish reasons. While many missionaries, Tom among them, supported Japan's desire to restore its sovereignty and take a place of honor among nations, they also feared a backlash against Christians and foreigners if Western countries refused to revise the treaties and treat Japan as an equal. Their fears would prove well-founded before long.

Whatever Itagaki's motivation in inviting them to his home region, Tom knew that his support and protection meant the missionaries could work in Itagaki's home province of Tosa without undue fear of attack by "barbarian" haters, who still lashed out against Christians and foreigners in Japan's more remote areas. But Tom and his fellow missionaries had to walk a fine line. While their spiritual role prevented them from getting directly involved in Japan's domestic politics, these men of the cloth clearly recognized the value of working with prominent individuals like Itagaki. Tom wrote:

> This was thought to be an unusually good opportunity, because Mr. Itagaki had promised to lend his influence in favor of the [Christian] movement and because the men of Tosa are among the best and most reliable as well as influential in the Empire.
>
> Mr. Itagaki (afterwards "Count" Itagaki),[8] together with his followers, had been very active in helping to bring about the restoration of the Imperial Government; and when that was effected, he became one of the Empire's privy counselors, a position which he afterwards resigned because of his pronounced liberal principles. He then became the recognized leader of a strong and growing party, whose first aim was to bring about a constitutional form of government. He was therefore in a position to exert a strong influence in favor of Christianity in his own part of the country where men of liberal views were very numerous.
>
> In October [1884], there was a meeting of representatives of the "Jiyūtō" from all parts of the land held in Osaka. The meeting was presided over by Itagaki-san and was attended by several hundred men. At this meeting, it was resolved to dissolve

the organization. The members did not, of course, propose to renounce their principles but only to disband the party, insofar as it was an organization.

About the time that this meeting closed, [my colleagues] Mr. Thompson . . . and Dr. Verbeck came to Osaka on their way to visit Tosa in compliance with Mr. Itagaki's request. Some 60 or 70 of the members of the Liberal Party who were still in Osaka came to our house, at our invitation, and listened to an interesting and instructive lecture from Dr. V. in our parlor. A few days after, Dr. V. and Mr. Thompson went on to Tosa and began Christian work there. This was the beginning of our work in Kōchi (the principal town in that province) of which I may have more to say at some future time.

It was under the banner of the Union Church of Christ's United Evangelistic Committee that Tom and his colleagues began their work in Tosa.

Notes

1. Tom's first visit to Ozu Church was December 9, 1885. He baptized thirteen people, four of which became evangelical workers. Tom also performed the church's first communion service, which was the first time those participating had ever tasted bread; Yamamoto, *Ozu Church*. Citation from Hikotoro Aoyama, *Arijigoku,* "Gentleman, or Saint Alexander," Japan: 1933; MG archives.

2. *Japan Evangelist*, Vol. X, No. 2, Feb. 1903, 6. Arima's first name is not given; initials were commonly used in mission records.

3. Information about Japan's political climate and Itagaki Taisuke drawn from Vlastos, "Opposition Movements," 247–49; and Cody, "Itagaki Taisuke,"134–45; Itagaki quotation at 145. For Itagaki's views on Shintoism, Confucianism, and Buddhism see Yanagawa, *Perry*, 126. See also Cody, "Itagaki Taisuke," 169–77 for discussion of Itagaki's views after his European trip.

4. The pastor's name was Yasukawa (first name unknown).

5. Itagaki's views on Presbyterian faith noted in article in *Doyo Shimbun*, Tosa newspaper, May 19, 1885. Kochi Church, *History*, "Establishment and Biographies." See also note 6. As to his belief that religion was one piece of the overall picture in building a Japanese spirit, Itagaki was not the only leader who held this view. As early as 1875, Confusion scholar and linguist Nakamura Masanao called for the adoption of Christianity as Japan's national religion, largely due to its strong ethical basis and its usefulness in promoting the Westernization of Japan. Scheiner, *Christian Converts*, 61. Other individuals also promoted this view. See Burkman, "Urakami Incidents," 193–94.

6. The Reformation, or religious revolution of the sixteenth century, is the basis for Protestantism as a separate branch of Christianity. The traditional date for the beginning of the Reformation is October 31, 1517, when German pastor Martin Luther posted his "Ninety-Five Theses" challenging key tenets of Catholic teachings. Frenchman John Calvin, beginning in 1536 with publication of his *Institutes of the Christian Religion*, also led the reform movement. After a controversy in 1539, followers of Luther began to call themselves Lutheran; and the name "Reformed" became associated with Calvin's teachings. Most Reformed churches use the Presbyterian form of governance. *Encyclopedia Britannica*, "World Religions," 911–12.

According to "World Religions," 883: "Presbyterian [is a] form of church government developed . . . during the 16th-century Protestant Reformation and used with variations by Reformed and Presbyterian Churches throughout the world. . . . According to Calvin's theory of church government, the church is a community or body in which Christ is head and all members are equal under him. The ministry is given to the entire church and is distributed among many officers. All who hold office do so by election of the people. The church is to be governed and directed by assemblies of officeholders, pastors, and elders chosen to provide just representation for the church as a whole." See also Smylie, *Brief History*, esp. 30–31.

7. *Japan Weekly Mail*, May 17, 1884, cited in Thomas, *Protestant Beginnings*, 169.

8. Leaders of the Meiji government established a new peerage system in 1884 in the belief that it would strengthen the position of the emperor. Itagaki disagreed, fearing that a new caste of aristocracy would stand between the emperor and the people. He initially refused the emperor's offer of the title of "Count" but, under pressure from colleagues and regime officials, accepted the title on July 15, 1887, rather than insult the emperor. Itagaki did insist, though, that the title should not be passed on to his heirs. Cody, "Itagaki Taisuke," 202–8.

CHAPTER 10

Planting Seeds

Itagaki's support of Christianity was paying off.

The year 1885 began on a high note. The four children were growing and adding light, laughter, and occasional worries to the Alexander household. Seven-year-old Ella, who always had seemed older than her years, began to shoulder some of the responsibility of caring for her younger siblings. Her five-year-old sister, Emma, devoted herself to books. Ella and young Emma were learning to read at the school for missionary children, taught by their mother and other missionary wives, but young Theron was a different story. "Theron did not give his attention very much to books in those days," Tom wrote. "He had too much mischief to attend to. He was, however, passionately fond of stories, and, no matter how busy Emma and I might be, did not hesitate to put in his plea, 'Tell me a story, Mama.' 'Tell me about you was little, Papa.' We were glad to observe that he gradually learned to cry less and to be more manly, but he always had a great aversion to anything like inconvenience; and like all other boys, was extremely fond of candy and of having his own way." Lois, though still an infant, delighted the whole family with her smiles and beguiling baby ways.

A bout of measles struck the household just before Tom was due to take a long-scheduled trip to the south.

> I had to postpone my journey for the time being, therefore, and turn the house into a hospital in which Emma and I were to be nurses for two or three weeks. Theron got on nicely and after being imprisoned for a week, or more, was well again. In the meantime, however, the three girls followed suit and were all sick together. Emma and I were busy enough in our new calling for a little while. She, being more skillful than I, was in greater demand day and night, so the burden of the work fell on her. Our care and labor were rewarded, in that the children all got

up well and strong, not having sustained any injury from their sickness.

On the work front, Tom was pleased with progress being made in all parts of central and southern Japan. Former samurai, professors, merchants, and other locals embraced the Christian message in greater numbers than ever. In Osaka, the missionaries' work was "abundantly blessed," as Tom put it, "with frequent additions of men and women to our number of native Christians." Two churches, the Osaka North Church and the Osaka South Church, were organized by the end of the year, and Tom was happy to see local Christians raise enough money to finance the churches without drawing on the mission's meager treasury.

Although he was a man of the cloth whose focus was supposed to be on spiritual, not worldly, matters, Tom was well aware of the important foundations he and his colleagues were laying in a rapidly changing Japan. He confidently predicted that the new churches, whose members included some of Osaka's leading citizens, would have a significant impact on Japanese politics, society, and business.[1] The church members' early decisions bolstered his optimism. "I felt some anxiety beforehand as to whom they would elect for elders," Tom confessed, "but I was highly gratified to see the very men put in, whom I should have chosen had the matter been left to me." Tom was equally happy to see a prominent Japanese preacher, the Reverend Yoshioka Koki, agree to serve as Osaka North Church's first pastor. Yoshioka had served as an aide to the emperor and had given up a senior foreign ministry position in order to become a Christian minister. His high-level connections and government experience added new luster to the faith community that was growing from the seeds Tom and other missionaries were planting.

By now, Tom's Osaka mission station was completely independent of the Tokyo station, giving him the freedom to manage it and plan for the future without seeking the approval of colleagues in Tokyo. That independence had not been given freely by his Tokyo brethren, though. It had been won only through Tom's consistent and principled insistence that a mission station serving such a vast territory should have the freedom and flexibility to manage its own affairs without second-guessing from people who were not on the scene. One thing had not changed, though. Tom still had to wrestle with the foreign mission board in New York City in his never-ending quest for more funds and workers to serve the needs of a growing mission field.

Osaka South Church kindergarten, cofounders Rev. Takeuchi Kokichi
and Tom Alexander, inset. Main photo 1894

Osaka North Church, Rev. Yoshioka Koki and
Tom Alexander, inset. 1888.

After the children had recovered from the measles, Tom took his long-planned trip to the south, visiting churches, installing new pastors, and preaching to large and small gatherings of Christians and non-Christians alike. As Tom passed through the countryside on this and other journeys, he could see why the Japanese had such a well-deserved reputation for industriousness: family members of all ages were bent over their work in the fields or labored at the many handicrafts and light manufacturing still done in the home. He also would have been exposed to old customs that had not yet died out in rural areas. Japanese riders approaching on horseback often would dismount and wait for foreigners to pass before mounting again and resuming their trip. The reason was that in the old days of warlords and elite samurai, lower classes would never ride by a superior. Despite lingering distrust of foreigners, many rural Japanese nonetheless considered them as belonging to a class above their own. Tom also must have been intrigued by the number of Buddhist pilgrims he passed on the roads, clad in simple robes tied at the waist and often carrying tall staffs with bells attached. These devout pilgrims from all walks of life were following a centuries' old tradition of paying homage to Buddha by visiting temples scattered throughout the country.

During his journeys, Tom also would have seen clear evidence of the many diseases ravaging Japan. Illness was never far from sight, either in the pockmarked faces of Japanese who had been afflicted with smallpox or in the open sores and phlegmy coughs of people suffering from various skin diseases and tuberculosis. Water-borne diseases were rampant. More than one hundred thousand people had succumbed to cholera in 1879, and thousands more died each year from typhus, dysentery, and malaria. It wasn't surprising that disease spread so easily. Rural dwellers used human and animal waste on food crops, lived in close quarters with oxen and horses, and shared common baths. Wells used for drinking water often were dug near latrines, and farmers waded barefoot in fields fertilized with human waste. Runoff from the fields flowed into streams used for washing clothes and cooking utensils. Farmers often washed night soil buckets in the same waterways. Unsanitary living conditions also meant that fleas, bedbugs, lice, blood-sucking worms, and other vermin plagued most villagers, who accepted them as an inevitable part of life.

Foreign missionaries were just as vulnerable to disease, as Tom was sorely reminded more than once when tragedy struck close to home. A doctor had diagnosed his Yokohama host and coworker, John C. Ballagh, with "nervous symptoms induced by the form of littoral malaria peculiar to this country," adding that "his state of health indicates the need of such change of climate as would be best secured by a return to America for a time."[2] And one recent autumn, Tom's former seminary classmate and good friend, Thomas Winn in Kanazawa, had lost his three-year-old son to typhoid fever, and Winn's wife also fell deathly ill with the disease. Lacking a doctor in Kanazawa, the Winns had traveled to Osaka, where, along with their young daughter and newborn son, they stayed with Tom and Emma. The Winns "were in great distress on account of the bereavement and found a melancholy relief in talking of the little one whom they had lost," Tom wrote. "They had been at our house about two weeks when Mr. Winn was prostrated by a severe attack of typhoid fever, which threatened to terminate his work on earth; but after lingering for many weeks, he finally recovered."

Typhoid fever, like malaria, was not a disease to take lightly, as Winn himself made clear. Describing the attack that felled him in Osaka, he wrote, "I had an acute headache which did not go away. On September 25th, I gave a sermon in the morning and I was going to give another sermon in the afternoon, but I could not bear the pain and laid on a couch, tied my head tightly with a handkerchief, and tried to stand the pain. For one month I could not remember anything. . . . I was without consciousness due to the high fever, yet I remember having dreadful dreams. It took me six months to get well. My eyes, lungs, and heart were quite weakened due to the high fever.[3]

As troubled as he had been about his good friends' illnesses and about the virulent diseases afflicting so many people throughout the countryside, Tom surely was grateful that serious illness had not struck his own family—at least not yet.

Tom paid close attention to work taking place in the southwestern Tosa region, where his fellow missionaries had journeyed following the surprising invitation from democracy advocate Itagaki Taisuke. Itagaki's support of Christianity was paying off, just as Tom had hoped and expected. Tom's colleagues traveling in the Tosa region found many locals to be keenly interested in the religion, "earnestly and even anxiously enquiring into the principles of Christianity," as they reported to the mission board in New York. "This is especially noticeable in Japan whose indifference to religion is so marked among the educated classes of the people. But in this district in every town visited, the missionary is beset with eager questioners anxious to learn not from mere curiosity but from real desire for knowledge."[4]

Public meetings were held in theaters or lecture halls in towns and villages throughout the region, with Japanese ministers and new converts taking the lead in organizing them. The meetings usually took up an entire afternoon and sometimes lasted well into the evening, with as many as a half a dozen separate lectures delivered one right after another. The buildings were packed to overflowing. Crowds of three or four hundred people, sometimes even including Buddhist monks, pressed into the lecture halls to hear about the new religion that had sparked so much controversy, concern, and curiosity in Japan. Some listeners came just to see what a foreigner looked like, since most of them had never seen an American or a European. They must have been surprised when they realized that Western missionaries did not all have shocking red hair and grotesque, bulbous noses, like the caricatures in newspapers and journals they had seen.

Missionaries who took part in these meetings were equally impressed with their experiences, especially the way audience members paid such rapt attention to lectures. In their report, they described a typical gathering: "The crowds, the men holding their pipes in their mouths without smoking, the silence unbroken except by the voice of the speaker, or the whisper at times of a mother hushing a child, and once I remember by the tones of a temple bell floating across the city."

The missionaries' biggest challenge was how to grab audiences' interest at the beginning, so they would want to return for more. They divided the lecture series into different topics, beginning with the sorts of scientific and religious questions that people have pondered for ages, including: the limitations of man's knowledge; the relation between science and religion; the existence of God; and is there life after death? Then they moved on to purely preaching meetings, where they delved into topics like: who is Christ; how to know God; immortality; and the second coming of Christ.

As listeners' interest grew, missionaries then offered small group gatherings designed to appeal to different audiences. For people who were interested in learning more about Western society and politics but were not ready to plunge into discussions about Christianity, the missionaries offered meetings designed for general conversation. In those gatherings, the remarkably well-informed Japanese participants asked about the relationship between the President, Congress, and the Supreme Court; the functions of the Senate and House of Representatives; methods of taxation; free trade and protection; the position of farmers in America; and other sophisticated questions. Missionaries, in turn, asked what Japan had been like before Commodore Perry had arrived with his coal-fired "black ships" in 1853 and

1854. They also asked about the reasons for the shogun's overthrow and the restoration of the emperor in 1868; about Japan's prison system; and about the popular belief that foxes could control people by entering their bodies and possessing their spirit.

Some men—and they invariably were men at the smaller gatherings— were ready to go further and delve into religious questions. Many of the younger participants were aware of the agnostic views of Western political philosophers such as John Stuart Mill and Herbert Spencer, while the older men were largely Confucian in background and training. Together, they posed questions that tested the missionaries' ability to explain and defend their own belief in Christianity. They asked such questions as, "You speak of God as Creator, but how can you prove that matter is eternal and thus was created by God? You speak of God and of knowing him; but may not the universe be an illusion; and if the universe, why not God? You speak of God as good, yet the world is full of pain and sorrow. You speak of conscience; what is conscience? And after all, how do you know that you know?" Some of the old samurai also wondered, doesn't the Christian belief in non-retaliation and in turning the other cheek make men cowards?

The missionaries' replies seemed to satisfy their audiences. On one memorable occasion, though, participants seemed as if they were ready to move on to a study of the Scriptures, but then the real trouble began. Using Paul's letter to the Romans as their text, missionaries talked about the guilt of humankind, the righteous judgment of God, and how God's promise is realized through faith. As soon as they got to the part about incarnation— God taking human form in the person of Jesus Christ—their Confucian listeners recoiled. Confucians never discussed the afterworld or the concept of a god; any notion of God coming to earth as a human was just too much of a stretch for them to accept. Hearing that incarnation was the cornerstone of Christianity made the religion seem as unbelievable to them as Buddhism. These men could not be convinced to go further in their study. Other participants, though, were more open-minded and continued their studies with the Gospel of John. While missionaries did not try to minimize the mystery of the incarnation, neither did the remaining Japanese students seem to object as strongly as the older Confucian gentlemen to the concept. Soon, eight men and then thirteen more were baptized.

After all the challenges Tom and his fellow Christian workers had faced in their efforts to plant their faith in Japan, the work in Tosa gave him every reason to be pleased. Together, he and his fellow missionaries were fulfilling one of Jesus' commands:

Go therefore and make disciples of all nations,
baptizing them in the name of the Father and
of the Son and of the Holy Spirit,
and teaching them to obey everything
that I have commanded you.

(Matt 28:19–20)

Notes

1. Osaka South Church, *Fifty Years*, 5. Yoshioka as emperor's aide in Higuchi, *Muromachi Church*.

2. Henry Faulds to BFM, September 17, 1882. PCUSA, "Correspondence." Information about disease and sanitary conditions in Hane, *Peasants*, 44–45.

3. Nakazawa, *Winn*, 46.

4. The quotation and subsequent description of public meetings in Tosa appear in PCUSA, "Annual Report," January 20, 1886.

CHAPTER 11

A New Badge of Honor

Many Japanese . . . viewed the sword as the soul of the samurai,
an emblem of his power and prowess.

Whenever they could, Tom's family loved to visit interesting places in and near Osaka. The grounds of the ancient Osaka Castle, site of many battles between Japan's old feudal lords, was a favorite playground for the children, with its vast open spaces, trees, and massive granite walls enclosing the moat. The iconic castle and most of its buildings had burned to the ground in 1868 after the embattled shogun fled from troops fighting to restore Emperor Meiji to the throne. High ramparts on its outer walls had survived, though, and offered tremendous views of the city. Long rows of barracks for imperial troops covered a portion of the grounds, clearly signifying the emperor's tight hold over Japan's important commercial city and the surrounding area.

Another favorite destination for family visits was Japan's first permanent capital, Nara, a small town nestled in the mountains east of Osaka. Buddhist temples, Shinto shrines, and spacious gardens were impressive, but they couldn't compete in the children's eyes with Nara's famous deer, which wandered freely through the streets and gardens—heavenly animals, according to Japanese legend, that protected the town and surrounding countryside. One of Tom's daughters remembered them as "tremendous creatures that came charging toward us to eat the *o-sembei* [deer biscuits] we held out to them. Strangely, they had shrunk unbelievably when I saw them on my return," she wrote as an adult.[1]

There also were weeks spent in various mountain or lake resorts to escape Osaka's heat and disease. Located in the subtropics, Osaka sweltered under blistering temperatures and high humidity in the summer. Tom, who worried about the effects of the oppressive heat on Emma and the children, sometimes rented rooms for the family in the town of Mino, located in the hills to the north, and sometimes in the scenic hot springs town of Arima near Kobe to the west, with its cooling waterfall and lush vegetation. Lake Biwa, Japan's largest freshwater lake northeast of Osaka, also was a pleasurable retreat. The whole family thrived in the cooler, cleaner air away from Osaka's mosquito-ridden canals and rivers that were increasingly polluted from the city's new industries and textile mills. Emma and the children generally remained in their vacation abodes for the duration of the summer, while Tom traveled to and from Osaka to keep up his work.

By the mid-1880s, former samurai were the core of the Protestant church. Although just 5 percent of the total population, samurai accounted for roughly 30 percent of church membership rolls.[2] Many of these new Christians were moving into top positions in government, business, and the new field of journalism. As Tom knew well by now, samurai warrior-statesmen had played a crucial leadership role during centuries of rule by Tokugawa shoguns. Under the class system observed in those years, samurai had ranked near the top of the hierarchy: below the emperor, shogun, and lords; but above peasants, artisans, and merchants. Their dress, swagger, hair tied in a topknot, and two swords prominently displayed on their hips had set them apart from other "common" classes. In those days, the shogun and Japan's local lords had relied on these elite, highly educated men to wield the reins of power and defend the nation.

Like English knights, samurai warriors of the Tokugawa era had adhered to a strict code of ethics—called Bushido, or "the Way of the Warrior"—a code that stressed honor, courage, truthfulness, loyalty, humility, and self-discipline. These warriors had been famously unafraid of death in combat for their lords. Samurai status and privilege had been inherited, flowing from father to son and to sons beyond. At age five, a young samurai boy had been clad in warrior attire, trained in martial arts, and given a blunt sword to wear in his belt. When he turned fifteen, the lad had received two finely crafted steel swords, one long and one short, which he tucked into the sash around his hips, giving him the distinctive aura of a samurai. Many Japanese of this era had viewed the sword as the soul of the samurai, an emblem of his power and prowess.

Nowhere was this truer than in Itagaki Taisuke's home region of Tosa. Famous not only for the role its leaders had played in the restoration of the emperor in 1868 and in the call for constitutional democracy, Tosa also was known for rugged sports like polo and archery, with arrows shot not only on foot but also on horseback at a full gallop. And "nowhere else, not even in Japan," wrote one of Tom's colleagues, "has the sword been held in higher honor. A sword once drawn could never be sheathed unstained; and in Tosa, even the farmers were swordsmen."[3]

As the missionaries' work in Tosa progressed, Tom had the chance to learn more about Itagaki Taisuke and his role in Japan's recent turbulent past. Son of a samurai family, Itagaki had taken the lead within Japan as early as 1874 in pressing for an elected national assembly, a constitution, and clear limits on the Tokyo government's increasingly arbitrary use of power. What made Itagaki's role as an opposition leader so remarkable was the fact that he was a military hero, who had led a large contingent of troops from his native Tosa region during the battle to overthrow the shogun's regime and install Emperor Meiji as the sole ruler of Japan in 1868. He had even joined the new government as a top-ranking councilor of state, becoming one of a handful of officials advising the emperor and helping run the government.

Itagaki had resigned his government position in 1873. One reason was his sharp disagreement with colleagues over Japan's policy toward Korea. Itagaki was among the conservatives pushing for military action that would force Korea to open diplomatic and trade relations with Japan, much as the West had forced such relations on Japan two decades before. His strong ally in this argument was another state councilor, Saigo Takamori, who had fought alongside Itagaki in the battle to oust the shogun and had resigned from government along with Itagaki in 1873. Saigo then had led the failed 1877 Satsuma Rebellion, the civil war that had ended with Saigo's beheading two months before Tom and Emma arrived in Japan.

Korea had not been Itagaki's main worry, though. He had been even more concerned about the Meiji regime's direction, first as it eliminated samurai privileges, including generous government stipends, and then as it centralized political control in Tokyo at the expense of regional authorities. Itagaki and other early supporters of the emperor watched with increasing concern as imperial advisors drawn largely from two prominent southern provinces used their positions to increase their own power and extend preferences and benefits to friends and supporters, all in the name of the emperor. Such misuse of power fueled popular discontent and bore an uncomfortable likeness to the corruption and dysfunction of the deposed shogun's regime.

Unlike his old colleague Saigo, though, Itagaki wanted to use peaceful means to achieve his goals for reform. In 1881, after the emperor refused his proposal to establish an elected national assembly to allow for greater regional input into national policies, Itagaki had formed Japan's first political party—Jiyuto, or "Liberal Party"—aimed at instituting democratic, constitutional government. By forming the Liberal Party when he did, Itagaki rode a wave of popular unrest over Meiji government policies. He attracted disgruntled ex-samurai, who were struggling to adapt to a rapidly changing Japan; and wealthy merchants, who resented centralized control in Tokyo and heavy taxation to support the regime's aggressive modernization program. He also attracted farmers and peasants suffering the dual burden of high taxes and low crop prices. Severe economic depression in the early 1880s added fuel to the fire as the rural economy collapsed, throwing even more uncertainty and upheaval into the lives of Japanese already reeling from radical changes imposed by Tokyo's new ruling elite.

As the Liberal Party grew, its members' interests splintered, with divisions forming between the wealthier, more educated members, who were doing well economically under the new regime, and poorer farmers, small merchants, and other groups who had suffered most from high taxes, sharply higher personal debt, unscrupulous moneylenders, and bankruptcies. Radical groups acting in the party's name launched violent anti-government protests that Itagaki and other party leaders refused to join or bless. Increasingly severe government repression followed these and other protests. Imperial troops violently suppressed public demonstrations; and top officials acting in the name of the emperor banned activities of a political nature and heavily censored or closed opposition newspapers, even arresting and jailing editors and reporters.

Itagaki and other party leaders not only recognized they were powerless to control the violent actions of some party members, but they also realized they could no longer function as a party in the face of growing government oppression. Thus, during a fateful meeting in Osaka in October 1884, the Liberal Party disbanded. This move was but a tactical defeat in the party's larger struggle for popular rights and government reform. It was immediately after that meeting when nearly seventy party members and leaders had gathered at Tom's Osaka home to hear one of their first lectures on Christianity and its tenets.

The work of missionaries and Japanese preachers in the Tosa region had progressed so well that by the spring of 1885, new converts began to talk of forming a church in Kochi. As the region's largest town and capital city, Kochi was the center of Tosa's political and cultural life. Kochi also was Itagaki's home town, a fitting location for the first Protestant church in the politically active province. On May 12, Tom began a journey to the island of Shikoku to help his colleagues organize and dedicate a new church. Located off the jagged southern coast of Japan's largest island of Honshu, Shikoku lay snugly tucked in the embrace of its larger neighbor.

Traveling from Osaka to Kobe by rail, Tom boarded a steamer along with some of his fellow missionaries from Tokyo. The steamer followed a well-plied southerly route through Osaka Bay and soon emerged into the open waters of the Pacific Ocean. Stiff winds often buffeted ships sailing along Shikoku's coastline, but the weather was fair on this May day and the voyage a pleasant one, giving Tom and his friends a chance to enjoy the view from the steamer's deck. Small towns and villages along the shoreline of the island's heavily forested hillsides resembled hamlets Tom had seen in other parts of Japan during his sojourns. Fishing boats dotted the sea, with sailors hauling in fresh catches for local markets.

At about noon on May 13, Tom's steamer rounded a sharp spit of land on Shikoku's eastern edge and headed toward Kochi, located in the middle of an arc formed by the island's southern coast. As the ship made its way through wide-open Tosa Bay and drew closer to shore, Tom could see the five-story keep of Kochi castle. The shogun-era fortress dominated the town from its perch high in the mountainous terrain that rose from water's edge.

As the boat docked, several missionaries who had spent weeks laboring in Tosa were there to meet Tom and his fellow travelers and escort them into town. This was the beginning of a week Tom would never forget. He later reflected on his experience.

> Mr. Itagaki had kept his promise and used his influence in favor of Christianity, though he did not care to accept it for himself. On the evening of the 15th, Mr. Knox baptized thirteen people—among them were Mr. Kataoka, Mr. Sakamoto and other men of influence. The church was organized on Sunday, the 17th with a membership of some twenty-five persons. I preached the sermon and Mr. Miller performed the ordination service.
>
> On Monday, we had a social meeting with the Christians. Some of the old samurai kindly favored us with an exhibition of the old-fashioned sword exercise in which men of that class were formerly drilled. The sight was a very curious one and full of interest to us.

The "men of influence" baptized that day included Kataoka Kenkichi, a samurai son who had collaborated closely with Itagaki and who later would serve as speaker of the national parliament, or Diet, and Sakamoto Nao-hiro, who had devoted himself to the liberal civil rights movement and also served in the Diet, ultimately resigning out of disgust with what he viewed as a corrupt, authoritarian Meiji government.

**Kochi Church elders, 1895. Middle row, center: Rev. Tada Shiroshi, first pastor.
Back row, third from left: Hosokawa Gisho; fourth from left: Sakamoto Naohiro.
Picture inset, upper right: Kataoka Kenkichi.**

Also baptized was Hosokawa Gisho, headmaster of a famous kendo martial arts school in Kochi, where he taught traditional swordsmanship to new generations of Japanese. Before the Meiji era, Hosokawa had also been a recognized leader in iaijutsu, a highly refined sword-drawing technique taught to samurai warriors. Even though the Meiji regime had ordered samurai not to wear their prized swords in public, that order had not pre-vented sons of old samurai families and other young Japanese men from seeking training in the traditional arts of elite samurai warriors. Hosokawa's long adherence to the strict samurai code of ethics, Bushido, had allowed him to accept equally idealistic Reformed Protestant tenets, making him a good example of the blending of old and new in a changing Japan. Ho-sokawa's adoption of the Christian faith had not changed his approach to swordsmanship, though, even during exhibition duels. His philosophy was simple: not to cut, and not to be cut. Everything else was fair game.[4]

At the social gathering following the church ceremony, Hosokawa joined one of his fellow samurai-turned-Christians in a display of swordsmanship, reenacting the ritual in the same way it had unfolded thousands of times before. The demonstration probably took place in Hosokawa's martial arts arena, located at the base of Kochi castle in the heart of town. Tom, as head of the mission station responsible for the Tosa region, would have been seated along with his fellow missionaries in a place of honor with a good view of the action. Surely filled with keen anticipation as the match began, Tom and his colleagues would not be disappointed.

The demonstration must have unfolded just as countless training exercises had in the years when the samurai had reigned supreme. Two warriors clad in leather and metal protective gear entered the arena. A deep drum sounded, its echo resonating through the hall. The two combatants turned to face each other. Eyes locked, they moved six paces apart, long curved swords angled at their sides. Bowing slightly at the waist, they eased slowly into a deep crouch; as they did so, they drew sabers from their scabbards, sweeping them in one fluid motion to the center of their bodies. Gripping their swords waist high, left hand held firmly at the base and right hand atop the shaft, each combatant pointed his blade at his opponent's eyes. Their gazes remained fixed on each other, the better to predict their opponent's intentions and moves. On a silent cue, both men rose to a standing position, distributing their weight equally between the right leg in front and the left one held slightly behind.

With a sudden lunge and a loud stamp of his bare foot, Hosokawa thrust his sword forward, shouting fiercely, as he tried to land a blow on his opponent's heavy armor. The other man parried his move, striking Hosokawa's sword with his own and moving quickly backward and away to prepare his own offensive move. One strike followed another in a seemingly choreographed set of moves, each combatant displaying a refined swordsmanship. The sound of loud guttural cries, feet pounding the wooden floor, and the echo of sword against sword filled the room. Overhead strikes, short thrusts and other well-practiced techniques awed the small group assembled to

4. Kochi Church, *History*, "Biographies of Important Members." The demonstration described in this scene is as I envision it, based on Tom's *Journal* and Kochi Church, *History*, and from discussions with the Kochi Church minister in 2009. The action is based on descriptions in Junzo Sasamori and Gordon Warner, *This Is Kendo: The Art of Japanese Fencing* (Tokyo: Tuttle, 1964), 81–86. Based on my research, I am highly confident that Tom received the sword—either Hosokawa's or someone else's—on this occasion. It is still in the Alexander family's possession.

watch this display of samurai prowess. Although this was just a demonstration, the ferocity of the battle left no doubt about the courage and tenacity of samurai warriors, Japan's ancient protectors. Upon another unseen cue, the fighting stopped. The warriors' intensity melted away as they relaxed into a neutral position. Standing face-to-face, they sank slowly into a crouch. Rising again, they bowed formally, first to each other and then to the audience.

Tom must have been as surprised as everyone else by the next move. Hosokawa walked toward the group seated in the arena and stopped in front of Tom, who rose to meet him, his slender, 6-foot frame towering above the powerfully built kendo master. Hosokawa balanced a short sword horizontally on the upturned palms of his hands. He then bowed at the waist, extending his arms straight out in front and offering his most treasured possession to the American missionary from East Tennessee.

Samurai sword given to Tom Alexander

Sword with case, dagger for committing seppuku (ritual suicide) inset in scabbard

Tom reached out his hands to accept this unexpected gift from a man who had just been baptized into Christianity. The symbolism of the kendo master's gesture surely touched him deeply. This proud former samurai no longer needed his sword as a visible emblem of his status. The Christian convert had a new badge of honor to wear deep in his heart, a religion that was among the forces reshaping Japan since its forced opening to the West three decades before.

Notes

1. Mary Alexander, "Japan Notes."

2. Thomas, *Protestant Beginnings*, 169.

3. Imbrie, *Church of Christ in Japan*, 92. Information about Itagaki in the following section is from Cody, "Itagaki Taisuke" and Vlastos, "Opposition Movements." Itagaki's Liberal Party was the predecessor of the Liberal Democratic Party, which has ruled Japan nearly continuously since its formation just after World War II.

CHAPTER 12

Home to America

In faith, humility and watchful care Mr. Alexander has been to
us Christians a bright example.

Tom was in high spirits after his return from Kochi, where the new church
was moving ahead on solid ground. In Osaka, too, the number of Christians
rose steadily, bringing total membership in the two churches to about 150
in 1885. Tom's mission station was reinforced by the arrival of more workers from America to serve in the south, and he himself traveled frequently
throughout the region, preaching to large groups of attentive audiences. Just
when it seemed that life couldn't get any better, tragedy struck.

Fires, earthquakes, and killer tsunami waves hit Japan's volcanic island
chain with unwelcome regularity. Tom and Emma already had experienced
the horrors of fire sweeping through Tokyo's tightly packed homes and
buildings. Osaka introduced them to the terror of another form of natural
disaster, as Tom described so vividly in his journal.

> The month of June is always a wet month in this country and we
> are usually prepared for two or three weeks of pretty steady rain.
> But this year the rainfall was unusually large, being about 22
> inches during the month of June alone. The region outside the
> city eastward was soon submerged in many feet of water and the
> rivers which run down through the city were swollen into swift
> and angry floods.
>
> On the evening of June 30th, I went as usual to attend
> prayer meeting at the native church [Osaka North Church]
> on Nakanoshima. I saw then that the rivers were beginning to
> overflow their banks and could not avoid feeling some degree of
> uneasiness. I expected that, by the next morning, the Conces-
> sion (Foreign) would be under water.

Alarm bells and drums were sounding all night. When morning came, however, I was surprised to find no water in our yard nor in the streets nearby. But the rain was still pouring down in torrents, and continued without stopping until after night. The result was that on the morning of the 2nd of July we found the Foreign Concession covered with water to the depth of from one to three feet.

The water continued to rise slowly through the day until jinrikishas could no longer pass through the streets, and we had either to go in boats or wade through the water. I went out twice during the day—once in the morning and again in the afternoon.

In the afternoon, the sight was really terrible. The rivers were covered with debris—broken bridges, parts of houses, all kinds of furniture together with boats which had broken loose from their mooring above and come down with the rest. The police were every wise busy trying to save bridges which were yet standing, rescuing people from the rivers and other places of danger, and making themselves useful generally.

We foreigners hardly knew what to do. If the stone wall along the river should give away, no one could tell just what the result might be. The whole Concession might be washed away, as the soil is very sandy. Some attempted early in the day to send their families off to Kōbe but found they were too late. The trains had stopped running. Most of us then hired boats to come and wait at our gates, expecting to take them if necessary.

During the day, officers came from the city government urging us to leave the Concession and go up to higher ground, whither we would be conveyed by the government and where we would be provided for. This generous offer was, however, repeatedly declined, because we did not apprehend any great danger and did not wish to put the government to unnecessary trouble and expense.

Emma and I retired that night at the usual time—10 o'clock—and went to sleep though the water seemed to be getting higher. At midnight we were awakened by the loud ringing of our door bell. I found at the door two high military officers who said that they were sent by General Takashima, Commander of the Osaka division of the regular army, to say that there was no means of knowing how much higher the water would rise, as Lake Biwa [northeast of Osaka] was overflowing upon us and that General Takashima united with the city government in urging us at once to leave the Concession and go up to a new hospital building near the castle, which would be put at our disposal.[1]

As most of our neighbors on the Concession were in favor of complying with this request, we thought it would be best for us to do likewise. Accordingly we awakened our children, dressed them, put a few necessary things in a trunk, got into our boat and went to the bridge in front of the "Fucho" [a stone carving by an artist of the same name], which we crossed double quick, as it seemed likely to give away at any moment.

We were detained for an hour or more at the "Fucho" while jinrikishas were being procured for us and our friends—in number amounting to some thirty people. About 3 a.m., however, everything was declared to be ready and we took to the jinrikishas which carried us through the flooded streets up to the castle.

The ride was one long to be remembered by us all. The water was in many places up to the axles. The people in the houses by the way seemed to be awake, all of them, and everything indoors and out looked desolate enough. We reached the castle about daybreak—July 3rd—and were given rooms furnished with rough beds, tables and chairs. We remained in these quarters until the 5th.

We were treated with the greatest kindness by the officials and by all who came about us. Mr. Tatino Gōzo, Governor of Osaka-fu [district], called on us and sent us a present of wine and beer—but when he found we did not use such things he took them back and gave us, instead, fowls and biscuits (in boxes). General Takashima also called and sent us a present of several fowls apiece.

When the water had gone down sufficiently we were sent back to our homes by the authorities. During our absence our houses were guarded by the police—an armed man being stationed at each house. While at the hospital we appointed three of our number to write letters to Gen. T. and to the Governor expressing our appreciation of their very great kindness.

The effects of the flood did not pass for months afterwards. The destruction of property was very great among the natives who lived in the flooded districts. Some eighty thousand people were rendered homeless. The government authorities took great pains to alleviate the distress. Contributions flowed in from every quarter both from natives and from foreigners. The Japanese never showed so much liberality before in endeavoring to aid the sufferers from a great calamity like this one. Indeed, no such flood had ever occurred in this region, at least, not for many years past.

As soon as possible after the flood, Tom took his family out of Osaka for the summer. Even in the best of times, people who suffered from breathing problems, as Tom often did, struggled to cope with Osaka's worsening pollution. Coal dust and wood smoke from stoves, fireplaces, and increasing numbers of cotton mills and factories filled the air. Fine particles lodged in lungs and blocked their tiny airways, often leaving permanent damage. And in the flood's aftermath, the risk of cholera, typhoid fever, and other diseases spawned by sewage-filled waters and mosquitoes was even higher than normal. Tom rented a house in Kobe, where they enjoyed the fresh sea air and swam in the warm, gentle waves that rolled to shore along the shallow coastline.

Tom returned to Osaka every Saturday to attend to his preaching and missionary work, which prospered during the summer with the addition of more Christians to the churches there. In mid-September, the family returned to Osaka, and Tom began making arrangements to visit the church in Hiroshima. He was just about to set out on October 8, his thirty-fifth birthday, when the American mail arrived and dealt him a crushing blow. A letter from his father brought news of the last hours of his dear sister, Becky. She had been ill most of the eight years since Tom had left America, and so her death did not come as a complete surprise; but losing her hit him hard. She had been one of his favorite sisters and had sacrificed her own education and freedom to remain home caring for their father. Tom mourned her passing.

> It was, to me, a very, very sad bereavement. I had hoped that she might recover and that I might be permitted to meet her again in this world, but such was not God's will. She died about 12 noon, August 5th, leaving the old home sad and desolate. My father wrote to me two days after her death, from whose letter I quote the following: "Emma is with us no more. She died day before yesterday about 12 o'clock. There was a change on her that morning that made us think she would not be with us much longer. So she asked me if she was dying. I told her that I did not think she was. She told me that when I thought she was dying, I must tell her. So in a little while I told her she was dying. She smiled and said it was all right. Then she prayed for me and her brothers and little sister here at home and then she prayed a most beautiful little prayer for her brother and family that are away in a foreign land."

"Time passes quickly by and the years crowd one upon another and we hardly have time to mark the change," Tom wrote early in 1886. Work consumed most of Tom's waking hours—with worries often robbing him of sleep—and his travels increased in frequency. Tom always enjoyed the week of prayer following Christmas and New Year,

> But this year I was called away to attend a meeting of Chūkai [Presbytery, or regional governing body] in Yanagawa which was to have been held Jan. 6th. I had therefore to leave on the last night of the old year and set sail from Kōbe bright and early. After enduring the extreme cold and encountering numerous other difficulties I reached Yanagawa about noon of the day appointed only to find that the meeting of Chūkai had been postponed. Thus I had to spend the week of prayer largely on the road and at the end meet with disappointment.

Never one to miss an opportunity to turn bad fortune to good use, Tom used the trip to visit towns along the way where he and Japanese preachers had labored hard to spread the Word. In Shimonoseki, Toyora, and other towns, he visited churches and preached to large and attentive audiences. After a brief return to Osaka, Tom traveled again in February, joining his Japanese brethren in Ozu and Iyo on the island of Shikoku.

> A native preacher, Mr. Sakurai, had been preaching there for some time and had met, at first, with great opposition, but afterwards many of the people changed their minds and became Christians.[2] And this was my second visit to them. Mr. Oshikawa met me there and we held numerous public preaching services which were well attended. Public sentiment seemed to undergo a change, and those who formerly hated Christianity began to regard it with favor, and many of them set about examining the Scriptures for themselves. I baptized eight persons who had been thoroughly instructed already.

Tom traveled on to Shimonoseki to attend the postponed Presbytery meeting, journeying from there to Hiroshima "to be present at the dedication of the new chapel of the Hiroshima church. The chapel, a very neat one, was built with money raised half by the church members and half given by [fellow missionary] Mr. Fisher and others interested. The dedication was followed by the observance of the Lord's Supper, on which occasion five persons were admitted to the church by baptism. Public preaching services were held in the church for two or three days and were well attended."

Even in Kanazawa, the conservative Buddhist stronghold where Tom had labored six weeks, his friend Thomas Winn had baptized one hundred people by 1886. Sadly, though, severe eye trouble forced Winn to depart Japan in April with his family. "It was with great reluctance that he consented to go, and we were all exceedingly sorry to part with him. His trouble seemed to be of so serious a nature as to make it extremely doubtful whether he would ever be able to come back again," Tom wrote. Despite his sorrow at saying goodbye to his old friend and the heavy demands of work and travel, Tom felt abundantly blessed by the positive results he and his fellow workers in Christ were witnessing throughout the region.

Tom also felt blessed by his family and took great comfort and joy from his growing children. All of them were healthy and lively. The eldest, Ella, took piano lessons twice a week and showed more talent than young Emma, learning quickly and playing reasonably well for a nine-year-old. Theron was well-mannered and loved playing ball and exploring outside. Lois continued to delight the family with her easy-going ways and baby-like charms. She seemed to love her nanny, O-Chise-san, more than anyone else, even calling her "Dada," which made Tom and Emma laugh.

Tom and Emma were expecting their fifth child in June, and on May 21, 1887, they had intended to celebrate their tenth "tin" anniversary in their usual quiet way. But Tom's colleagues and friends had other ideas, as Tom wrote.

> The Osaka Recreation Club, of which I was president at the time, had appointed a picnic for that day, which took the form of a boat excursion down to the sea. About thirty persons attended. Emma was not able to go, but I went and took with me the two older children, Ella and Emma.
>
> Immediately after the boat left the landing at Kawaguchi, the Hon. Secretary, the Rev. G. H. Pole (Church Missionary Society), called the company to order and, requesting me to take the chair, said it had been thought good to give the president and his wife a present on occasion of their "tin" wedding. He then presented me with a large number of tin toys on behalf of the club. We took our lunch along with us, and the following is a copy of the bill of fare:

Osaka Recreation Club
Spring Picnic
21 May 1887

Bill of Fare

Roast Beef   Oxtail Jelly
Meat Patties
* * *

Bread, Butter, Pickles
Pepper, Salt & Mustard
* * *

Mince Pies   Plum Cake
Cream, Chocolate,
Silver & Golden Cakes
* * *

Tea & Coffee

I was sorry that Emma could not go, for I felt sure that she would have enjoyed the trip very much. Well, we felt on this, the tenth anniversary, that time had passed very rapidly indeed. And although we had experienced some trials by the way, we could really rejoice in all the way in which God had led us. Our affection for each other had grown stronger as the years passed by, and we felt that this was something for which we ought to be profoundly thankful, for such is not always the case. It was about this time that we learned, with sorrow, of the death of Prof. T. J. Lamar, who married us ten years before.

The Alexander family was blessed early in the morning of June 22 with the birth of another girl, a strong and healthy child from the first. Ella and young Emma were given the honor of naming the new baby. They chose "Mary" without hesitation. "Then," Tom wrote, "it occurred to them that the baby was born right in the midst of Queen Victoria's Jubilee festivities, so they suggested 'Jubilee' for a second name; but concluded that that did not sound quite right and changed it to 'Victoria.'" Tom bought a silver medal, coined in honor of the queen, for the new baby and for his wife, too. "With every addition to our family, we had mingled feelings of gratitude to God and of the increased responsibility laid upon us."

Tom and Emma had been in Japan for ten years now, and the mission board in New York and their more seasoned colleagues in Japan strongly advised them to return to America for a sabbatical. Although the family's health was good and Tom's energy and dedication to duty were as strong as ever, they agreed that a one-year break was a good idea.

We accordingly laid our plans to start as soon as Emma should get strong enough to make the journey. We found it hard to leave our many friends in Osaka. We had warm friends among the English missionaries, as well as among the American, whom we were very sorry to leave. The ties of friendship formed on mission grounds are often very close; but they are peculiarly liable to being broken. When one leaves the field for what one supposes to be only a brief period of rest in the homeland, it may very likely turn out in the end that he will not again return to his post and, should he return, some among his friends may have gone. Indeed, such is very apt to be the case.

The native Christians in our churches also showed us the greatest kindness. They all expressed sorrow at having to lose us even a brief season. Many of them brought us presents—some very nice ones. About a fortnight before the time set for our departure, the members of the two churches in Osaka had a farewell meeting at Mr. Fisher's house at which nearly two hundred were present. Speeches were made by different ones among them, speaking in the kindest terms of us and the work we had been instrumental in doing.

They presented us with a pair of Kakimono—very fine hand paintings by Nagasawa, a celebrated artist. Mr. Iwa presented them in the name of the two churches, at the same time giving us a farewell address, a translation of which is given below. To this I responded as best I could. My heart was full as I spoke to so many people, nearly all of whom I had baptized and to whom I had so often preached both from the pulpit and in private. They had a photographer take a picture of the whole company present, including the members of our mission station—Fishers, Hearsts, Miss Garvin and Miss Warner.

Farewell Address

Osaka, Sept. 16, 1887

The Fall wind blows and the leaves and twigs fall to the earth, and the branches are left bare and lonely. So in this Fall of the year for the return of our dear Mr. Alexander to his native land, we are left in sorrowful loneliness. Looking back over the past, we remember that six years have gone since Mr. Alexander came to Osaka. At that time, there was no church organization, the Christians were few in number. Since that time, their numbers have greatly increased and there are now two organized church-es. There are now more than two hundred Christians in these churches.

If it is asked how this large fruitage has been secured, we must say, first by the grace of Christ, our Savior, and secondly by the abundant labors of Mr. Alexander. We desire gratefully to thank Mr. Alexander. But not only among us has he labored. In Chūgoku, Kyūshū and Shikoku are also many evidences of his faithful work. In faith, humility and watchful care Mr. Alexan-der has been to us Christians a bright example.

Neither tongue nor pen can express the gratitude which we feel for this. We desire, upon parting, to present, as a small token of our gratitude, this pair of "Kakimono" and this photograph. We humbly ask you to remember us in your prayers, and further that without long delay you will come again to us, with earnest labor to seek the salvation of the 38,000,000 of our brethren and sisters in this land.

We remain,
Sincerely yours,

The Members of the North and South Churches of Osaka.

In addition to the generous farewell gifts and moving speeches, Tom was flooded with letters from Japanese with whom he had worked and from many other acquaintances as well, all of them expressing their goodwill and kind wishes. The outpouring of love and affection moved him deeply. On October 6, 1887, many of Osaka's Christians accompanied Tom, Emma, and their five children to the train station, where they bade farewell to the family with many tears and prayers for their safe and speedy return. Then the trav-elers were on their way. After arriving in Kobe, they boarded a small coastal steamer bound for Yokohama. As the vessel got underway, Tom's hopes for a smooth voyage faded quickly.

The evening was stormy and gloomy. . . . The steamer was crowded so that we were all put into one stateroom. The weather was squally and finally developed into a regular typhoon, which lasted several hours. We were tossed about fearfully and were in danger of being dashed upon the rocks. We, however, escaped with our lives—but were worn out with fatigue and seasickness.

After a few days' rest in nearby Tokyo, they left Yokohama on the *Parthia*, a steamer owned and operated by the Canadian Pacific Line that had begun service just a few months before. The autumn ocean crossing to Vancouver lasted a seemingly interminable fifteen days.

The voyage was unusually rough. Emma and the children—Ella especially—were very seasick; only the baby was free from seasickness. After being at sea for about ten days, we encountered a severe storm which gave us a better idea of the power of Old Ocean than anything we had ever experienced. We were extremely glad, therefore, when at last we arrived safely in Vancouver. Emma was so weak that we felt it necessary to rest for a few days before beginning the trip across the continent. Ella was also too weak and ill to walk. We spent about three days in Vancouver—and finally reached Emma's old home at Maryville, Tennessee, November 12.

Notes

1. Probably National Hospital today. General Takashima Tomonosuke (1844–1916) was the son of a samurai from Kagoshima in the southern Satsuma domain. He fought in the war leading to the toppling of the shogun and Restoration of Emperor Meiji as Japan's sole ruler in 1868. He joined the Imperial Army upon its formation in 1874 and served as Emperor Meiji's chamberlain, managing the imperial household. Takashima led an imperial army division opposing the forces of Saigo Takamori of Satsuma during the 1877 Satsuma Rebellion. He was appointed lieutenant general in 1883 and given the title viscount in 1884. Takashima later served as Army Minister in the first and second cabinets of Prime Minister (and Finance Minister) Matsukata Masayoshi, also from Kagoshima; as vice-governor general of Taiwan; as Minister for Overseas Affairs; and as privy councilor, a title he held until his death. Keene, *Emperor*, 174, 528; and National Diet, *Portraits*.

2. The Reverend Sakurai Akinori began his evangelical work in February 1885 in Ozu. Information provided in personal email from one of Sakurai's descendants. Winn's right eye suffered a retinal hemorrhage from a snowball thrown by a boy at Eiwa School in Kanazawa. After two years in America and a difficult recovery, Winn returned to Kanazawa in 1888. Nakazawa, *Winn*, 47–48.

CHAPTER 13

You Can't Go Home Again

Mount Horeb no longer felt like home.

After the grueling Pacific Ocean crossing and long transcontinental train journey, Tom, Emma, and the children reached Knoxville, Tennessee, on November 12, 1887. Emma's sister and brother were there to meet them and accompany them to nearby Maryville. The trip had sapped the family's energy and spirits, and they were relieved when the horse-drawn carriages, heavily laden with people and trunks, finally arrived at Emma's old homestead. Her mother welcomed them home and joyfully swept her grandchildren into her embrace, delighted to meet them for the first time. Emma was thrilled to be home again, but her joy was tempered with sorrow over the fact that her dear father had died during her absence, never to be seen again, at least not in this life.

She soon received more bad news. Not long after her homecoming, Emma learned that her older sister, Ella, had died in childbirth at her home in Ohio, leaving behind a grieving husband and four young children. "Emma felt this bereavement to be doubly sad because Ella was the one with whom she was most intimately associated while growing up," Tom wrote, "and because she had not been able to meet her since returning from Japan. Ella's body was brought home and interred in Magnolia Cemetery, near the grave of her father. Previous to this time, Emma had anticipated a reunion of her brothers and sisters at the home of their mother at Maryville. But when Ella was dead and it seemed difficult for some of the others to come, she reluctantly gave up the idea, saying 'We will have the reunion in Heaven.'"

Despite their fatigue and grief, Tom and Emma soon rebounded and began settling into life at home in Maryville, gradually adjusting to the changes they found. The children were enthralled by their new surroundings, as Tom noted in his journal.

> The children were full of wonder at the many strange sights and sounds. The fields, the fences, the houses, everything were so different from what they had been accustomed to. Theron and Lois attracted attention everywhere by talking to each other in Japanese—which they spoke in preference to English.
>
> At first we noticed many changes. Those whom we left ten years before had, many of them, moved away to other parts, and many were dead and gone forever, while the children and young people had grown altogether out of our recognition. We had not been at home long, however, until it began to seem as if we had not been away at all. It seemed rather that we had been dreaming for a while and waked up to find things changed, somewhat to be sure, but on the whole very much as they formerly were.

Maryville scene and campus, 1895

Soon after their arrival, Tom made his way—alone—to Mount Horeb to visit his father, leaving Emma and the children in Maryville. It would be a full six months before Tom would take his family to see his father. Upon his homecoming, Tom found that his siblings had grown and changed so much that they seemed almost like strangers; his father was the only one in the family he recognized. Other changes confronted him, too. His father had sold the old farm and bought an adjoining one, tearing down Tom's childhood home in the process, the home where he had been born and raised. In addition, Tom's beloved sister, Becky, had died while he had been away in Japan. Mount Horeb no longer felt like home. After a few days, Tom headed back to Maryville.

Never one to sit still, Tom visited churches throughout East Tennessee, speaking about mission work in Japan and preaching an occasional sermon. "I am always at the service of the [Foreign Mission] Board, ready to go anywhere and do anything as far as I am able," Tom wrote to the Board secretary in New York City.[1] He also accepted an honorary degree of Doctor of Divinity from his alma mater, Maryville College, an honor that he accepted with his typical humility. Life proceeded smoothly until Christmas, when Tom caught cold from exposure and then suffered an attack of what his doctors called "muscular rheumatism and nervous prostration." His illness confined him to bed, and he did not leave his room for several weeks. Being laid up frustrated him greatly, since there was so much work to be done in the home mission field. And as Emma struggled to care for him and the children, Tom worried whether she would hold up under the strain. Fortunately, the children remained healthy. Tom took the time to reflect on them and their developing personalities.

> The children all soon began to show the good effects of the pure air and outdoor exercise. They were everywhere admired and treated very kindly by everyone. They soon became so attached to America and their surroundings that they did not have any desire to go back to Japan.
>
> Ella was large for her age, with dark hair and eyes. In disposition generous and impulsive. Her quick temper was her greatest fault and gave her and the rest of us much trouble.
>
> Emma also was large—her hair and eyes much like Ella's. Her disposition, as well as her face, was very different. She was less fond of books than Ella but more useful in taking care of the baby and in doing turns [household help]. Her greatest enemy was an inborn love for teasing her sisters and brother.

Theron had large dark eyes, fair skin and light brown hair, with
fine features. He was sensitive and somewhat girlish in disposition. He gave us more trouble than any of the others on account
of his ill temper and his stubbornness. Music had a peculiar
effect upon his nerves, often making him cry. He said to me one
day, "I love Mama more than God, and I don't know what to do
about it."

Lois was perhaps more universally admired than any of the others; indeed, she was too much admired for her own good, and
her naturally sweet and gentle disposition was somewhat spoiled
by the constant attention of friends. Her eyes were large, dark
and expressive. She was full of funny sayings. I was driving with
her one day soon after our return from Japan. I told the horse to
"get up" when Lois said very seriously, "He am getting up."

Mary had not developed sufficiently for us to judge very well
what she would be like. She had, however, grown old enough
for us to see that her disposition was not any better than that of
some of the others—indeed she seemed more like Theron than
any of the rest, and that meant trouble all around.

The year closed with me confined to bed and suffering severely,
but the rest were well, and all felt that it was good to be in the
homeland once more.

Although small town life in Maryville had not changed much during Tom and Emma's absence, other parts of America were struggling with
post-Civil War turmoil and changes brought about by industrialization.
Immigrants from Europe and Asia, freed slaves, and farm workers seeking
new opportunities crowded into dark, dirty tenements in Northern cities,
where crime, racial and ethnic conflict, and disease flourished. Hydroelec-
tric and steam power, telephones, and railroads were changing the face of
America, fueling economic growth but also widening income inequality.
So-called "Robber Barons" in mining, railroads, oil, and steel monopolized
industries and bought off politicians, worshipping to a new gospel of wealth
in a Gilded Age. Political corruption and dangerous, abusive work places
spawned populist politics and radical labor unions. Religion wasn't immune
from change, either. The rise of science, including Darwin's theory of evolution; social sciences like psychology, sociology, and comparative religion;
and secular universities challenged organized religion's hold on American
values, as more and more Americans pursued a new rationalism and ques-
tioned the literal truth of what was written in the Bible.

As Tom lay suffering in bed at the close of 1887, the US Navy opened a new base in the Kingdom of Hawaii, where it had secured a long-term lease for the exclusive use of Pearl Harbor as a coaling and repair station for warships, locking England, France, and other Western naval powers out of this strategically important Pacific outpost. America's naval expansion and growing military might did not go unnoticed by Japan's leaders as they continued their efforts to strengthen and modernize Japan.

Tom's symptoms eventually eased enough for him to begin traveling again, not only to churches throughout Tennessee, but also to larger church gatherings in Kentucky and North Carolina. In May 1888, he attended the Presbyterian Church's General Assembly as the Japan Mission's official representative. His first exposure to the church's main governing body, meeting in Philadelphia on the occasion of its centennial, taught him a great deal that he had not known about his own church and how it worked. The meeting and informal side conversations also exposed Tom to the heated emotions surrounding Darwin's theory and other challenges to traditional orthodoxy. Tempers sometimes flared as delegates confronted issues dividing the church and fueling the rise of secularism in America. Tom would become entangled in some of these same controversies after his return to Japan.

Tom had planned on returning to Osaka after just one year in America, but recurring illness forced him to change plans. He and Emma debated whether to remain in Maryville or go to California, where a sizable population of Japanese immigrants would allow Tom to put his language and missionary skills to good use. "After much serious deliberation, we decided on the latter course. We were afraid if we should stay in Maryville that circumstances would combine to keep us longer—or to induce us to separate for a time, Emma remaining to look after the education of the children, while I should go back to Japan alone."

In November 1888, exactly one year after returning to Maryville, Tom and Emma gathered up their children and made their way to Oakland, California, staying for a few weeks in a hotel they realized they could not afford for long. Then, Tom wrote, they "were very fortunate in finding a neat cottage of seven rooms ready furnished and in a good locality. . . . I said we were fortunate in finding so good a place; but in truth we did not feel that we were merely <u>fortunate</u>, but that God had guided us. We committed ourselves to his care and guidance when we left Maryville. We felt that we were going out into a strange country and that we needed divine direction. We were thankful, therefore, when we found a house to suit our needs so well." After they were settled, and as 1888 drew to a close, Tom reflected on the year just past.

It has been like all the years of our lives, fraught with many cares and some trials, but God's goodness has far outweighed everything else.

It was a great trial to us to leave our home friends. Emma could not help but feel that in all probability she was saying her final farewell to her mother. Her mother is in feeble health and if we should be gone another ten years, we can hardly hope to find her living when we return. The same may be said in regard to my father, who is already more than seventy-two years old.

These partings are hard for us all. But we gladly pass through them for the sake of the cause to which we have long since given our lives and our all. My own greatest desire and most earnest longing is to get back to Japan, that I may spend and be spent in making known the Gospel of Christ to those who know it not. Than this I crave no greater joy.

The year 1888 is now numbered with the past.

Swift to its close ebbs out life's little day;
Earth's joys grow dim, its glories pass away;
Change and decay in all around I see;
O Thou, who changest not, abide with me![2]

While in Oakland, Tom had more time on his hands than he was accustomed to. He busied himself writing letters to the mission board in New York City, some of them typewritten for the first time, lobbying for more missionaries and money to help the Osaka station respond to the growing interest in Christianity in central and southern Japan. He outlined his vision for a line of mission stations located in all the largest cities, from Osaka in central Japan to the southernmost island of Kyushu, in order to handle the growing workload in the region. He also took time to comment on changes taking place in Japan.[3]

The latest papers from Japan announce that the Japanese Government has at last concluded a treaty with some one of the Western powers (what one is not stated) on terms of perfect equality. If this be true it is an important step in the advance, and one that will greatly facilitate the formation of Mission stations in the interior. But whether it is true or not, the country is practically open to us as matters now stand. By going through with a sufficient amount of red tape we can occupy almost any point in the Empire.

As it turned out, Japanese news reports were not true, and the unequal treaties had not been renegotiated, despite years of painstaking effort and patience on the part of the Japanese. The Meiji regime so far had resisted nationalists' calls for unilateral abrogation of the treaties, which would have invited Western retaliation, preferring instead to pursue their lawful revision through negotiation. Frustration in Japan was mounting, though, and the regime's critics were pressing for Japan to take matters into its own hands and renounce the treaties, with or without treaty partners' approval. How long could a proud nation continue to endure the West's disrespect and discriminatory treatment, these critics asked, especially when Japan had done so much to remake itself in Western fashion? When Tom returned to Japan, he would find out just how deeply this animosity against the West ran.

In his letters, Tom also noted the widespread use of English in Japan, not only in the world of commerce and at court, where the emperor and empress both spoke English and had adopted Western dress, but among ordinary citizens as well.

The young men and women throughout the land, in the towns and cities not only, but also in the remotest mountain districts, are extremely eager to learn enough English to be able to read, and many are ambitious to speak the language, as well. . . . Missionaries have not been slow to avail themselves of this desire. English language teaching was an early way to reach people, through boys' schools especially. But ten or twelve years ago, it was very difficult for girls' schools to sustain themselves. Children had to be given board and room in order to get parents to send them. But girls' schools now are crowded out, and parents pay all expenses, with even Buddhist priests being willing to take the risk of their daughters becoming Christians in order to have them get an English education.

As widespread as interest in English was, though, Tom challenged the view held by some of his fellow missionaries and other observers that the Japanese soon would adopt English for everyday use in place of their native language.

The Japanese have a wonderful language of their own, with a most copious vocabulary and with an idiom that admits of the greatest variety—and accuracy—of expression. It is an extremely difficult language to acquire, but once acquired it becomes even in the mouth of a foreigner a most beautiful and powerful instrument. It is not probable that such a language will be pushed to the wall by English, at any rate for a long time to come.

Time passed, and New Year's Day of 1889 not only ushered in a new year but also treated Tom to his third eclipse of the sun, an event that still impressed him as an adult. The children were growing rapidly, which made Tom and Emma feel old, even at the relatively young ages of thirty-eight and thirty-three. The four older children thrived in their studies at a highly rated Christian school. The owner charged them a reduced tuition, Tom explained, "because in so doing she would be indirectly aiding the great cause of Foreign Missions." Then, on April 30, the family welcomed a sixth child into its midst: little Eva, whom they called Evie. She was "a bright and healthy girl," Tom wrote. "We all thought her resemblance to Theron quite strong."

Not all news was equally good, though. Tom's health was so bad that he spent much of the year in bed. Not only did he suffer physically, but he also was plagued with guilt because he couldn't work, even as the mission board continued paying his $200 monthly salary. The ailment that doctors in Maryville had described as "muscular rheumatism and nervous prostration" was actually a far more serious illness. Tom had caught a strep infection, and it had progressed to rheumatic fever, whose effects are as damaging as they are debilitating. Fever, painful, swollen joints, chest pain, heart palpitations, fatigue, and shortness of breath all combined to wring the energy from Tom's body. Left untreated—and no drugs were available in the 1880s to fight this or many other diseases—Tom's rheumatic disease continued its attack, leaving his heart valves and heart muscles permanently damaged. Tom would never be completely free of the disease's symptoms.

Ill or not, Tom was anxious to return to Japan after a two-year absence, and he and Emma began to prepare for the long voyage. "I felt but little regret at the thought of leaving America a second time," Tom wrote. "I found little there to attract and hold me after having been so long in a foreign land. Emma felt much the same, though she had considerable regret in bringing our children back to Japan, where there are so few educational advantages and so many things to demoralize even older people than they."

At three o'clock in the afternoon on August 3, 1889, Tom, Emma, and the children, including three-month-old Evie, boarded the steamer *Belgic* bound from San Francisco to Yokohama. Precisely fifteen days, fifteen hours, and sixteen minutes later—"a very short trip," according to Tom—the family landed once again in Japan. "We received a very warm welcome from our missionary friends and especially from the native Christians," Tom wrote. "Our welcome here was far more cordial than that which we received on our return to America." Tom and his family had come home.

Notes

1. To Arthur Mitchell, December 12, 1887. PCUSA, "Correspondence."

2. Hymn "Abide with Me," by Henry Francis Lyte (1793–1847).

3. Letter to Arthur Mitchell, BFM, February 13, 1889. PCUSA, "Correspondence."

CHAPTER 14

A Death in the Family

One last little sigh and the dear life was gone forever.

Even though leaving family and friends in America had been hard, Tom and Emma were glad to be back in Japan. The voyage across the Pacific had been smooth and pleasant, with just a few days of rough weather, but Emma had suffered from seasickness most of the way, just as she had on her maiden voyage across the Pacific. The ship's rolling and pitching had upset the children's stomachs, too, but they had been able to go up on deck almost every day when the weather was good. Upon their return to Osaka, Tom and Emma soon had their house in living condition again, and they resumed life much as they had known it before leaving two years before.

Just as Tom had anticipated when they had left, many of the faces in the mission station had changed during their absence. Some missionaries had moved on to other posts, and others had come to take their places. He welcomed visitors from America, including the Secretary of the Board of Foreign Missions in New York City, Dr. Arthur Mitchell, who was on a tour of Asian missions. While in Osaka, Dr. Mitchell baptized little Eva, prompting Tom to write, "She was very good while the ceremony was being performed. It may be interesting to her some future day to know that she was baptized by so good and great a man as Dr. Mitchell."

Japan, too, had changed during the family's absence. Itagaki Taisuke's pro-democracy activists, bolstered by a groundswell of support throughout the empire, had seen one of their main goals fulfilled. On February 11, 1889, Japan had adopted a constitution, becoming the first country in Asia to take such a momentous step. The new constitution, as Itagaki and his Liberal Party had proposed, named the emperor as head of the empire, but it also granted rights to the people and their elected representatives and created an independent judiciary. Although the constitution did not give as many rights as the activists had hoped, it still was a major step forward in Japan's transformation from a loose collection of semi-autonomous domains ruled by hereditary lords to a modern, democratic state. As the emperor had first promised in an 1881 Imperial edict, a representative parliament, or Diet, was elected and convened for the first time in November 1890, a year after Tom's return to Osaka. Japan's first election gave just 1 percent of the population—the country's wealthiest men—the right to vote, but it nonetheless allowed at least some citizens to experience the most fundamental right in a democracy: the right to choose.

The Japanese were taking their cue from the West in more than just the political realm. The late nineteenth century was an era of might makes right. Western powers were expanding their economic and military reach into the Asia-Pacific region, as well-known military thinkers, most notably America's Alfred Mahan, stressed the importance of naval power to extend and protect legitimate national interests overseas, especially—for America—in the Pacific. The early Meiji regime's slogan, "rich country, strong military," took on a new urgency in the face of the growing challenge from the West, and government leaders redoubled their efforts to build up Japan's industrial base, export capability, and economic strength. Future industrial giants, including Mitsui, Mitsubishi, and Sumitomo, operating with strong government support, gained control of large swaths of Japan's domestic market. Osaka's cotton mills churned out large volumes of yarn and fabric, allowing Japan to reduce its costly import bill for items essential for military uniforms. In this high-stakes competition they were engaged in, Japanese leaders also tried to bolster national pride and encourage popular support for the notion of Japan as a great power.[1]

Japan's strong independent streak also extended to church matters. Foreign missionaries had played a key role in laying foundations for the Japanese church, but by now, many of Japan's churches were well-established, self-financing bodies. Japanese preachers and lay church members alike sought greater freedom from day-to-day control by missionaries. Tom not only understood this desire but supported it, too. He admired the Japanese preachers and elders who governed the churches he had helped establish and had full confidence in their abilities. "No one could fail to be impressed with the intelligence, the orthodoxy and the piety of . . . the native ministers and elders," Tom wrote following a meeting of missionaries and Japanese Christians. "The church is safe in the hands of such men, and this feeling is greatly strengthened by my personal acquaintance with most of the men, many of whom I regard as warm personal friends."[2]

Tom was prepared to cut the apron strings and allow Japanese Christians to stand on their own, without missionary support. That goal was one he had worked toward since his earliest days in the field. In 1886, long before leaving Osaka, Tom had established a Home Mission Board, with an equal number of Japanese and foreign members, to help shape the direction of mission work in his region. He also had encouraged Japanese churches to raise funds from among their own members and reduce their reliance on missionary funds, a step that would guarantee their true independence— not to mention ease the financial burden on the Japan mission and the home mission board.

The arrival in Japan of Unitarians, who denied the existence of God as a Trinity and thus the divinity of Jesus; and Quakers, who lacked a specific creed and looked to the Holy Spirit for guidance, had sparked tremendous confusion among Japanese Christians and hurt mission schools throughout the country. Nonetheless, Tom was heartened by progress being made in the mission's evangelistic work. "The churches in connection with our Western Japan Mission are now on a firmer basis and in better condition, on the whole, than at any time in their past history," Tom reported to the foreign mission board in February 1891.

> It also is a remarkable fact that, while there is a widespread reaction against foreigners and everything foreign, public sentiment has steadily grown more favorable toward Christianity. In many places where one year ago persecution against Christianity was very strong, the tide has turned and a generally favorable feeling has taken possession of the hearts of the people. And I think it may be said that throughout <u>Western</u> Japan, at any rate, public sentiment is more decidedly in favor of the Christian religion than ever before.
>
> This is owing largely to the fact that the lives of the Christians are generally so much better than those of the people by whom they are surrounded. A religion that can so transform and elevate commends itself to the judgment of intelligent and thinking men in Japan, as well as elsewhere throughout the world.[3]

Tom also took an unprecedented step for a foreign missionary in Japan. He was a man who lived out his beliefs, and his belief in the Japanese Christian church was unshakable. Japan's new constitution had granted freedom of religion to the country's citizens, with the proviso that its practice be "within limits not prejudicial to peace and order, and not antagonistic to their duties as subjects." And for the first time, Christianity was completely legal in Japan. How better to celebrate this milestone than to join the very church he had spent so much time and effort to build up? In April 1891, Tom applied to change his membership from Union Presbytery in Tennessee to the Chinzei Presbytery on Japan's southern Kyushu Island, the furthest location from his home base of Osaka and one of Japan's more remote islands. The Japanese Presbytery voted to accept Tom as a member, making him the only foreign missionary, or one of a very few, ever to join the Church of Christ in Japan, as the Union Church of Christ had been renamed in 1890.[4]

* * *

On July 17, 1892, Tom wrote: "Almost three years have passed away since I last wrote in this fragmentary record of our married life. They have been years of toil and care, with their lights and shadows. We have much to be grateful for, a fact which we never forget." Although he had much to be grateful for, Tom found it almost impossible to accept the tragedy that had struck his family.

> On the 28th of October 1891, occurred the great earthquake of the Nagoya-Gifu region, which was felt severely in Osaka. Many thousands of lives were lost in this great disaster, mostly in the region just named, though in Osaka a cotton factory was shaken down in which a considerable number of people perished.
>
> I was absent from home, attending a meeting of the "Chinzei" Chūkai (Presbytery) in Hiroshima. I did not feel disturbed by the earthquake, as it was comparatively light west of Osaka. Emma and the children, however, were very much alarmed, not so much perhaps by what had actually taken place as by anxiety as to what might happen at any time. Emma's nerves were so shaken that she did not get rid of the feeling of insecurity and anxiety for months—indeed, I doubt whether the effect upon her nervous system will ever pass entirely away as long as she lives. Our house was considerably damaged and one chimney was so badly unsettled that it had to be taken down and rebuilt from the foundation.
>
> But serious as the earthquake calamity was, and as important as other events that have taken place within the last two or three years are, I have no heart to dwell upon any of them. One single event has just recently occurred which overshadows all others in our minds.
>
> I allude to the death of our dear Ella. My pen almost refuses to record so sad an event. Our hearts are rent and torn with grief, while our sense of loss is inexpressibly great.
>
> Since our return from America in summer of '89, Ella had been growing and developing very rapidly. In stature and size,

she was almost the same as her mother, and until the early spring of this year her health seemed almost perfect. It was in the latter part of April that we noticed at times that she seemed slightly unwell, and somewhat less interested in her studies than usual. But we thought nothing of it, supposing that her listlessness and paleness, as seen occasionally, were due to the approach of warm weather or some such cause.

On Sunday, May 15th, she went with me to the South Church, where she was accustomed to play the organ on Sunday mornings at the church service. We rode up to the meeting, dismissed our jinrikishas, and after service walked home together. But Ella was not well, though she did not complain and seemed to enjoy the walk. It was her last walk, and that her last Sunday at the South Church.

Now when I go to the same church I go alone, the organist's chair is empty and the organ silent; and I cannot easily restrain my tears. But I must not anticipate.

During the week that followed that, to me, memorable Sunday, our dear girl continued to grow worse, though at times we thought her better. On Tuesday afternoon, May 17th, she seemed rather bright and went over to the recreation ground just across the street. But next morning found her worse again. She kept her bed nearly all that day, though in the afternoon I carried her downstairs where she sat upon a chair in the sitting room for an hour or so.

We summoned the best medical aid within our reach—Dr. W. Taylor of the American Board of Foreign Missions and later Dr. H. Lanning of the American Episcopal Mission, both of them excellent physicians. But the disease proved too stubborn for their skill. We did not feel any great alarm until Sunday, the 22nd.

In the morning of that day I went to the North Church and preached from the text, "Speak unto the children of Israel that they go forward." I felt a burden on my heart even while trying to inspire faith and courage in others. It was an anxious day for Emma and me. The day previous was the fifteenth anniversary of our wedding day, and when we greeted each other in memory of the occasion we both involuntarily burst into tears. Already our hearts were beginning to feel, though unconsciously, the shadow of the coming event.

Late in the evening of the Sunday just referred to Dr. Taylor called me to one side and told me that he had done everything he could and with absolutely no result and that the case was very serious indeed. Though in a measure, as I thought, prepared for the sad intelligence, the shock was fearful.

My limbs trembled under me; my head grew dizzy; and I had to sit down to keep from falling. I, however, summoned up courage enough to call Emma, at the doctor's request, and consult her in regard to a proposition for a surgical operation by the Doctors Taylor and Lanning—I may say in passing, that the operation was never performed, and that it could not have been successful, as we afterwards learned.

That Sunday night was a trying one for us all. Ella had been unable to sleep for several nights, and Emma and I had taken turns in watching with her, Emma doing most of the watching. On that night, though I retired I could not sleep, and Emma stayed by the sickbed until morning striving to comfort and relieve the patient sufferer.

Ella urged her mother to lie down and rest, which she did occasionally during the night though she did not go beyond call. I was in the sick room frequently during the night; and early next morning—May 23rd—was dressed and by the sick bed again. It was becoming more and more evident that the end was approaching. The hour for breakfast came and I urged Emma to go down and at least take a cup of coffee.

While she was gone, I sat holding Ella's hands in mine. They were already growing cold. The doctor soon came in and gave a hypodermic injection of morphine to allay the suffering which was intense and increasing. In the meantime, Emma had returned to the room.

Ella asked how long it would be until the morphine would begin to take effect. When the doctor answered, "Ten or fifteen minutes," Emma took out her watch and she and Ella counted the minutes until the partial relief came.

I can never forget the scene, so pathetic, so inexpressibly agonizing to us all. Emma then sat and held the hands of the departing one, and we two watched her young life as it ebbed away.

No one else was in the room until the very last when Dr. Taylor came in. Ella was conscious almost to the very end, except for the influence of morphine. My tears came and went as I sat and watched the approach of death, but Emma's eyes were dry and her face unmoved. She preserved her ordinary demeanor in order that the dying one might not discover any sign of alarm.

One last little sigh and the dear life was gone forever—(As a Japanese friend afterwards expressed it, "like the single note of a cuckoo among the green leaves of spring")—and our first born lay before us a lifeless lump of clay.

Not till then did Emma show any sign of emotion, but then the floods broke loose and a torrent of grief overwhelmed her soul—from which she has not yet recovered and perhaps never will, though the day may come when things will look different to her and to me.

None of the other children knew the end was near. I let them go away to the playground as soon as they were through breakfast, where they remained till sometime after their sister was gone. Then at Emma's request, I went down and called them home and she sat down and told them that Ella had gone to heaven.

They were surprised and shocked beyond measure as the terrible truth gradually took hold upon them. Little five-year-old Mary's heart seemed almost broken. She hardly ceased to weep aloud all through the long, gloomy day that followed. I say "gloomy" because the day was dull and cloudy without and our hearts were so sad.

But Emma was especially careful that the children should not get too gloomy impressions of death. After the body was dressed and they were all looking at it, she called their attention to the pretty hands and pretty dress, and always spoke of Ella as having "gone to Jesus" and as being happy.

It was with this impression in mind that, a morning or two later when we came to the table, Mary voiced the sentiments of us all, when she said: "I am not crying because Ella is happy, but because I am sorry." Again she said, "I am sorry Ella is dead; I would rather have died myself than to have her die."

"The 23ʳᵈ of May" is indelibly inscribed upon our memories in characters of blood. The month of May is fast becoming an eventful one to me. My mother died on the 5th, 1867. My sister, Emma, was born on the 13th, 1856 (?). We were married on the 21st, '77; my father died on the 6th, '91; and now this last event on the 23rd, '92.

But I must not digress. The news of Ella's departure spread rapidly among our missionary friends, and among the Japanese Christians. Everybody seemed to vie with everybody else in showering us with kindness. Ella was very popular, and no face was more familiar than hers. She had a smile and a cheerful greeting for everyone. She was especially kind to children, and the little ones on the concession knew, admired and loved her.

Her many friends, young and old, literally overwhelmed the coffin and filled the rooms of our house with wreaths and crosses of the most beautiful flowers; and in many other ways showed their love for her and their sympathy for us.

We could not keep the precious clay near us long, so the coffin had to be closed before many of her friends could get one last look at her face. Before it was closed her sister Emma placed a little bunch of flowers in the cold but pretty hand. Oh, how our hearts ached for this sister, so near Ella's own age! They two were always together; were affectionately, though not demonstratively, fond of each other, and the younger one was very dependent upon the older.

The funeral was conducted by the Rev. Messrs.' J. P. Hearst, Ph.D., and Geo. E. Woodhall, members of our mission, in our sitting room. The meeting was attended by all the missionaries who could be present and by many of the native Christians. The funeral took place on the day following her death, May 24th, in the afternoon, and we proceeded at once to Kōbe where preparations had been made for the internment.

In the Foreign Cemetery at Kōbe, near the seashore where the restless sea surges back and forth, we laid her to rest. There her fair young form will molder back to dust again, while numerous pines keep solemn vigil over her grave.

This first great sorrow, this first break in our family circle, has made a deep and lasting impression on all our minds. We miss the loved one at every turn and all the time. Even little Eva talks about Ella and mourns her absence. One night, recently, after Emma had put Mary and Eva to bed and as usual sat waiting for them to go to sleep, Eva suddenly asked, "Where is Ella?"

Emma said, "She has gone to Jesus' house." Then, after a pause, Eva said, "I don't like Jesus. I wish he wouldn't 'vite (invite) us there." "But," Emma replied, "Jesus is very good to us and loves us, and we ought to like him." To which Eva answered, "Well, I do like him a little, and I would like to go and just look inside the gate and come away."

But the mother feels the loss more than anyone else. Perhaps that is natural, and always so. But Ella had of late years grown to such maturity and was so well read that she had become a constant and most helpful companion for her mother. When the children's clothes were being made, Ella was ready with her assistance and suggestions.

And this reminds me that just before Ella's last illness began, Emma had bought some white material with which to make her (Ella) a new dress. Both Ella and her mother had already done some work on the dress, but it was unfinished when she died. It was her shroud. Little did the fond mother anticipate for what a sad purpose that white material would be used.

But so it often is. We cannot see a step before us, and it is well we cannot. Emma is inconsolable in her grief and her sense of loss is unspeakable, though she is upheld by her faith in the Heavenly Father.

How we miss the absent one I cannot begin to tell. There is an empty chair at the table. The piano which Ella used to play at morning worship now stands silent, while our hearts are too heavy to sing without it. We often catch ourselves listening for a footstep that never comes and looking for a form that never appears. . . .

We feel sure that God took her to Himself, and that for some good and wise purpose though we do not see what the purpose was. Deep questionings arise in our minds as we try to realize her present state. Why was she taken away in the very beginning of what seemed such a fair and promising life? Of what use was it that she was ever given to us at all? We cannot tell, where is she now? What is her state? What is her relation to us? What to her former self?

We strain our eyes and try to see beyond the veil, but we see nothing. The only comfort is in what Christ and Paul teach us. The many mansions we know are there, whatever that may mean. "We know that if this our earthly tabernacle be dissolved, we have a house not made with hands eternal in the heavens." "And death is swallowed up in victory!" "That the sufferings of this present time are not worthy to be compared with the glory that shall be revealed in us!"[5]

The Bible in many places takes on a new meaning to us in the light of this great affliction. When we think of the blessedness of her present condition we would not recall her to this world of sin and pain though our hearts are sad and lonely without her. . . . It is with difficulty that we can bring ourselves to realize the sad truth that we shall see her no more in this life.

Notes

1. See Iriye, "Japan's Drive," 294–312, and Jansen, *Modern Japan*, 414–55.

2. To Arthur Mitchell, BFM, December 22, 1890. PCUSA, "Correspondence."

3. To Arthur Mitchell, BFM, February 21, 1891. PCUSA, "Correspondence." In his letter, Tom mentioned Unitarians and Quakers as being hurtful to mission work.

4. Yanagawa, *Chinzei Presbytery*. "Record of 19th Chinzei Presbytery of the Japan United Christian Church, April, Meiji 24th [1891]." In 1893, after moving to Tokyo, Tom transferred his membership from Chinzei Presbytery to the Second Tokyo Presbytery.

5. "The many mansions," John 14:2; "We know that if this," 2 Cor 5:1; "And death is swallowed," 1 Cor 15:54; "That the sufferings," Rom 8:18; all King James Version.

CHAPTER 15

Nationalism on the Rise

Backlash against foreigners, especially Christians, rose sharply.

Following Ella's death, Tom and Emma moved through life in a daze. They managed to perform day-to-day tasks and attend to important family and church matters, but every time Tom returned from a trip, he expected Ella to be among the children running out to the road to greet him. He recalled how his normally restless and impatient daughter had been so wonderfully patient during her illness despite the unrelenting pain and how grateful she had been for the smallest of favors.

"For every little service that we rendered, she invariably said, 'Thank you.' The last words she spoke to me were these. I think it was less than an hour before she died that I turned her pillow for her, when she thanked me as usual. I wonder if today she is not engaged in expressing her gratitude to the Great Father for us all!" Even though Ella had not professed her faith publicly before she died, Tom was confident that she had been a committed Christian. Her death preoccupied his thoughts, and this man of the cloth, who had consoled so many mourners in their grief, found little comfort and few answers in the words of the Bible.

May 24th, 1893

Yesterday was the anniversary of Ella's death and we all went down to Kōbe in the afternoon and put flowers on her grave. I could not help wondering all the time whether she could see us, or know anything of what we were doing. There is nothing in the world so absolutely silent as the grave.

The sea is restless and noisy, the air we breathe, though itself voiceless, is yet stirred into motion by unseen causes, and is made vocal with the sounds of life; but the grave utters no voice, gives no sign that we can possibly interpret.

What, however, may we say of the spirit that took its flight one short, sad year ago? I confess I do not know, nor does it seem possible to me to get anything out of the Bible on the subject which will set the mind at rest. The year has gone by with the empty chair in our family circle, and the aching void in our hearts.

The wound is not healed, nor can we feel that we yet have any light as to why our dear one should have been taken away. Still we are not without faith. We believe that we shall yet know the reason, or if not, we shall be let to see that all was for the best. We doubt not that God is a Father who cannot err in his wisdom nor do anything but that which is best for his poor, wayward children.

The grave in the Kōbe cemetery is neatly kept and is a pretty spot. We have had it enclosed and a suitable stone put up, with Ella's name and the dates of her birth and death inscribed—also the following lines from Longfellow's poem, "The Reaper and the Flowers."

> And the mother gave in tears and pain,
> The flowers she most did love;
> She knew she should see them all again
> In the fields of light above.

It is a spot around which our affections will hover as long as we live, no matter how long the time may be nor where we go in the years to come, and yet we know that

> She is not dead—the child of our affection—
> But gone unto that school
> Where she no longer needs our poor protection,
> And Christ himself doth rule.

— — — — —

> We will be patient, and assuage the feeling
> We may not wholly stay;
> By silence sanctifying, not concealing,
> The grief that must have way.[1]

Ella's death—from a burst appendix, they later learned—had largely overshadowed that of Tom's father a few weeks before hers, on May 6, at age seventy-five. Tom may not have been close to his father, but he nonetheless felt a son's devotion to the man who had raised him.

> He had seen much trouble during his long life. His domestic afflictions were greater in number than usually fall to the lot of man. Having been married four times and having had born to him twelve children he lived to see all of them buried except five children. . . . His last illness was brief—pneumonia being the trouble. He was a man of little education so far as schools were concerned, but had read much and was consequently well informed. His faith was strong. The Bible was his constant companion especially in his later life. . . . He died as he had lived, in faith. When asked on his deathbed how the future appeared to him he invariably replied "Bright" or "Very bright." As from this distance I look back over his life, as I knew him, I see very little to condemn and much, very much, to admire and that I would gladly imitate. I can hardly realize that he is gone and that I shall see him no more on earth.

By the 1890s, Japan's efforts to catch up to the West were bearing fruit, as the country's army took shape along Prussian lines, exports and export earnings surged, and foundations were laid for heavy industries like steel and shipbuilding. The country's leaders were convinced from the West's example that the road to great power status lay in expanding Japan's own reach, not only militarily, but also through trade and emigration. By 1893, nearly twenty-two thousand Japanese were living in Hawaii, then an independent kingdom; and Japan's leaders considered other Pacific and Asian destinations to be equally promising places for colonization. Japan still did not boast much of a navy, though, and even with its growing economic and military strength, the country still was no match for better-armed Western powers.[2]

In the eyes of Japanese military strategists, Japan sat uncomfortably in the middle of the world's great powers, whose commercial and military interests were expanding more and more deeply into East Asia. Although Japan's island status gave it some protection, Russia's completion of a six-thousand-mile Trans-Siberian Railway in 1891 and of a naval base in Vladivostok on the Sea of Japan in 1892 convinced Japan's military leaders that Russia soon would move into China and then Korea, putting Russia in a perfect position to invade or slowly strangle Japan through control of sea lanes. Other European powers—Germany, Britain, and France—also loomed as threats from the west. Looking east, Japan saw America, whose industrial might, transcontinental railways, and growing naval strength were fueling its expansionist reach across the Pacific.

The question was how could Japan ward off the growing threat from these Western powers and, at the same time, unify the Japanese people at a time of badly fractured domestic politics following the election of Japan's first parliament? The answer would not be long in coming.

Life goes on for the bereaved, and so it was for Tom and Emma. In July 1893, the Board of Directors of Meiji Gakuin College in Tokyo—successor of the boys' school Tom and his fellow missionaries had moved to the capital from its first home in Yokohama—voted unanimously to call Tom as the chair of Systemic and Biblical Theology, a prestigious position in the school's theology department. Although honored to be asked, Tom hesitated, uncertain of what his duty was. Ultimately he decided to accept.

> I did so with a deep sense of my unfitness for the place and with much sorrow at the thought of leaving Osaka. It is a great personal sacrifice to us. Here we have lived for more than eleven years (including the time spent in America during which period we of course regarded this as <u>home</u>). The place is dear to us in many ways and beyond expression. We do not expect that any other home, this side of heaven, will ever be to us anything like what this one has been.

Once their minds were made up, though, Tom and Emma turned their faces toward their new calling and prepared to move once again. Even the mundane task of moving was complicated by Japan's growing anger over Western powers' continuing refusal to renegotiate the unequal 1850s treaties. In an effort to pressure Western governments to come to their senses and begin treating Japan as an equal, authorities had begun to slow the issuance of inland passports for foreigners. Tom and his family felt the effects. For weeks, they sat surrounded by bare walls and in the midst of boxes and bundles, "hanging by the eyelids," as Tom put it, waiting for documents authorizing them to relocate to Tokyo. The passports finally came, and, because the weather was extremely hot in Osaka, Tom sent Emma and the children ahead to Tokyo, where at least the nights were cooler. He remained behind for a few days packing up the last of their belongings.

Tom left Osaka on July 19 at 10:46 p.m., "riding off alone in a jinrikisha in the moonlight. I felt sad at what I was leaving behind and apprehensive as to what lay before me. Certainly he was right who said, *Tempora mutant et nos mutamur.*" ["The times change and we, too, are changed."] Tom went in faith, certain that God was guiding him. "I have but one object now in this world," he wrote, "and that is to serve the Master as best I can in the sphere where I am most needed."[3] While awaiting delivery of their household goods in Tokyo, the family spent several weeks in the Metropole Hotel in the Tsukiji foreign district. Finally, they moved into their own home, first at No. 27 and then at No. 42 Tsukiji.

In November, Lula Christine was born, bringing the number of children up to six again "as it had been previous to Ella's going away. But we shall never cease to count her, too, as one of the number. And our children will always insist that 'we are seven,' though 'one in the church yard lies.' The new baby had a warm welcome. Especially, Mary and Eva were delighted to have a little baby sister. They could hardly believe their ears when I assured them that she was ours and had come to stay. They thought I must be joking." Between the new baby and the other children's illnesses—Mary fell ill with a light attack of typhoid fever and Theron with scarlet fever—Emma had her hands full as they settled into their new home.

Farewell gathering of Osaka North and South Churches, June 9, 1893.
Tom Alexander back row

Young Emma, Eva (author's grandmother), Theron, ca. 1893

Tokyo had changed since the last time Tom and Emma had lived there. Soot and pollution from the city's coal-fired furnaces and heavy industries darkened the skies and obscured the view of Mount Fuji most days, while new electric lights warded off the darkness and gloom of urban nights. Missionaries teaching at Meiji Gakuin had brought some of America's favorite pastimes with them. The school's baseball and rowing teams were among the first in Tokyo, but new teams were cropping up among the Japanese. Missionaries also brought some of the same deeply held convictions that divided their brethren in America, with conservatives and liberals facing off over Darwinism and other controversies that were challenging religion's place in society and complicating the teaching of Christianity in Japan.

A cloud had fallen over Tokyo's political atmosphere, too, complicating missionaries' efforts to maintain religious teachings in their schools and universities. Nationalism was on the rise, fueled not only by popular resentment against the West and against changes made by leaders seeking to build up Japan as a world power, but also by some of the tenets of Japan's most important political documents. The 1889 constitution had enshrined the notion that the people existed to serve the emperor and the state. Any individual rights that the people enjoyed were a gift from the emperor, the country's sacred sovereign, who ruled over his subjects much like a father rules over his family.

Japan's educational system offered an effective and efficient way to instill the correct views in the Japanese citizenry. The 1890 Imperial Rescript on Education, an official edict that governed Japan's approach to education, stressed the importance of loyalty, filial piety, and harmonious relations among citizens. It also called on the emperor's subjects to "respect the Constitution and observe the laws; should emergency arise, offer yourselves courageously to the state; and thus guard and maintain the prosperity of Our Imperial Throne coeval with heaven and earth." Army drill masters were provided free of charge to schools to lead students' physical education, resulting in an increased intermingling of military and civilian attitudes and customs. Near-universal conscription gave military leaders further opportunity to shape the views of Japan's young men by teaching them to be loyal, devoted citizens.

Backlash against foreigners, especially Christians, rose sharply. *The Japan Evangelist*, a missionary publication, reported in 1894 on the deteriorating conditions.

> Within the last two years the opposition to Christianity has become more thoroughly organized throughout the entire country. Buddhist sects, otherwise mutually hostile, are united against the common foe, and, wherever it is possible, the Buddhists stir up also the Shintoists. Opposition takes sometimes the form of social ostracism, sometimes, in local government institutions, the form of a ban on those who would investigate [explore] Christianity, and universally the form of charges against Christians as being unfilial, unpatriotic, and disloyal. In some instances, there have been disturbances at Christian meetings by the rowdy element.[4]

Reactionaries in the Diet and the public at large took aim at foreigners' land holdings. The law prohibiting foreigners from owning property in Japan had been skirted for years by missionaries and other foreigners working and doing business in Japan. The method was simple. Foreigners found Japanese individuals whom they trusted and asked them to buy land, which the Japanese owners then leased back to the foreigners on a long-term basis. The foreigners had to hope, of course, that the real landowner would not sell the land out from under them. Japanese Christians had long played this intermediary role for missionaries, since there was no other way to obtain land for residences or mission schools. Some newly elected Diet members threatened to toughen the law or to confiscate the land entirely. These draconian steps were never taken, but Japanese Christians who leased land to missionaries feared the effect of the growing backlash on their businesses and, for some, even on their personal safety.

Mission schools and missionary activities also suffered. Even as early as 1890, while still in Osaka, Tom had worried about the future and expressed his concerns in a letter to the mission secretary in New York City.

> No doubt you hear more or less of late about the reaction that is taking place in this country. This reaction is likely to prove to be a serious matter. Together with other causes, it may, and I think undoubtedly will, affect our work materially. Indeed, its influence is beginning to be felt most decidedly in connection with our mission schools. Some of our most experienced missionaries are convinced that we are not to have, for some time to come at any rate, the prosperity which has been ours for years past.
>
> In addition to the reactionary movement, political agitation occasioned by the recent promulgation of the National Constitution and the consequent election of members of the Diet to be opened next autumn is in some quarters causing so much excitement as to seriously interfere with missionary operations.[5]

Many young men attending Christian schools believed, with good reason, that Japanese authorities would discriminate against them after they had graduated and were seeking jobs in the civil service or in government-sponsored universities. Men employed as teachers learned that professing their belief in Christianity often led to their dismissal. One bright spot that remained for missionaries were the schools and Bible studies for girls and women. Although female enrollment dropped modestly, many women prized the education offered by missionary schools for themselves and their daughters and worked hard to support them. And bravely, too, in the face of such strong public and official backlash, many Japanese Christians and churches redoubled their commitment to prayer and the Christian life. Although conditions were tough, they would not turn their backs on their new-found faith.

Most political struggles are about power, and so it was in Japan after the first parliament took office. Gone were the days when the emperor and a few key advisors could suppress popular opposition to their policies, although they continued to try by closing opposition newspapers and dissolving the Diet, forcing three elections in the space of just four years. They more than met their match in some of the new parliamentarians. Savvy politicians like Itagaki Taisuke of the Liberal Party and others had been elected to the Diet, and they lost no time in pressing for change in Japan's domestic and foreign policies.

Itagaki Taisuke, President of Liberal Party

Topping their list was treaty revision. Japan's public was fed up with the West's arrogance, and so were its politicians. In their view, Japan needed to take a hard line with Western powers and demand Japanese control over its own tariffs and over foreigners breaking the law in Japan; otherwise, why shouldn't Japan unilaterally abrogate the treaties and refuse to live up to their terms? In 1892, the new Diet's House of Representatives passed a resolution calling on the throne to do just that.

Japan's growing defense budget also was in the opposition parties' sights. Because the treaties in place with Western powers barred Japan from raising tariffs on imported goods, the tax burden fell most heavily on Japan's largely rural population. Fully 60 percent of the government's revenue came from taxes on farmers. Less money should be spent on Japan's military,

Itagaki and other politicians argued, so the crushing burden on farmers could be reduced and more could be spent for regional development. Finally, Itagaki and other conservatives demanded that Japan take a tough stand against China over the status of Korea, revisiting an issue that had led him and his fellow councilor-turned-opposition leader, Saigo Takamori, to resign from the emperor's inner circle in 1873.

Jockeying between Japan and China over the Korean peninsula had intensified in recent years. Lying just 120 miles off the coast of Kyushu, Japan's southernmost island, Korea had long been an important trading partner and was viewed by Japanese strategists as falling within Japan's natural sphere of influence in Asia. China also had designs on the country, and domestic factions in Korea had learned to play one country off against the other. By 1894, civil war in Korea offered the perfect excuse for Japan to send its military to Korea, in order to "protect" the forces begging for Japan's help against their China-backed foes. After China sent its own troops to Korea in June, Japan responded, first by sending a division, and then, in August, by declaring war. Wounded soldiers quickly flowed back into Japan.

That summer, Tom had sent his family to a house they often rented on the shore of Lake Hakone, a mountain resort southwest of Tokyo and a favorite missionary retreat to escape Tokyo's heat and pollution. Disabled and wounded soldiers, numbering over one thousand by late August, began pouring into town for rest and recuperation. Tom arrived on August 1 and was asked to preach to the village's small company of believers in the little chapel founded by the Church of Christ in Japan. Arriving at the chapel the following Sunday, he was surprised to find forty or fifty people assembled for the service, about half of them soldiers.

Seeing their interest, the missionaries later asked local military authorities if they would object to soldiers attending regular services. Not only did the authorities not object, they said they would encourage soldiers to attend. Their response surprised the missionaries, who had grown accustomed to official hostility. Local military authorities clearly were taking their cue from Tokyo, where war department officials indicated they would let local commanders decide how to handle missionaries' requests. In addition, Prince Komatsu, the emperor's cousin and commander-in-chief of the army, actually invited missionaries in Tokyo to give Bibles to imperial soldiers and talk to them about Christianity. What could explain this unexpected turn of events? One possible explanation was that because some senior military officials were Christian, they were open to missionary activities among imperial troops. More likely, though, the prince and war department officials were trying to win Western support or at least neutrality during Japan's conflict with China. Being seen as hostile to Christianity would not help their cause.

Tom and his colleagues in Hakone never did fully understand the reasons for military authorities' support, but they accepted it gratefully as a sign of God's grace. Until his return to Tokyo on September 19, Tom preached one service each day and two on Sundays, attracting as many as sixty soldiers, who listened with interest and respect. "But what about the results?" Tom asked.

> Of course, we cannot say definitely how much of the seed sown will bring forth fruit. But this much can be said: some hundreds of men were brought under the impression of Gospel truth for the first time. Among these I should say as many as fifty or sixty were brought to a determination to study carefully for themselves the truth they heard and to accept it.
>
> Many hundreds of Scripture portions, as well as books and tracts, were distributed and eagerly received. Sometimes those who attended the meetings would ask for books or tracts to carry to their friends who were sick and unable to attend. Altogether, those of us who were permitted to engage in the work felt that we had met with an exceptional opportunity, and we availed ourselves of it with thankful joy.
>
> I cannot close this hasty letter without a word of admiration for the Japanese soldiers. Although there were so many in Hakone, the village was quiet and orderly. The men were as unobtrusive and inoffensive as it is possible for men to be. I did not hear of a single act of rudeness or impoliteness toward any one during the whole summer.[6]

In the end, a good many soldiers were baptized and joined the church. And in addition to the soldiers' good conduct in Hakone, Tom had another, more personal reason to be favorably impressed by their behavior, as he explained. "Theron was playing one day while we were there with some other boys, and one of them accidentally struck him on the head with a stone, making a large and ugly scalp wound. A surgeon of the Japanese army at once sewed it up most skillfully and declined remuneration for his timely services."

Tom's positive view of soldiers in Hakone contrasted sharply with outrage felt by the Western world, when reports of Japanese soldiers' conduct during one key military campaign reached their newspapers. After landing in Korea, Japan's well-prepared army had routed Chinese forces, quickly moving north and into China itself. Japan's military strategists viewed Port Arthur, a well-fortified outpost on China's southern coast, not only as their toughest challenge but also the key to controlling Manchuria and the sea lanes between Korea and China. As naval guns pounded the port, Japan's eighteen-thousand-strong army had massed into the city and overwhelmed its twelve thousand Chinese defenders.

Despite military leaders' orders for strict discipline and good treatment of enemy soldiers and civilians—orders which had been followed reasonably well up to this point—Japanese soldiers went on a rampage when they entered Port Arthur, slaughtering and mutilating thousands of mostly defenseless civilians, including women, children, and elderly men. Official army accounts alleged that some Chinese soldiers, who were notoriously brutal toward enemy fighters, had changed into civilian garb and were fighting Japan's oncoming forces. Other anecdotal accounts said that Japanese soldiers had been enraged by the sight of a Japanese soldier's head displayed on a wooden stake when they entered town. Whatever the reasons, Western countries were appalled by the atrocities, which occurred even as senior Japanese diplomats were in Western capitals seeking revision of the treaties.

In March 1895, just nine months after the war had begun, China capitulated, and a treaty was signed in Shimonoseki, one of the towns in southern Japan where Tom had labored long and hard to establish a now-thriving church. At the end of its first war fought with modern weapons and strategies, Japan emerged victorious and with its own colonies: Formosa (Taiwan today), the Pescadore Islands, and parts of China. Patriotism fueled by the war also had unified the Japanese people in a way that no imperial edict could have. Japan's Diet soon voted for large increases in the military budget, reversing earlier opposition to bloated military spending. Japanese pride over its wartime victory soon turned to renewed anger and resentment against Western powers, however. Because Japan's holdings in China threatened other Western powers' claims, Russia, France, and Germany pressured Japan to give up its hard-won territory in Manchuria. Japan's leaders grudgingly agreed in the face of such united opposition by stronger powers.

That bitter medicine was sweetened by the fact that Great Britain in 1894 had agreed to a new treaty, which granted Japan immediate legal authority over British nationals in the country, to be followed by full tariff authority in five years. Before long, all Western powers had agreed to new treaties, placing Japan on an equal footing with them at last. Tom saw reason to be both pleased and concerned about Japan's wartime victory. "The war had put Japan not merely in the forefront of oriental nations," he wrote, "but has shown her in some respects to be one of the leading nations of the world. This fact will not make it any easier for us ordinary missionaries." Events soon would prove him right.[7]

Notes

1. From "Resignation," by Henry Wadsworth Longfellow in *The Seaside and the Fireside* (1850).

2. For politics under Japan's new constitution and the period leading up to and including the war with China, see Jansen, *Modern Japan*, 414–41, and Lone, *Modern War*. These two sources form the basis for much of the information presented in this chapter.

3. Letter to Dr. Gillespie, BFM, July 13, 1893. PCUSA, "Correspondence."

4. Rev. Henry K. Miller, "Summary of Dr. Hail's Report, read to the Recent Council of the United Missions in Japan, in Session at Tokyo, July 3–10, 1894," *Japan Evangelist*, Vol. I., No. 6 (August 1894), 351. The report does not specify which Dr. Hail prepared and read the original report, but it probably was J. B. Hail, who wrote many mission reports. His brother was A. D. Hail. Both were friends of Tom Alexander and his family.

5. To Arthur Mitchell, BFM, May 28, 1890. PCUSA, "Correspondence."

6. "Work among the Soldiers at Hakone," *Japan Evangelist*, Vol. III, No. 1 (Oct 1895), 48.

7. Account of massacre in Port Arthur from Lone, *Modern War*, 154–63. See also Keene, *Emperor*, 494, with a description of firsthand accounts. Quotation from letter to Dr. Gillespie, BFM, May 28, 1895. PCUSA, "Correspondence."

CHAPTER 16

Unsteady Ground

Japanese Christians were deeply loyal citizens but felt they
were under assault.

The big news in early 1896 was the earthquake and tsunami tidal wave
"which swept over a large district in the northern part of the main island,
engulfing whole villages and destroying tens of thousands of human lives
and millions of dollars' worth of property," Tom wrote. "This appalling calamity was so far from us that we did not feel the awfulness of it as much
as of those smaller calamities that had occurred from time to time in our
midst." Although Tokyo had not been hit by that northern earthquake and
tidal wave, Tom had lived through another bad trembler two years before,
in 1894. He had been on his way to teach at the college in the afternoon
of June 20.

> I was in a jinrikisha on my way to the Meiji Gakuin. Owing
> to the motion of the jinrikisha I did not feel the shock very
> severely. And I was at first puzzled to know what was taking
> place. The first thing that attracted my attention was the sharp,
> crackling sound of the wrenching and breaking of the timbers
> in the houses along the street where I was passing. The sound
> was like that of sharp peals of thunder in very hot weather, and I
> instinctively looked around for a black and angry cloud, but the
> sky was cloudless, with a hazy appearance around the horizon.
>   Then I saw the houses on all sides being violently shaken,
> and the tiles falling from the roofs, while crowds of people were
> rushing from their houses into the streets, laughing in a half
> hysterical way, as the Japanese do when under the influence of
> any emotion like grief, or fear. As I was not far from the Meiji
> Gakuin, I went on till I got there. But as soon as I saw the dam-
> age done to the foreign buildings there, I hurried back home to

see how my family, and others in Tsukiji, had fared. Fortunately all were safe, though greatly excited and frightened. One, or two, Japanese, however, had been killed at a neighboring house, and several friends had narrowly escaped death.

The damage throughout the city was very great and many people lost their lives. The consternation excited by a severe earthquake is peculiar, in that it arises so largely from the sense of helplessness—no one knowing in the least which way to turn for safety.

The foundations of Tom's life and of the church in Japan also were being shaken. Teaching and academic life did not come naturally to Tom. Not only did he feel heavily burdened by his work, but he could not bring himself to enjoy it either. Because he felt he was shortchanging the students, he offered to resign just six months after he had arrived. "But during all this discouraging and very laborious time, President Ibuka and Mr. Uemura, with other Japanese brethren, gave me their encouragement and urged me to hold on. In response to their earnest entreaties, and from a stern sense of duty, I continued my work. Notwithstanding the pressure upon me in the school work, and despite a large amount of committee and general work, I preached one hundred and seventy one (171) times during the year."

Uemura Masahisa, 1920s

Ibuka Kajinosuke, 1922

Meiji Gakuin President Ibuka Kajinosuke and the Reverend Uemura Masahisa were leaders in the Church of Christ in Japan and men of great influence among their compatriots. Because of Ibuka's high standing among Japanese colleagues and foreign missionaries, he had been appointed as Meiji Gakuin's second president and as the first Japanese to head the prestigious Protestant college. Like Tom, he had studied at Union Theological Seminary in New York City. Uemura, eldest son of a samurai, had seen his world collapse with the overthrow of the shogun and the installation of Emperor Meiji in 1868. He had resorted to raising and selling pigs to ward off starvation. He also had studied with Protestant missionaries in Yokohama to prepare himself for the future in a rapidly changing Japan.

Tom probably had met Uemura during his initial stay with the Ballaghs after arriving in Yokohama in 1877. He also had encountered him on a number of occasions during his frequent trips from Tokyo to teach at the boys' school in Yokohama. Later, while posted in Osaka, Tom had often welcomed Uemura into his home, even selling him a book on theology that Uemura had begged to buy. Over the years, even though Uemura had little use for most missionaries, he and Tom had formed a solid bond. Tom liked and admired his Japanese friend and strongly defended him against other missionaries, who criticized Uemura for being too independent and even abrasive.

In one lengthy letter to the Foreign Mission Board, Tom defended the missionary publication *Fukuin Shimpo* (*Gospel News*) and Uemura, the paper's publisher, against critics in missionary ranks.[1] Tom urged the board to continue financial support of the paper, saying, "I am far from being alone in the opinion that if the Board decides not to continue aid to the 'Fukuin Shimpo,' it will thereby cripple one of the most influential agencies now at work in favor of the evangelical faith in Japan. Great injury will be done to the cause which we all have at heart, and that, in more ways than one." Not willing to risk the loss of this important voice for Christianity, Tom also quietly supported the paper out of his own pocket.

As to his colleagues' criticisms of Uemura, Tom acknowledged his friend's independence, self-reliance, and sometimes abrasive character. These traits, he wrote, "have led to a dislike of him on the part of some of the missionaries, so strong as to prevent their being able to do him justice." Noting that he knew Uemura better than any missionary then in Japan, Tom wrote:

> He is of the intellectual, rather than the sentimental, type. His piety does not trickle down his cheeks, but it is real. His prayers are fervent. He takes a deep interest in spiritual matters and regards the great lack of the church in Japan at present as a want of spiritual life. So far as the man is concerned, therefore, I regard him as a safe leader, and one who is determined to exert a still wider influence for good.

Tom's defense of his friend stemmed from his dispassionate assessment of Uemura's faith and of his positive role in the church in Japan. In addition, the two men both held progressive views on some of the most controversial theological issues of the day, including evolution. But another factor also undoubtedly helped explain the bond that had grown up between the two men. Uemura had lost a teenaged daughter to sudden illness in 1892, the same year that fourteen-year-old Ella had died. The two men's painful losses surely forged an unspoken understanding in a way that only shared sorrow can.

Tom's feeling of inadequacy in his professional life was not the only reason for his frustration and discontent. Long-simmering controversies within the church had erupted into a full boil in the 1890s, threatening to split Christians in Japan just as in America. Publication of a Japanese-language version of Darwin's famous treatise on evolution in 1895 poured fuel on the fire.

In 1893, the year Tom had joined Meiji Gakuin's faculty, one of his former professors at New York's Union Theological Seminary had been ousted from the ministry by Tom's own Presbyterian Church.[2] The Reverend Dr.

Charles Briggs, one of America's most noted biblical scholars, had chaired Hebrew and related language studies at the seminary until his appointment in 1891 as chair of Biblical Studies. What had gotten him into trouble was his inaugural speech in 1891. The Bible contains errors that cannot be explained away, and some traditional interpretations of the Bible cannot be accepted as the literal truth, Briggs argued. He also believed that church teachings should be brought up to date in order to reflect modern scientific discoveries, especially those related to creation and evolution.

Briggs' head-on challenge to long-accepted church teachings enraged conservatives and traditionalists alike, with churches throughout the country calling for action against him. The Presbyterian Church's main governing body tried and convicted Briggs of heresy, not only ousting him from the ministry but also trying to veto his academic appointment. The seminary rejected the General Assembly's authority and appointed Briggs as chair, despite the fierce opposition.

The bitter divisions opened by Brigg's heresy trial made their way to Japan, where Tom's conservative colleagues cheered his former professor's conviction, leaving Tom as a minority on the faculty supporting Briggs' views. Everything Tom had learned in Osaka from Dr. John Gulick, his naturalist colleague, had convinced him that Darwin's theory of evolution was consistent with the notion of God as creator: that evolution was simply God's way of bringing about change in species. Tom also believed that because Scripture had been written by people, it should be seen as a human effort to interpret God's will and not be taken literally, although he hoped that any imperfections were few in number. And, like Briggs, he argued that Scripture should be interpreted in the light of new discoveries that increase our knowledge of the world around us. Otherwise, he felt, religion would lose its appeal to thoughtful, educated people.

The theology taught by Unitarian Universalists, recently arrived from America and Europe, also had complicated life for more traditional Protestant churches operating in Japan.[3] The newcomers' message—that Jesus was a prophet but not the Son of God; and that God is a single entity, not a trinity of Father, Son, and Holy Ghost—thoroughly confused many Japanese Christians. Doesn't Christianity embrace just one set of beliefs, they wondered? If this new group calls itself Christian but directly contradicts what we have been taught, what and whom are we to believe?

The deepening split between denominations, all of them fighting to attract and retain members in the face of growing secular trends in society, coupled with the emergence of a new, untraditional theology, led many believers within and outside of Japan to call for greater unity of Christians, possibly even under the umbrella of a single religion based on the Golden

Rule of "Love your neighbor as yourself." Tom advised his brethren in the Church of Christ in Japan not to attack the new beliefs head-on, but rather to keep preaching their own message of faith clearly and firmly. He was worried, though. He was a strong believer in Apostle Paul's message to the Corinthians, that together we are the body of Christ.[4] After witnessing the harm done by conflicts among the various denominations, he told more than one colleague that if ever there were a single, unified church, he would be the first to join.

Tom's progressive views made him the target of vicious attacks by his colleagues, who saw him as extremist and destructive of their more traditional teachings. But in the mind of Meiji Gakuin President Ibuka, those critics misunderstood Tom and his motives. Tom's heart, Ibuka believed, lay in building up the church in Japan, not in destroying it. Tom showed how far he had moved away from his strict Calvinist upbringing in a speech to the Church of Christ in Japan. "I do not believe one can take a theology of the seventeenth century and apply it to today. It must be adapted to today's ideological currents." He concluded by saying, "My policy is study of the truth, and nothing but the truth." Of course, not everyone saw truth in the same way.

Ever since Japan's resounding wartime victory over China in 1895, nationalist fervor had grown to a fever pitch. In the eyes of many Japanese, Japan had proven to the world's great powers that it, too, possessed the military strength and popular backing to support an expanded world role for the country. While patriotic pride and a sense of national superiority were widespread, conservatives and nationalists exaggerated the country's sense of unity. There were plenty of Japanese, especially rural residents whose sons were filling the emperor's army of draftees, who were indifferent or even opposed to Japan's military build-up. Eventually, politicians like Itagaki Taisuke resumed their fight against Japan's growing defense budget, even though he, like his compatriots, welcomed a more prominent role for Japan in Asia and the world.

As national pride swelled and appreciation for traditional Japanese values rose, life for missionaries and Japan's new Christians grew more difficult. Nationalists attacked Christians as being un-Japanese and their religion as being incompatible with patriotism and loyalty to the emperor. Anti-Christian sentiment intensified after a Japanese Christian schoolteacher refused to bow before a picture of the emperor and a copy of the Imperial Rescript on Education during a ceremony celebrating the emperor's birthday, believing instead that he should bow only to his Lord above. His action flew in the face of widely accepted practice. At the beginning of class each day and at all school gatherings, teachers or administrators read aloud from the emperor's decree on education with its emphasis on loyalty and traditional values. Then students or audience members bowed to the emperor's picture and imperial decree displayed prominently at the front of the room and shouted banzai three times for the emperor.[5]

The Christian teacher's refusal to take part in this show of respect for the emperor enraged critics of the foreign religion. He was fired from his job and shunned by family and friends alike. In desperation, he sought and found shelter at Muromachi Church in Kyoto, then ministered by Yoshioka Koki, who had served as the first Japanese pastor of Osaka North Church. Although it was very risky to take in such a prominent fugitive, the Reverend Yoshioka may have enjoyed some immunity from official retribution due to the fact that he once had held a senior position in the Meiji regime's foreign ministry.

In response to growing pressure from this and other highly publicized incidents that fed suspicion about Christianity, the Ministry of Education banned the teaching of religion in all private schools, including those, like missionary schools, that sought government recognition and the privileges for students that went with it. Tom wrote about the severe disadvantage this edict conferred on private Christian schools.

> Students of private schools are not exempt from military conscription and hence may be drafted into the army at any time; they cannot enter government schools except by examination, and when they have graduated from the private schools they are forever excluded from the civil service, so that no public career can ever be open to them, no matter how great their abilities or attainments. Hence the number of students, particularly of boys, in Christian schools is kept down to a comparatively low figure; even Christians preferring to forego their natural preference for a Christian education in order to secure for their sons the advantages which the government schools alone can give.[6]

Plummeting enrollment at Meiji Gakuin College and every other Christian boys' school in Japan put more unwelcome stress on faculty and administrators at a time when tensions already were running high.

Japanese Christians were deeply loyal citizens but felt they were under assault. Many of them were sons and daughters of samurai families, whose ancestors had played prominent roles in the old Japan. Many now held high-ranking positions in government, business, and the church itself. Pressure built within their ranks to distance themselves from foreign missionaries in order to prove their loyalty and patriotism. In addition, some prominent Japanese Christians criticized those missionaries—too many, in their view—who neither spoke the language nor engaged directly in evangelistic work. What use were they, their critics asked, the Reverend Uemura Masahisa among them. Better that they return to America or Europe and leave Japan's own Christian workers to sow the seeds of faith.

Tom agreed. Unlike many of his colleagues in Tokyo, he had labored hard in the mission field, spoke Japanese fluently, and had given up church membership in America to join the Church of Christ in Japan. Too many missionaries, he felt, were focused more on self-promotion and on building their own bureaucratic empires than on tending to the needs of the church in Japan. "Tokyo is literally swarming with missionaries," Tom wrote to the mission board at home, even as his colleagues pressed for more men and women to bolster their ranks. Instead, he argued, more of the work and responsibility should be handed over to the Japanese. "In my judgment, what we need is . . . more of the spirit of the Master to see in our Japanese brethren fellow-laborers and in every way to help them go forth and preach."[7]

Tom's disagreement with fellow missionaries extended to the halls of Meiji Gakuin College, too, where he discovered just how vicious academic politics could be. Many of the foreign teachers were well-ensconced in their jobs, comfortable and secure in positions they had held for years. Few of them had served in the field, struggling to juggle money and resources to support the demands of mission work. When members of the mission board in New York City—who were aware of Japanese Christians' desire for greater autonomy and who faced serious financial constraints of their own in supporting the large number of overseas missions—proposed cutting the number of foreign faculty members at Meiji Gakuin, Tom agreed wholeheartedly. His support for a thorough reform of Meiji Gakuin and for cutting the number of foreign teachers by half, from six to three, pitted Tom against nearly all of his fellow professors.

Little by little, as each year passed, Tom's roots within the Japanese church and his relations with Japanese Christians grew deeper, while the divisions between him and some of his missionary colleagues widened. He was sticking to his principles, though, which he considered more important than popularity.

Tom (center, top row) with colleagues in Tokyo

Fatigue, aching joints, and heart palpitations plagued Tom more and more as his rheumatic heart disease worsened. He didn't have as much energy as he had in the past, and sometimes he just couldn't eat, even though he was losing weight. Yet he had never worked as hard in his life. He had hit a groove in his teaching and enjoyed it more, but in addition to his teaching, he also carried a heavy administrative load at the college and pursued other outside activities. He served as dean of students, attended countless faculty and committee meetings, was treasurer of the West Japan Mission, and continued his extensive writing and preaching in both English and Japanese.

As many trials and troubles as Tom faced, none compared to the shock that hit him in December 1896, when Emma's doctors determined she must leave Japan as soon as possible for the sake of her health. Tom had worried in recent years as Emma had suffered from severe headaches, mysterious body pains, and a general malaise that had worn her down steadily. In addition to teaching at the children's school, entertaining, and performing all the other duties of a missionary's wife, she also had struggled to cope with the endless demands of motherhood. Tokyo's oppressive summer heat and its cold, damp winters had not helped her ailments. Now Tom and Emma faced the worst prospect they could imagine—the break-up of their family.

They had known a separation was coming at some point. The older children were rapidly outgrowing the educational facilities available to them in Japan, and schooling in America was the only real option. They had planned to take the children home together when Tom began his second sabbatical in August 1897, after which Tom and Emma would return to Japan with the younger ones in tow, leaving the three older children in school in America. Now they faced an immediate separation, with Tom destined to remain alone in the field, for how long no one could tell. The year 1896 came to a close with this cloud hanging over their heads. Early in the New Year, Tom reflected on the sad parting with his family.

> The new year came on apace. So true is it that time and tide wait for no man. We would fain have stayed the advance of time and so have prolonged the few remaining months that we were to be together. The children continued going to school, Emma was more busy, if possible than ever. She made many of the children's clothes with her own hands and prepared for the journey.
>
> I contrived to spend most of my evenings with her and the children around the fireside. I felt that I could not long have the pleasure of such evenings. At our family worship, and always, we prayed that God would direct us aright. . . . I engaged passage on the *Doric*, which was set to sail from Yokohama, via Honolulu, on April 13th. It is needless to say that, as the weeks went by and the days began to seem very few that we were to be together, our hearts grew heavier, and we felt very tenderly toward each other.
>
> What we were about to do, had often been done by friends and acquaintances of ours, and to us it seemed a very natural and proper thing for them to do. Yet this did not make it any easier for us. Then, too, it was something that we had long looked forward to and for which were in a measure prepared, but this even did not afford us much relief. There was no denying that it was a fearful ordeal through which we must pass.
>
> I was able to preserve a calm exterior in the presence of the children until the long looked for 13th of April came. It was a day long to be remembered. I lay in bed weeping for some time before the rising bell and could not control my feelings at the breakfast table; and as to conducting family prayers in the usual manner, it was simply out of the question. I could not bring myself to undertake it.
>
> Emma seemed calm and collected, but the children's faces were long. Mary was always tender-hearted and affectionate, and she soon began crying and kept it up nearly all day. She ascribed her grief to her toe, which she said was being pinched

by her shoe. But Emma and I thought we knew the pain to be in her heart, rather than in her toe. She did not want to leave "Papa" behind. No doubt, they all felt the same way, but the others were able to conceal their feelings till the time for parting drew nearer.

We left Tokyo, to take the steamer in Yokohama, early in the forenoon and the steamer sailed about 3:30 p.m. Quite a number of friends accompanied us to Yokohama, many of whom went out to the ship also.

The last I saw of any of them was as I was rowed away from the ship toward the shore. Emma and the younger children stood on the upper deck and waved their adieus to me until I could not distinguish their forms from others around them. They have now, May 18th, been gone just five weeks, and I have not heard how they fared on the voyage, but am expecting a letter in another day, or two. Notice was in the paper some time ago that the *Doric* arrived in San Francisco April 28th.

I came back home late in the afternoon of the memorable 13th to take up the burden of living alone. So far as the mere fact of being by myself is concerned, I am not nervous about it and do not mind it, as some people do. But the trial is very great. No one knows how much I grieve over it, nor how lonely my heart is. The next morning after they all went away, it took about all the courage I could command to come down the stairs and go to the breakfast table alone.

All their empty chairs in the sitting room and at the breakfast table were so many mute reminders of those who had so lately left me. Christine had been accustomed for some time to ride downstairs every morning on my back and was thus the first to be at the table with me. It is needless to say, I missed her more than tongue can tell. And now they all seem so far away, almost as far, and as really gone out of my life, as Ella.

Notes

1. To Arthur Gillespie, BFM, February 22, 1894. PCUSA, "Correspondence." See Appendix II for full text of letter.

2. Longfield, *Presbyterian Controversy*, 22–23.

3. Dohi, "First Generation," 21–24.

4. 1 Cor 12:12. Information about Ibuka's views in following paragraph from Ibuka

eulogy of TTA, in Akiyama, *Tales of the Great*. Alexander quote from "Report on the Conference of Church of Christ of Japan," synopsis of TTA speech. In *Fukuin Shimpo*, No. 78, late 1890.

5. Jansen, *Modern Japan*, 466–67. See also http://www.uchimurakanzo.net/Kanzo/Welcome.html. The teacher, Uchimura Kanzo, became a prominent Christian leader and proponent of a non-denominational "non-church." His refusal to bow took place in 1891. In March 1926, he wrote about the incident and its effect on his life. "My refusal to bow to the Imperial Rescript on Education, not only deprived me of my situation in the Dai Ichi Kotogakko [school], but sent me out into Japanese society as a vagabond, wherein for some 20 years, I had not a place where to lay my head on. But I was more successful in book writing and journalism." Uchimura became famous for his self-professed love for "two J's," Jesus and Japan.

6. "The Problems before the Church of Japan." In *The Church*, September 1896, on "Japan Christians' History" website by Hugo [no last name]. Online: http://japanschristianheritage.com/2011/09/obstacles-of-the-church-in-japan-and-doshishas-falling-away-1895.

7. Letters to Arthur Gillespie, BFM, January 27, 1897, and January 14, 1898. PCUSA, "Correspondence."

CHAPTER 17

Worlds Apart

There was often an unmistakable something in his look and carriage
that cast a shadow over my mind as I walked back alone.

With his family back in America, Tom tried to carry on with his life in Tokyo as normally as he could, but he found it hard to cope with his family's
absence. He certainly was used to being alone. His travels had put him on
the road for weeks at a time, often by himself; and he had often sought ref-
uge in his study when he needed time by himself to reflect on parishioners'
problems or to prepare a sermon, Bible study, or funeral service. But nothing had prepared him for the terrible void he faced every day of every week.
No children rushed to greet him as he returned home from a day's work
or a long journey. Emma wasn't there to ask how his day had gone or to
offer words of comfort when his troubles weighed him down. He felt alone,
utterly alone. He hid his misery from colleagues and friends, but the pain of
separation burned below the surface like a hot ember that even time could
not extinguish. The tightness in his throat and heaviness in his chest never
completely left him.

To fill the empty hours, Tom plunged even more deeply into his work.
In great demand as a speaker, preacher, and scholar, he kept up a busy schedule of teaching and preaching, along with a heavy load of writing, including
a number of books in Japanese: *Men of the Old Testament*, *Commentary on
Philippians*, and *Studies on the Book of Amos*. He wrote eighty articles, also
in Japanese, on the Bible and its meaning for Uemura Masahisa's *Fukuin
Shimpo*—a real tribute to Tom, since Uemura largely shunned foreign missionaries and rarely invited them to preach in his church or contribute to
his journal. Together with an Episcopalian missionary, Tom launched a

new Japanese-language magazine, the *Biblical Expositor*, and contributed to other journals and magazines in both English and Japanese.

A recognized scholar of Japanese Christian literature, Tom also served on the Literary Committee of the Japan Tract Society, which wrote and distributed Japanese language religious materials for use by missionaries and Japanese Christian workers. For the General Conference of Protestant Missionaries in Japan, he wrote an English language article entitled, "The Preparation and Spread of Christian Literature: Past Work and Present Need." His busy schedule did not lead Tom to neglect his teaching or duties as dean of students at Meiji Gakuin, though. He often took eager and inquisitive young men studying for the ministry to mission gatherings in Tokyo and Osaka and to other meetings and events that offered good learning opportunities for future church leaders.

Despite Tom's heavy workload, thoughts of his family pressed into his mind at all hours of the day and especially at night as he lay in bed, hearing not the gentle sounds of breathing or of children quietly calling out in their dreams, but the ghostly creaking and settling of the silent house. Pictures of the family's last days at home and of their journey to America played in his head, and he tried to deal with them in the best way he knew, by writing.

> A few days before they left, Lois and Mary saw some Japanese boys trying to drown a little dog in the canal nearby our house. They promptly flew to the rescue and brought the poor little puppy to the house and begged permission to keep him till they could find someone who would take him and care for him. Emma and I, though we did not want the ugly little thing on the place, gave our consent on condition they should find somebody to take him.
>
> But this was not so easy to do. Indeed, they finally failed to find an owner for him and had to leave him here when they went away. Christine was telling the story of the poor little dog's wrongs one day, and she said, "The naughty boys were throwing stones at him, so he was like Stephen, wasn't he?" After that we always called him Stephen. Stephen still stays with me and is growing into a very respectable looking specimen of the canine species.[1]
>
> For some time before going away, Christine had tried to console me, in view of her approaching absence, by promising me that the "Limb baby" would stay with me. "The Limbs" were an imaginary family of people whom she herself originated

---

1. Stephen, the first martyr of the Christian church, was stoned to death by a mob after false witnesses accused him of blasphemy against Moses and God. See Acts: 6–7.

and of whom she often talked. One day I expressed doubt as to whether the "Limb baby" would be big enough to afford me much company. She said, "O yes, he is big enough, he is bigger than Goliath!"

This statement afterwards gave her a good deal of trouble. For I teased her by saying that I couldn't do anything with such an enormous baby. I would be afraid he would knock me over, or get out of humor sometime and kick over the dining table and smash all the dishes, etc., etc. So, she finally admitted that she had overstated his size.

Well, in due course of time letters came stating that they all arrived safely in Maryville on the 8th of May. The voyage as far as Honolulu was fairly good, but rather uncomfortable from there on, I judge. In one of daughter Emma's letters speaking of the overland journey, she says: "One day on the train we were surprised by a great bump, and soon the train stopped, and we found that six feet of track had been taken out, and the train had jumped it, because we were going so fast." This was certainly a narrow escape. It makes me shudder to think of it.

Dec. 31st. New Year's Eve has come and I am getting used to being separated from my family, somewhat as a man gets used to a boil, or to any other great trial. . . . I pray continually that this separation may be overruled for the good of us all, and that we may all be permitted to come together again sometime.

Maybe it was pangs of loneliness, failing health, or unending disputes with his conservative colleagues, but for whatever reason, Tom felt increasingly dissatisfied with himself and his work at the theological school. And despite his prodigious writing and frequent preaching, he also felt he was not accomplishing much of any worth outside of the academy. When his predecessor as Chair of Systemic and Biblical Studies, Dr. William Imbrie, returned from America after an absence of five years, Tom resigned in Imbrie's favor, but continued teaching the same amount as before. Imbrie's presence was a great comfort to Tom at this difficult time in his life. The two men spent many hours together at the school and at Imbrie's home on campus. Imbrie later recalled the times he had spent with his friend.[2]

It was our frequent custom on pleasant afternoons when his work was done to walk together to the railway station; and that road to the station from the point where it turns to the left and winds through the shade will always in my memory be associated with him and the things that he said:—Of the Church of Christ in Japan; of the Christianization of the people; of the changes come and coming in men's apprehension of God and the things of God; of what God was to him and prayer; and once of the thoughts that ruled his mind not long before when he could not sleep at night—thoughts of God and of Christ.

He was fast growing older then and I could not but notice that his step had lost its former spring; and when we parted at the station there was often an unmistakable something in his look and carriage that cast a shadow over my mind as I walked back alone. Then came his visit home [to Maryville], as I half knew at the time and as later I felt sure, simply to say goodbye to those whom he loved.

Tom also forged another friendship that helped smooth the rough edges of ongoing conflict at the theological school. The Secretary of the Board of Foreign Missions in New York City, Robert Speer, visited Japan in 1897 during his tour of world missions. Tom had corresponded with him many times in the course of his duties. When he met him, he took an immediate liking to him and happily discovered that Speer shared his open-minded views on the most contentious issues of the day. The two men forged a lasting bond that was reflected later in the warmth of their correspondence and in the help Speer gave to Tom and his family when Tom's heart problems finally forced him to leave Japan.

Frequent letters from Emma and the children kept Tom abreast of his family in America. Their lives had settled into a mostly comfortable routine, although Emma drew little satisfaction from fulltime housework and child care. Even though her duties as a missionary's wife had sometimes weighed on her, she now missed the greater sense of purpose she had felt though her work in the mission. Tom recorded the family's progress in his journal.

> The older children were in college, or in the preparatory department, while Mary and Eva attended a small private school. . . . Emma's health was not good, but better on the whole than for a year, or two, previous. She gave herself up wholly to keeping house, making the children as comfortable as possible and helping them in their studies. No work could be more important and yet much of it was the merest drudgery. Christine stayed at home and "helped" her mother, while the rest were in school. The children seem to have gotten along well in their studies and to have made considerable progress in music—Emma and Lois on the piano, Theron with the cornet and Mary with the violin.

In the summer of 1897, not long after their homecoming, the family had joined one of Emma's brothers and his family on a visit to Nashville, taking in exhibits and rides at the Tennessee Centennial Celebration. After she

returned home, four-year-old Christine proudly displayed to her family and
friends the little gift her mother or uncle had bought for her: a delicate, blood
red cordial glass with her name written on the side in neat, flowing script.

Early in 1899, Tom began a journey to America on his second sabbatical.
He booked passage through the Holy Land, where he planned to travel with
several other missionaries. "It may seem strange that, after having been
separated from wife and children so long, I should take this round-about
way to get to them. But Emma had written urging me not to lose so good an
opportunity, and although not fond of travelling, nor yet of sight-seeing, it
seemed that it would be foolish of me not to avail myself of it. I was unen-
cumbered, had only myself to look after and had an excellent, and what was
more to the purpose, a <u>congenial</u> set of companions with whom to make the
journey. And so altogether I decided to go the longest way round." After so
many years of studying and teaching the Gospels, Tom looked forward to
visiting the Holy Land and witnessing for himself the places where Jesus had
walked during his journey on earth.

Tom and his fellow travelers sailed from Japan via Hong Kong, Singapore, and Colombo in British Ceylon; through the Gulfs of Aden and
Suez, and on to Ismailia and then Cairo, Egypt. Visits to the pyramids and
the Sphinx, museums and their mummies, and the fertile Nile Valley, while
interesting, were just a warm-up for the real purpose of their visit. After a
rough sea voyage across the Mediterranean and a precarious landing, the
small party finally set foot in the Holy Land. Tom filled his journal with page
after page describing their journeys by foot, horseback, and rail to all the
sites a cleric could hope to see in a lifetime: Jaffa and Caesarea, Jerusalem
and the Damascus Gate, Jericho and the Dead Sea, Bethlehem and Hebron.
He later wrote articles about his trip for the *Fukuin Shimpo*.

While surveying the countryside surrounding the Holy City of Bethlehem, Tom recalled the words of Psalm 48:2, "Beautiful for situation, the joy
of the whole earth, is Mount Zion." He drank rain water that had collected
in Jacob's well, where Jesus once had asked a Samaritan woman to give him
a drink. By the time of Tom's visit, the Palestine Exploration Society of
London had reopened the well to a depth of about five feet after removing
debris that had largely sealed it shut over the years. A long horseback ride
to the Sea of Galilee took Tom and his companions to the biblical town of
Tiberius, where they arrived at noon.

We heard the call to prayer from the Mohammedan mosque just as we entered the town. On the way to the lake, and soon after leaving Nazareth, we passed through Cana of Galilee. There in a church we were shown two water pots of stone, said to have been of the number used at the wedding when Christ turned the water into wine. . . .

The way from Nazareth to the lake lies across a rolling plain, or table land. Just before reaching the lake, the road descends rapidly to the level of the water which is some 700 feet lower than the level of the Mediterranean. We spent the afternoon and night at Tiberius, taking a boat ride on the lake. The heat was, however, too great to admit of our enjoying the ride.

Finally, the time came for the travel partners to go their separate ways and for Tom to make his way to Maryville and his waiting family. He had sent letters to Emma and the children along the way but, given his nomadic schedule, had not received any replies. So he had no more reason than usual to worry about Emma's health. After traveling through Italy, over the Alps into France, and on to Dover and then London, Tom sailed on May 15 from Southampton, England to New York City, arriving on May 25 and going straight to his overnight lodgings.

At the Foreign Mission Board rooms, I found a letter informing me that Emma was recovering from her illness. That was the first I knew of her being ill. The children had written me of the fact, but the letters failed to reach me. I reached Maryville on the evening of May 27th, having been just three months and ten days on the journey from Tokyo.

I found Emma just getting up from a very serious attack of typhoid-malarial fever. She was able to be up when I arrived but was still very weak. She had been ill for several weeks and daughter Emma had been her only nurse. The latter must have had a pretty hard time of it, but she made a good, faithful and careful nurse.

Emma improved rapidly and was soon about as well as she had been for several years. It was certainly a very glad day for us all, when I at last got home. It had been a little more than two years since my family had left me in Japan. We were very thankful that our lives had all been spared, and especially grateful that the wife and mother had come through her illness safely.

It was a warm, pleasant evening when I reached Maryville. Only Theron and Christine were at the station to meet when I got off the cars. The former I recognized at once. He had grown much larger, but was little changed from what he had been when he left Japan.

But Christine had changed so much that I recognized her only by her being with Theron, and from her resemblance to the other children. She did not know me at all. She said to her mother afterwards, "I am awfully sorry I didn't know papa." It was a happy family that gathered that evening at the tea table.

Tom's three-month sojourn through the Holy Land left him just five months to spend with his family, and he wanted to make the most of it. But his appearance shocked and worried his wife. He was thin, almost to the point of emaciation, and very pale. Even though Emma tried to get him to rest, he remained restless and uneasy. She did convince him to spend five weeks vacationing in the resort town of Montrale Springs near Maryville, where the family boarded at a guest house. While he and Emma enjoyed some relaxed time with each other and the children, Tom continued to mix work with recreation, visiting churches in the area to speak about foreign mission work and preaching some Sundays. Hanging over their vacation, too, was a difficult question they had grappled with for some time: whether Emma and two or three of the youngest children should return to Japan with Tom, leaving the oldest ones in school in Maryville; or whether all the children should remain together with Emma in Maryville, while Tom returned to Japan alone.

Although Tom and Emma both hated the idea of being separated again, they finally decided it would be best for the children, and probably for Emma's health, too, if the family remained in Maryville. After their return from vacation, Tom bought a roomy, two-story house and lot on High Street, next to Emma's brother, also named Tom, and near Maryville College campus. The large family was much more comfortable there than they had been in the small rental they had occupied for two years. Tom and Emma spent much of his remaining time at home fixing up the house and making it into a home.

Tom Alexander home on sabbatical, 1899

Maryville home on High Street. Theron, Young Emma,
Christine, and Lois on porch

Tom took Emma with him on some of his visits to country churches in Rockford, Ensebia, Lloyd's Creek, and elsewhere. "We went always in a buggy and both enjoyed the rides very much, as well as the meetings with the people. Emma's father had at different times in his life ministered to all three of the churches just mentioned, and she herself had sometimes gone with him to meet his appointments, when she was yet a mere girl. She was everywhere welcomed for her father's sake as well as on her own account."

During his home stay, Tom also drew comfort from get-togethers with former professors who had played a large role not only in rebuilding Maryville College from the ashes of the Civil War but also in shaping his own life. He enjoyed long conversations with the Rev. P. M. Bartlett, former president of the college, still hale and hearty at the age of eighty. "He was very fond of children, which made him a favorite in our family. He said one day, just before I left home, that when he looked at the children, he believed he felt my coming separation from them more than I myself seemed to feel it. I wish we might follow his example, and become more charitable and Christ-like as we grow old."

Tom was due to sail from San Francisco on November 9 and planned to leave Maryville by train on November 2. But he took the time to arrange a last outing with his family.

> Just a few days before leaving Maryville to return to Japan, on Saturday, October 27th, I hired a hack and took Emma and the children (excepting Theron, who preferred to stay at home) on a picnic to Montvale. We had a delightful day—the coming and going, that is, the trip itself, through the country was pleasant. Then, after eating our lunch at the springs, we spent an hour or two in the woods, gathering nuts and otherwise amusing ourselves. It was raining when we got home, but all agreed in pronouncing the picnic a success. The memory of it is grateful to me, as, no doubt, it is to Emma and the girls.

As pleasant as the day had been, Tom must have been hurt by Theron's decision to remain home rather than join his father on what surely would be his last picnic with his family. As he did with other difficult emotional matters, though, Tom most likely walled off his feelings about this incident and hid them even from himself. As much as Tom loved his family, it seemed that the strained and rather distant relationship he had had with his own father had been repeated with his son. Perhaps, too, young Theron was rebelling from subtle but unmistakable pressure on him to pursue a career in the church, rather than in science, where his real interests lay. If Tom did feel disappointed by his son's decision to stay home, he never expressed it. But Tom did not hide the emotions he felt about his departure day.

> That day became the one to which I looked forward with mingled sadness and dread, and many were the tears shed in secret as I knew the day to be swiftly coming on. One morning Emma said: "You seem to perspire at night. Your pillow is wet every morning!" I did not tell her that it was tears, and not perspiration, that wet my pillow, but such was the fact, nevertheless.
>
> Outwardly I tried to seem calm and unmoved, and the effort made me nervous and irritable, and even cross sometimes, for which I was then, and am still sorry. The 8th of October was my 49th birthday. I received little presents from each member of the family. In the evening we had dinner, at which Dr. and Mrs. Boardman, with Martha and their daughter, and Mrs. Lamar, were guests. I was given to understand beforehand that we might be going to have chicken for dinner, but I suspected it would be turkey, and sure enough it was. The evening passed very pleasantly and soon my birthday was at an end.
>
> When finally the 2nd of November came, I busied myself all the forenoon with all sorts of little things in order to keep from breaking down completely. The children all went off to school in the morning as usual. But Mary, Eva and Christine did not take lunch with them, as they were wont to do, but came home at noon. The older children were at home always for the noon meal, and on that day Emma's mother was with us, so we all had dinner together. There was an effort on the part of all to be cheerful, but evidently it <u>required</u> effort. The atmosphere was funereal, in spite of everything.
>
> At half past two p.m., I said goodbye and walked away to the station alone. It was raining, and the only persons at the station to see me off were Drs. Boardman and McCulloch, Mr. Eugene Webb, and my old friend, Capt. W. H. Henry. I crossed the continent alone, reached San Francisco late in the afternoon of Nov. 8th and sailed on the *China* early in the afternoon of the next day. The voyage was uneventful, excepting that it was broken by a stop of twenty-four hours in Honolulu.

Tom reached Yokohama just before daylight on November 30, Thanksgiving Day, and took the train straight to Tokyo and his house at No. 27 Tsukiji. He found his old servant, Etsu-san, waiting to receive him. She had prepared his rooms, and Tom resumed life in the old manner, alone again. Letters soon arrived from Emma and the children. Tom had missed Christine's sixth birthday but had left money for her to buy an "Express Wagon" that she had wanted. He also learned that on November 12, Mary and Eva had professed their faith and joined Maryville's Providence Presbyterian Church. Tom and Emma were gratified to see their maturing daughters pledge themselves to God's service.

The problems Tom had left behind in Tokyo had not disappeared; rather, they were there to greet him with open arms. Conservatives in Meiji Gakuin's theological school did not want Tom back on the faculty and combined forces to block his return. Meiji Gakuin President Ibuka, who admired his American colleague and shared his progressive views on theology, discovered that even a college president was not powerful enough to override the wishes of determined faculty members. So instead of returning to Meiji Gakuin College as he had hoped and expected, Tom accepted a position in Japan's old imperial capital of Kyoto, where a fellow missionary had been forced to abandon his post and return to America due to his wife's illness.

Trusting that the Lord had good work for him to do, Tom maintained a positive outlook and even looked forward to doing evangelistic work again. In the years before his sabbatical, he had journeyed occasionally from Tokyo to Kyoto at the invitation of regional government officials to take part in their prayer meetings. Tom had brought many of them into the fold of Christianity himself, so he was familiar with the territory.[3] As the year 1899 came to a close, Tom packed up his belongings for yet another move and reflected on the future.

> As I write these closing lines of another year's record, night is settling down upon the world and darkness comes on apace— the last night of the old year is already here. But it is the eve of a New Year and hope beckons us onward to higher and better things. May the year to come be one of blessing to all our household; and doubtless it will be in one way or another, for we are the children of an Heavenly King—a bountiful and gracious Father.

The changes in Tom's life were not the only ones taking place at the turn of the century. England, France, Germany, and Russia had moved into China, claiming parts of the war-weakened country as their own possessions, including some of the territory they had forced Japan to give up after its defeat of China in 1895. The Japanese bristled at this blatant slap at their power and prestige, and militarists pushed for an even greater Japanese presence in Asia. Europeans were not the only powers encroaching on Asia; the United States also was expanding its reach into the Pacific. In 1893, US sugar magnates, diplomats, and local politicians, backed by US Marines, had engineered a coup deposing Hawaii's Queen Lili'uokalani and establishing a republic, whose first president was an American, Sanford B. Dole. America annexed Hawaii in 1898, and the islands became a US territory in early 1900.

Also in 1898, America had defeated Spain in war and had taken the Philippines, Guam, and Wake Island as new possessions in the region. Only a prior Chinese commitment to Japan had prevented the United States from establishing a naval port directly across from Japanese-occupied Taiwan. From Japan's perspective, the world's great powers were constructing a noose around the island nation that they might seek to tighten in the coming years. Unlike the first time Japan had felt threatened by Western powers—in the 1600s—this time, Japan would not choose seclusion as a way to protect itself.[4]

Tom settled into his new life in Kyoto, living in a rented home on Muromachi Dori. For the first time since coming to Japan in 1877, Tom had not needed an inland passport giving him permission to relocate from Tokyo. Through treaty revision, Western powers had restored Japan's sovereignty over judicial matters and, mostly, over tariffs (the United States granted Japan tariff autonomy only in 1911). In response, Japan in 1899 had granted foreigners the freedom to live and travel anywhere they wished in the empire.

Although Tom's health troubled him more and more, he defied doctors' orders and resumed a heavy schedule of preaching, traveling throughout Japan's southern and western regions where he had evangelized for many years, and teaching at Doshisha University's theological school in Kyoto. Established by one of Japan's leading Christians—Niijima Jo—as the country's first theological school operating outside of missionary control, Doshisha's independent streak fit well with Tom's own independent spirit. He volunteered his time to teach there, offering his services on top of his official mission duties.

Kyoto would be Tom's last posting in Japan.

Notes

2. Eulogy for TTA during memorial service January 31, 1903. *Japan Evangelist*, Vol. X, No. 2 (February 1903) 6–9.

3. Higuchi, *Muromachi Church,* Ch. 1, Sect. 2, "The Founding of the Muromachi Church (1889–1894)."

4. Jansen, *Modern Japan*, 436–39. See also, Wikipedia. Online: http://en.wikipedia.org/wiki/History_of_Hawaii.

CHAPTER 18

An Independent Spirit

If I had ten times 25 years to give to His service on earth, I would
gladly give them all to Japan.

On the day her father left Maryville for the last time, nineteen-year-old
Emma ran upstairs to her room to cry, crushed at the thought of living
without him again. "I know that there is not a better, wiser and more unselfish, modest man in this wide world than Papa," she wrote in the diary she
had begun that year while still a senior at Maryville College.[1] Other people
outside the family shared young Emma's admiration for her father. She and
several other Alexander children had benefited from free college tuition
and free music lessons courtesy of anonymous donors, whose gifts had been
made to honor their father, as well as their mother, the first Maryville College graduates to serve overseas as missionaries.

Young Emma was like her father, full of idealism and a sense of purpose.
Like him, too, she had set her sights on becoming a missionary and hoped
to serve alongside him in Japan. A serious student, she excelled in school
and earned her peers' respect. Selected by her classmates to work with two
male students in preparing the college graduation ceremony, young Emma's
head was filled with thoughts of speakers to invite, food for the reception,
and all the studies she would have to complete in the coming months. An
honor student, she also wrestled with various topics for her own graduation speech and finally settled on one suggested by her father, "Japanese
Folklore". In January 1901, as her twenty-first birthday approached, she was
thrilled to receive a package from Japan.

> When I came home to dinner today, I found a surprise which
> made me so happy that I reminded myself of old Scrooge when

---

1. Unless otherwise noted, this and other quotes are from young Emma's diary, all five
volumes of which are in my possession.

he woke up Christmas morning. It was a birthday present from Papa—a white crepe dress to graduate in and a most exquisite piece of pale blue crepe for a waist [dress]! They are both figured, and are just too pretty to wear. The white crepe will make a most excruciatingly beautiful dress. To make it safe he is sending the dress in two packages at different times and paying letter postage on them—only one package has arrived yet. He says he will send money to have them made up later. Was there ever such a kind father? Lois said, "He acts like a millionaire."

Young Emma as college student

As the eldest surviving child now on the verge of adulthood, young Emma shouldered much of the labor around the house and tried as much as possible to ease her mother's burden. Adding to her mother's cares was Theron's extended illness, another bout of malaria that kept him at home for more than a month, bedridden much of the time and eating little more than buttermilk and cornbread due to a swollen liver and raging fever. Young Emma also worried about the effect of her parents' separation on both of them. She knew how much they loved each other and how hard it was for them to be apart, but there didn't seem to be any alternative that she could see to the family's current living arrangements. And the time was fast approaching when she, too, would be leaving home.

As the spring wore on, young Emma occupied herself with the heavy load of her last semester of college and taught Sunday school to young children at Providence Presbyterian Church. She also found herself growing more and more irritated with a fellow student, Reading Beatty, who seemed to appear everywhere she went and was always asking to accompany her to church, lectures, or other events. "He treats me with too much familiarity, and he doesn't seem to have much respect for anybody, and yet I, Emma Alexander, go with him—but I will not do it again. . . . He is so big and strong and seems to like me, but I hope that I shall be doing right by sending him away."

Young Emma's excitement grew as graduation approached. Like her mother many years before, she had been elected to serve during her senior year as president of the prestigious Adelphic Union literary society. And then came May 29, "the great and notable day," when young Emma received her diploma after playing a piano duet and delivering her oration on Japanese folklore. Her ardent suitor remained a presence in her life.

> It is over! At last I have accomplished something. I have accomplished my college education. Although I have not done brilliantly, I can truly say that I have done my best—and what more could I do. . . . I wasn't one bit scared—not one bit. Prof. Wilson said after it was over that I spoke better and put more life into it than I ever did before. I recognized people over the audience— Mr. Beatty for instance standing over by the door with a look of great interest and concern on his face. I felt very composed and was so happy when I came down from the platform—so relieved my face felt like it was beaming with joy. I felt as if I had done something greater than I had ever done in my life. Of course, I have received many compliments all day—and very sincere ones too.

Thinking ahead to life after college, Emma had written that spring to the Board of Foreign Missions asking to be accepted for service as a missionary in Japan. They had agreed but felt she would benefit from a year of study beforehand, particularly given her young age and relative lack of experience. Although reluctant to wait another year before joining her father in Japan, young Emma grudgingly acknowledged the wisdom of the board's thinking. So in October 1901, with her tuition, room and board, and travel expenses paid by the board, she began her studies at the Training School for Christian Workers at 128 East 10th Street, New York City.

In New York City, young Emma learned about the role and duties of a female missionary and school teacher. Students' skills were honed not just in class, but also during frequent mission visits to the city's poorest tenement dwellers, an experience that opened her eyes to a side of life she had never seen. She also learned more about her father during her stay in the city. At a large gathering of Christian youth groups, she introduced herself to the keynote speaker, Dr. William Newton Clarke. Clarke was a well-known liberal theologian, who believed in the use of reason and in bringing religion closer to people by adapting its teachings to reflect modern knowledge and science. "I plucked up the courage and marched up to him standing among the big men. I told him that I shook hands with him in Japan—that my father was a missionary there. He asked who he was, and I said Dr. Alexander. His face lighted up and he was very cordial and said he was glad to shake hands with me again, and asked to be remembered to Papa. Papa is a great man."

Young Emma also contacted Mr. Robert Speer, Secretary of the Board of Foreign Missions and her father's kindred spirit, whose friendship had been forged through years of correspondence and cemented during Speer's fact-finding trip to Japan in 1897. Speer was a rising leader in the American Presbyterian Church. After meeting him for the first time, young Emma wrote, "If he is as well pleased with me as I was with him, he thinks me a pretty fine girl, but of course I cannot think that. He was exceeding nice to me, and spoke so nicely of Papa, that I approve of him very much." Later, one of Speer's colleagues, Dr. Halsey, told Emma that "Mr. Speer considered Papa one of the best missionaries on the field anywhere, and from all he, Dr. H, knew of Papa, he thought the same."

New York City, with its mix of glamour and squalor, wealth and poverty, and so many people and places to see enthralled young Emma as much as it had impressed her father during his studies there twenty-five years before. On May 20, 1902, young Emma had the good fortune to take part in another unforgettable event. "This evening in Carnegie Hall at the Centennial of Home Mission of the Presbyterian Church, I heard Theodore Roosevelt, President of the United States of America! Oh! It was a sight for an American! How they did cheer! And the Maryville College quartette sang and was encored!"

As the daughter of an independent-minded man of the cloth, young Emma was not one to shrink from debates on controversial theological issues of the day, the hottest of which was evolution. She had encountered the divisive topic in college when one of her professors compared people who believed in evolution to atheists. "But he doesn't take into consideration the evolutionists who believe in God and are Christians; he doesn't see how they can be consistent," she had written. But she tackled Darwin's theory head-on in New York City one day, as she and her fellow missionary students sat talking in her room. "Somebody happened to mention evolution and I got off onto the first tirade I have had on the subject since I was young in college. Of course, none of the rest of them believe in it—that is, as far as man is concerned. If I do say it, I know more about the subject than any of them, and that is not saying much. We had some pretty warm talking; I always get hot on evolution and I 'spect I say some rash things; but people are so inconsistent and unreasonable. . . . My views shock and amuse them, as much as theirs amuse me."

Her father's letters from Japan made it clear that the atmosphere there, too, was just as charged as it ever had been. "From what he writes, he is getting to be a terrible heretic. I hope when I get there he will put some wisdom in my head and expound a few things to me."

In Kyoto, Tom waited anxiously for his daughter to join him, glad to think she would be working by his side but also worried that "some rake" might try to sweep her off her feet. He did not let his anticipation or concerns distract him from his duties, though. Church work in the city progressed well, and in the summer of 1901, Tom helped lead extended Bible studies for several hundred young men who had traveled to Kyoto for that purpose. He also kept up a busy teaching schedule at Doshisha Theological Seminary, above and beyond his official missionary duties. Although the school was officially independent of missionaries, neither Tom nor the school's leaders had any misgivings about his sharing his knowledge and experience with the school's dedicated students.

Kyoto's sweltering summers sapped his energy, but winter took an especially heavy toll. Tom's living quarters were cold and poorly heated, and his health deteriorated badly in the city's damp, penetrating winter weather. Only his iron will and strong sense of duty propelled him forward as his heart grew weaker. A fellow missionary spent a day with Tom in Kyoto and described his visit. "In the afternoon, we took a short walk together. On our return home, when about two blocks from the house, he came to a sudden standstill and was obliged to rest for a time, before he could proceed. But even though his heart action was so seriously affected, a few days later he went on an extended preaching tour to the heart of Kyūshū [four hundred miles south]. This was his last missionary journey."[2]

Tom tried to ignore his ailments, but his health went downhill so fast that he could no longer hide from reality. In the depths of winter 1902, he mustered the courage to compose a letter to Speer at the foreign mission board. It was the hardest letter he had ever had to write. He sent it from the home of his fellow missionary and friend, Thomas Winn, now living with his family in Osaka, where Tom had journeyed to consult doctors about his condition. Winn and his wife had been happy to return the favor that Tom and Emma had extended years before, when they had opened their Osaka home to the Winns after their son's death and while Winn had battled typhoid fever.

> Osaka, Japan
> Feb. 6, 1902
>
> My dear Mr. Speer:
>
> I fear this letter will give you some disappointment, and confirm to you the statement which I made to you in my letter, *viz.* "that I have been an expensive man." I have been painfully conscious for three months past that I have been losing strength rapidly and that my health is giving away. For a month, I have been unable to sleep more than three or four hours a night, hardly so much on an average. And, although I have been going on with my work, it has been at a decided disadvantage.
>
> A few days ago, I came down here to Mr. Winn's, where I am enjoying their kind hospitality. I have in the meantime consulted both Dr. Laning and Dr. Taylor. . . . Both doctors say I must leave Japan at once and for good, and they say I cannot go to Tennessee where my family is; that I must go to a warm, dry and equable climate, and that Honolulu would be a good place. . . .
>
> I expect to sail from Kōbe on the 26th of this month by the *Peking*. A certificate will be forwarded later on to the Board, one from each of the above named physicians.
>
> I need not, indeed I <u>cannot</u>, tell you how much pain this decision gives me. I can hardly bear the thought of leaving Japan, especially now that the work is so promising. But I must not dwell upon this now. . . . I am not allowed to see Dr. Taylor's certificate, which is the only one in hand as yet. But Dr. Laning told me that going to Honolulu might prolong my life for several years. . . .

Please think it over [the matter of my duties in Honolulu] and forgive me for being so good-for-nothing physically and otherwise.

As ever,
Yours sincerely,

T. T. Alexander

The reason Tom was not allowed to see his doctor's certificate was because of the stark message it contained. Both doctors were so alarmed by his condition that they believed he might drop off at any moment. They ordered him to quit working, but Tom continued accepting invitations to preach and lecture, until finally he could no longer drag himself out of bed.

Tom's friend, Winn, also weighed in, urging Speer and the Board of Foreign Missions to keep Tom in its employ, even in Honolulu:

Osaka, Feb. 6, 1902

Dear Mr. Speer,

Dr. Alexander has given me permission to put a few lines into his letter. You can little realize how sad it makes us feel to hear the decision of the physicians yesterday in regard to Dr. Alexander. He has been during his 24 years one of the very best missionaries that the Board has had in Japan, and I think in the whole Orient. Our Mission, and the Japanese church, sustains a heavy loss in his departure from Japan, which is about decided upon!

I want to add a word today concerning Dr. A's future. If the Board can continue him in some such work as that suggested in Honolulu . . . he will probably yet do good work for Japan, which he loves as few missionaries do.

For the past splendid work that he has done and for the securing of the good work he will yet be able to do under better climatic conditions; I hope the Board will if possible continue him in its employ. . . .

Please consider this question most carefully yourself and secure its careful consideration by the Board.

Yours sincerely,

Thos. C. Winn

Tom was distressed beyond words at the thought of leaving Japan. "I had expected to go on with my work and to die in the harness," he wrote to Speer in another letter.[3] But, he added, "It was only after the doctors had given their verdict that I began to think it was my <u>duty</u> to seek a change of climate. My family are dependent upon me, and in an important sense it is a man's first duty to provide for his own household. So, altogether, I am reconciled, though I told Dr. Laning I would rather stay here and die than to take his advice and go elsewhere." Tom tried to convince Speer that, despite his illness, he would be able to shoulder a good amount of work in Honolulu, pointing out that "I have not ceased to accept calls to preach and to give talks; to serve in committees. Both last Sunday and the Sunday preceding, I preached here in Osaka (in Japanese), and have made a number of short addresses and speeches in the meantime. . . . I commit my way unto the Lord and ask you and the Board to do what you think right." Tom proposed that he be allowed to continue his evangelistic work among the Japanese in Hawaii.

By the turn of the century, nearly seventy thousand Japanese lived in the Hawaiian Islands, many of them concentrated in and around Honolulu. The first Japanese laborers had been recruited by an American businessman to work on Hawaii's vast sugar plantations in 1868, the first year of Emperor Meiji's reign and a year of great turmoil in Japan. Hawaii's king also had actively sought Japanese workers for the islands, possibly as a counterweight to the growing American presence. Although initially reluctant to cooperate in securing workers for Hawaii, the Japanese government eventually saw the benefits of sending its citizens to populate the islands. After watching waves of emigrants flow from Western countries to overseas outposts and colonies, expansionists in Japan pushed emigration as a way of enlarging Japan's influence through peaceful means. By the 1890s, large numbers of government-sponsored emigrants began to leave Japan to work overseas and send money back home to their families. Hawaii was the destination of choice.

The first Bible classes for the mainly Buddhist Japanese immigrants in Hawaii had been started in 1885 by a Japanese theological student from Doshisha University with assistance from an American minister. By the time Tom was contemplating his move in 1902, a vibrant Japanese Christian community flourished in the islands.[4]

As news of Tom's imminent departure spread, his friends, colleagues, and large circle of acquaintances, both Japanese and foreign, mourned their impending loss. The scenes that accompanied his farewell visits were reminiscent of Apostle Paul's departure from church elders in Ephesus, as described in Acts 20:37–38: "There was much weeping among them all; they embraced Paul and kissed him, grieving especially because of what he had said, that they would not see him again. Then they brought him to the ship." The sound of weeping filled one church when Tom announced he had to leave. A Japanese minister with whom he had worked closely, Hattori Shozo, broke down completely and prayed that God would take him instead and spare Tom for Japan. Kyoto's Doshisha Theological Seminary presented Tom with a pair of fine cloisonné vases with wooden stands made and signed by one of the first artisans in Japan to make such fine keepsakes, Kodenji Hayashi.

Cloisonné vases, now in Smithsonian Institution's Freer Gallery.
(Birdlike images at top are reflections of light)

But leave he must. In late February 1902, after traveling from Kyoto to Kobe and then by inland steamer to Yokohama, Tom spent one day at the Club Hotel before boarding an ocean steamer, the *Peking*, bound for

Honolulu. Countless friends and colleagues came to say farewell. "It was a hard, <u>hard</u> day," he wrote to his family. He barely had time to eat, and his hands and pockets were filled with letters sent by those who could not come in person to say goodbye.

One of his visitors that day was Meiji Gakuin President Ibuka Kajino-suke. Ibuka had been in his office in Tokyo when a colleague brought him the news of Tom's forced departure. Shocked and dismayed, he had broken down in tears at the news. Ibuka liked and respected Tom and felt his critics badly misunderstood him. Tom's views were never extremist or destructive, Ibuka believed; he was just more open-minded and progressive than many other clerics. Ibuka also was deeply grateful for Tom's early and unwavering support for granting the Church of Christ in Japan full independence from missionary control. Sitting with Tom in his Yokohama hotel room, the two men prayed together and talked about the future of the church. As they did so, Tom seemed to forget his illness. Tom counseled Ibuka and his fellow church members not to become defensive or rigid in the face of extreme theologies and destructive criticism then confronting the church, but rather to remain confident that their faith was sufficiently well-grounded and forward-looking to weather the storm.

Another friend and former colleague from Meiji Gakuin College, Dr. William Imbrie, also visited. Tom had talked to him in the past about how weary he sometimes had been, not only during his first years at Meiji Gakuin, but especially on his extended evangelistic tours throughout the country. Sometimes, Tom had told him, he had been so tired that he could hardly make it home from his journeys. Imbrie later recalled that as he spoke to Tom on that last day before his departure, "he smiled, and his eyes filled with tears; and I thought as I looked at him that already he had caught a gleam of the light that shines from the towers of the City of Rest."[5]

The Reverend Uemura Masahisa, editor of the *Fukuin Shimpo,* for which Tom had written eighty articles and which Tom had quietly supported out of his own pocket, wrote in its pages:

> T. T. Alexander, gentle, upright, and fond of learning, suffering from heart disease and being unable to live here longer is about to leave. He has been the best friend of the Fukuin Shimpō, and one of the most faithful workers in the Church of Christ of Japan, whose Missionary Society owes him the greatest debt of gratitude. His fellow workers can never forget his help and sympathy. We can but say that his humble nature and pious character have greatly influenced Christian life in Japan.

Tom in Kyoto, 1902

Uemura later described Tom as "very humble and unassuming, always courteous, a model missionary, giving great influence with his noble personality." Tom undoubtedly would have been embarrassed to hear these accolades from his friend and colleague.

As weakened as Tom had been before he left Kyoto, he had continued to focus his thoughts and concerns on his life's work—that of planting his faith in Japan. One of his biggest worries had been the fact that the city's Christians were struggling to raise enough money to build a church. In the same February 6 letter he had written to Speer from Osaka, Tom had expressed his hopes for the future of the Muromachi Church, along with his regret at leaving.

> P.S. I have left Kyoto for good. It was a severe trial to me to go away and leave my field of labor. I am glad to say, however, that the church there is in a better condition than for a long time. The members are actively engaged in trying to raise money to pay off a debt on their church lot. The debt is yen 700. In addition to this, they hope to get yen 1,000 to erect a church building. All

this they are hoping to accomplish inside of the present year. The effort they are putting forth is doing them good, so that a renewed interest is manifest through the church.

What Tom did not tell Speer was that the week before he had written the letter, members of Muromachi Church had met in an effort to raise funds from among themselves. Tom had pulled himself out of his sickbed and tottered to the meeting. When he realized the local Christians were falling short of their goal, he stood up and in a wavering voice offered to give 500 yen, or one-half the total needed for the building fund. The astounded believers had pledged then and there to raise the rest of the money. Inspired by Tom's generosity, they did so within a very short time and constructed one of the most beautiful and solid churches in all of Japan.[6]

Never one to hide his actions from his wife, Tom wrote to tell her the news of his gift. At home, when they received letters from him, the children would gather excitedly around their mother to hear what he had to say. This time was no different as Emma read the letter aloud. When she realized that Tom had given away two-thirds of their life's savings, plus the money he had earned through the sale of his furniture, she exhaled sharply but quickly recovered her composure. She never uttered a word of complaint or concern to her children. Even though she was trying to make ends meet on a small allowance, she didn't feel she should complain; for Tom had written that not only was it the right thing to do, but also that "Never have I seen the righteous forsaken nor his seed begging for bread."

Alexander family at home in Maryville, 1901. Front L–R: Emma; John Alexander (Tom's brother); Jane Alexander (John's wife); Eva (author's grandmother). Back L–R: Theron; Young Emma; Mary; Christine; Lois.

Tom ended his last letter to Speer from Japan with a postscript containing his thoughts about the future and his feelings toward Japan after twenty-five years of service.

> As I wrote you some time ago, we were all planning for another campaign of aggressive evangelism work in the city of Kyoto and vicinity. But in the midst of all this, I am called away; and as far as I can read the indications of God's providence, He has no further need of me in Japan, however great need He may have for others. I have only to acknowledge the infinite mercy to me and thank Him that He has permitted me to engage in His service for so many years.
>
> If I had ten times 25 years to give to His service on earth, I would gladly give them all to Japan.
>
> As I look back over the years that have past, I can say that I have found them to be years of joy; and although I have met with trials and bereavements and have been unworthy, and sometimes less than faithful, still I have every reason to be grateful to the Master, whose yoke I have found to be easy and whose burden has been light.
>
> Yours sincerely,
> T.T.A.

Notes

2. Curtis, "Testimonial."

3. February 18, 1902. PCUSA, "Correspondence."

4. Kimura, *Issei*, 3–5, 157. See also Iriye, "Japan's Drive," 308–9.

5. William Imbrie, "Eulogy," 9. Uemura quote from *Fukuin Shimpo*, November 1902. Cited in *Japan Evangelist*, Vol. X, No. 2 (February 1903), 5. Description of Tom from *Uemura Masahisa and His Age*, 450. [In Japanese.] Excerpt translated and sent to me by Uemura's grand-daughter, Nakamura Taeko, in a letter dated May 9, 2007.

CHAPTER 19

A Happy Reunion

He was thin and pale, and his evident weakness made my heart ache.

Honolulu, Hawaiian Islands
March 18, 1902

Dear Mr. Speer:

I arrived here on the 11th, just one week ago today, having endured the somewhat rough voyage very well, so well in fact that I was better at the end than at the beginning. I have been improving since my arrival, so that I am much stronger than when I left Japan. I consulted a doctor this morning for the first time since coming here. He tells me that this is undoubtedly the climate for me, that I could not find a better. I have engaged a room and board by the month and am waiting as patiently as I can to know wherefore the Lord has brought me here, or whether it is all a blunder of my own, and to no purpose at all.

There is plenty of work to be done among the Japanese here in the islands. The whole number of the Japanese population is now said to be 67,000. The Hawaiian Board and the Methodist Society are doing the work, as you know. On inquiry, I find that I am acquainted with half, or more, of the Japanese preachers employed by these two Boards. Some of them would be glad to have our Board begin work here. So would the leaders of the Church of Christ in Japan. . . .

I do not know whether I am doing right, or whether I am playing the part of a Jonah in running away from the field of labor appointed me. The whole situation is something I had not counted upon, for I had thought to stay at my post until released by death, or called away by such a condition of ill health as would unfit me for service. In the latter case, I expected of course to be sent to America. My coming here, therefore, is a surprise to myself, and seems to add to the perplexity of the situation. I can only wait for guidance, and pray, as ever, "Lead, kindly light, Lead thou me on."

I hope to hear from you soon.

Very sincerely yours,

T. T. Alexander

Tom hoped the board would allow him to remain in Hawaii to work among the Japanese and also to retain his connection with—and salary from—the Foreign Mission Board. He sympathized with Speer and other board members, though, who had to deal with "such a case as mine, in the midst of so many other cares and anxieties. I greatly regret the necessity thus laid upon you. It must be hard to know what to do with such a man," he wrote.[1] But as he contemplated his possible activities in Hawaii, he was gratified to realize that he knew so many of the Japanese brethren laboring there. One of them, the Reverend Motokawa Gennosuke, had been a theological student at Meiji Gakuin in Tokyo and now served as pastor of the Japanese Methodist Church in Honolulu.

Tom with Japanese ministers at his home, 723 King Street, Honolulu 1902.
Front L–R: Nagayama Manji; Tom Alexander; Inouye Tanefumi;
Middle L–R: Yajima Ukichi; Motokawa Gennosuke; Kodama Shokichi;
Back L–R: Fukao Tanji; Fujisawa Genkichi; Ishida Keikichi.

At home in Maryville, Emma was beside herself with worry and despaired at being so far from her husband when he was so weak. She also knew how disappointed daughter Emma would be to embark on her career as a missionary in Japan, not at her father's side as she had hoped, but alone, with her father lying deathly ill in Hawaii. Adding to Emma's shock was the fact that Tom's frequent letters from Japan had not hinted at the sharp downturn in his health. Perhaps to shield his family from worry, Tom had, until the last, told his family of his good health. Letters flew between Emma in Maryville, Tom in Honolulu, and Robert Speer in New York City, debating whether or not Emma should join her husband in Hawaii.

Maryville, Tennessee
March 8, 1902

My Dear Mr. Speer

Your very kind letter reached me this noon. I also received two letters from my husband, which were encouraging. I suppose you would also receive word by this steamer. Of course, I have been and am still very anxious but am able to hope for the best. I know that God makes no mistakes.

Emma will feel greatly disappointed but she is showing a very brave spirit and a trustful spirit, I think. I want to go and be with my husband as soon as it seems best for me to go. If I can take the two younger children with me, who are respectively twelve and eight; Emma would not stay at home; the others can get on without her.

I am very glad to have the check you sent, and I am indeed grateful to you and to the kind friend who gave it to you. It will be a very great help to me.

I am grateful to you for your sympathy and kind offer of help.

Yours very sincerely,

E. E. Alexander

Emma wanted desperately to be with Tom but had no money for travel. Tom, ever practical and unselfish, felt that the matter of his own future should be settled before Emma made any plans to join him. He also believed the children needed Emma at home more than he needed her in Hawaii. Plus, he hated to cause any more trouble or expense for the Foreign Mission Board than his hasty departure already had caused. In the end, Emma resigned herself to remaining in Maryville, although she was prepared to leave for the islands if Tom should need her.

As the board contemplated Tom's fate—whether to keep him on salary, and, if so, whether he would remain in Hawaii or be assigned someplace else—an anonymous benefactor had stepped forward and donated a substantial sum of money to help cover the family's living expenses in Maryville. Or, quite possibly, knowing of their dire straits, Speer had given the money himself. Tom and Emma never did learn the donor's identity, but they both asked Speer to convey their heartfelt gratitude to the kind and generous soul. Before long, and without deciding Tom's ultimate assignment, the board agreed to continue Tom's salary as he worked among the Japanese in Hawaii, as well as the family allowance for Emma at home. "I thank you for your kindness," Emma wrote Speer. "I received your kind letter concerning the continuation of my allowance and the continuation of my husband's salary. I am sure he is worthy of some consideration, but whatever I receive is grace."[2]

Robert E. Speer

Young Emma, still in school in New York City, was just as distraught as
her mother and poured out her sorrows in her diary as the drama surrounding her father unfolded.

> March 3 [1902]. A never to be forgotten day. I don't like to put
> it into words. This morning I got a letter from Mama enclosing
> one from Papa—and since reading them, the world seems dif-
> ferent. Papa must leave Japan; he was to have left Feb. 26. The
> doctors told him he could not live in Japan or Tennessee; he
> must go to Honolulu. I guess he is on his way now. Mama must
> go to him. I have had letters from Mama, Lois and Theron, all
> full of distress, but brave. Mama was full of sympathy for me,
> and Theron bravely tried to cheer me.
>
> It was a little bit before I could get it thru' my head. It
> seems as if I cannot bear it. Mama tells me to stay and finish my
> course, but how can I! Miss Smith is the only one who knows
> my trouble; the others think I am homesick. My grief is for Papa
> and Mama—but I am glad they are to be together. I went to the
> Board rooms to see Mr. Speer, but he was not there. I have cried
> till I feel very badly.

The grief that others mistook for homesickness soon was replaced by
real sickness. Young Emma was felled by an attack of typhoid fever that kept
her bedridden or confined to her boarding house for nearly four weeks. A
small, handwritten sign reading, "No Admittance—except the doctor," was
posted on her door. Exasperated by her poor medical care—she was examined by a doctor who was "blind and deaf and as old as Methuselah and
hasn't a grain of sense"—and by the indifference of her housemother, Miss
Smith, Emma "rose up in wrath and began to abuse the old man and said to
Miss Smith he was worse than no doctor." Her outburst finally brought her
the medical care she needed from another, more competent doctor. Under
his care, young Emma gradually regained her health.

In early June, as she finished her studies, young Emma received her
official appointment to the East Japan Mission. Under ordinary circumstances, the news would have filled her with delight, and she would have
rejoiced at the prospect of working with her father in Japan. But these were
not ordinary circumstances, and she didn't know yet just what her future
held. One thing was certain, though: it wouldn't be the future she had en-
visioned. And just before she left New York City, an old friend made an
appearance.

> Well, Mr. Beatty must appear upon the scene again. I had been
> receiving a great many letters from him; they were all very much

love letters. I did not write to him while I was sick. . . . He be-
seeched me to come to his home—he would pay my way; then
he wanted me to stop on my way home. I told him that if he
wanted to see me he would have to come to me. So he came on
Sunday, June 15; I gave up the day to him. We went to Central
Park in the afternoon and to the Central Presbyterian Church
in the evening.

He is very much changed. He is quiet and thin and sad—
lovelorn, I suppose. He stayed over Monday and went to the
[missionary] conference with me. We spent the evening in the
library at 128 [East 10th Street]. An evening which I shall long
remember and after which I was exhausted—neither of us ate
dinner. We were there for three hours, and a more grief-stricken
person I have never seen; it took him an hour to say goodbye—
he would put his arms around me and kiss me. Finally I was so
worn out and angry with the struggle that I told him that if he
did not stop and go, I would leave the room myself.

He said, "God this is hard," but he did not go. If I must tell
the absolute truth, I must say that it was a temptation to stay in
his arms and be loved, instead of going forth to the ends of the
earth alone. But I really do not think we suit each other—he
never calls forth my deeper thoughts and I doubt if he could appreciate them. But he has not lost hope—he wants me to marry
him at the end of seven years; by that time, he will be a minister
and ready to marry. He will come to Japan if I wish it. He is not
the careless person he was when I first knew him; he is admi-
rable in many ways.

Before leaving New York City on June 19, 1902, young Emma paid a
visit to Mr. Speer on the eighth floor of the Foreign Mission Board offices at
156 Fifth Avenue. She asked him if she could travel to Japan via Hawaii so
she could visit her father, even though that route would mean extra expense
for the board. Speer readily agreed, and young Emma boarded a train that
afternoon bound for home in Maryville.

I took a long last look at New York as we crossed [on] the ferry. I
have that picture with me yet in my mind—a wonderful picture
it is; those tall buildings looming up in the mist. I shall never
forget. I enjoyed the journey home. I changed cars at Washington at 10:30 p.m., then went to bed and slept the sleep of the
just to wake up in Dixie! Like sweet music in my ear was the
drawling speech I heard. Theron was in Knoxville to meet me. I
could not express if I tried all day my joy when I saw home and
Mama standing on the porch!

After a summer at home getting reacquainted with family and friends, sewing and mending clothes to take to Japan, picking and canning fruit, and worrying about her anxious and ailing mother, young Emma began to prepare for her long journey. Although she dreaded leaving her care-worn mother, she looked forward to spending a month with her father on her way to Japan. But before leaving, there was one important matter she had to attend to. On September 3, young Emma wrote to her devoted suitor, Reading Beatty, "telling him that I would give up the struggle—that I would marry him when he got ready, if he were still of the same mind. But if either of us changed our minds in the meantime, we would be free."

On September 19, 1902, at age twenty-two—the same age her mother had been when she had left Maryville as a new bride—young Emma left home, taking a train across the continent that largely retraced the route her parents had followed twenty-five years before. Although she traveled alone, she made friends along the way with a young teacher, a cowboy, a college student, and other voyagers bound for various western destinations. After an overnight stay in San Francisco at the Occidental Hotel, young Emma boarded a steamer headed for Hawaii.

> About one o'clock the steamer started, and I was moving away from my country. It filled me with a sort of rebellious grief. I was glad that none among the crowd on the wharf were my loved ones—it would have been too harrowing. I stayed up on deck that night till I nearly froze, afraid to go down. It was pretty choppy. Sure enough when I did go down the stuardess [sic] had to help me to bed. . . . The stuardess was awfully good to me. She said I was a "dear little girl." I smiled to myself but did not tell her that I was a dignified missionary.

Twenty fellow passengers helped her pass the time by playing ping pong, sharing meals, and carrying on friendly conversation. She was glad that her assigned table for meals placed her in the company of "a party of globetrotters and not with the missionaries." Then, on the morning of September 25, they sighted land. Young Emma was thrilled.

> Early in the afternoon, things began to be very beautiful—the water took on exquisite shades of blue and green, and the island of Oahu was lovely to behold. Honolulu, stretched out on a flat place with the hills rising up behind, looked very pretty. As we drew near, my heart began to thump like it was trying to get out.

It was four o'clock before we were alongside of the wharf. It took such a long time to get alongside!

The natives diving for pennies had no interest to me—I strained my eyes to see Papa. I recognized him a good while before we got up and waved and waved but he could not recognize me until he could see my features. He said he thought it might be I, but he could not be sure. I crowed my way down the gangway as soon as I could. He was thin and pale, and his evident weakness made my heart ache. We drove to the Cookes, a smiling and happy pair—and how much we had to talk of!

Young Emma loved Oahu: the ocean, with its exquisite shades of dark blue and emerald green; palm trees; exotic-looking banyan trees and other tropical foliage waving gently in island breezes; green hills surrounding Honolulu; hedges of night-blooming cereus; colorful birds; and the peculiar flavors of mangos, guavas, papayas, and other strange-tasting fruit. A US territory for two years since 1900, Hawaii nonetheless hosted a mix of cultures, which fascinated young Emma. "Honolulu is a strange place. One could not tell what country one was in by the appearance of the city or citizens. There are Japanese, Chinese, Portuguese, Hawaiians, Americans and Europeans all in their native dress." Her main complaint was the cockroaches and other insects that burrowed into every fold and crevice they could find, but she quickly adjusted to shaking these unwelcome pests from her nightgown before going to bed each night.

The Reverend and Mrs. Cooke, fellow missionaries living at 723 King Street, had opened their home to Tom, and they welcomed young Emma just as warmly. Despite his bad health, Tom had tried to make the most of his few months in Hawaii. He regularly led Japanese immigrants in Bible study; had mustered the strength to teach two week-long training classes for missionaries from around the Asia-Pacific region; and preached occasionally with Meiji Gakuin graduate, the Reverend Motokawa of the Methodist Society. Motokawa, who often visited Tom at home, asked young Emma to speak to a group of Japanese women who gathered regularly at his home for study. Tom went along and acted as interpreter.

Emma's greatest delight came on those occasions when Tom felt well enough to take her on excursions around Honolulu. One day, Tom took her by trolley to a Japanese tea house at the top of Pacific Heights that offered stunning views of the sea and the green hills rising from its blue-green waters. Another day, Mr. Cooke took young Emma to the harbor to see the cable ship *Anglia*, whose crew was laying the first trans-Pacific telegraph line from Australia to Vancouver, Canada. The ship's holds contained massive cable-laying machinery and two-thousand miles of cable rolled into enormous coils. After a tour of the ship, the captain gave Mr. Cooke a little section of cable as a souvenir. These welcome diversions helped young Emma forget that she soon would be leaving Hawaii and her father. Shortly after her arrival in Honolulu, she and her father had booked passage for her on the *Coptic*, scheduled to depart for Japan on October 29.

The steamer would sail without her.

Notes

1. Higuchi, *Muromachi Church,* Ch. 1, Sect. 2, "The Founding of the Muromachi Church (1889–1894)."

2. Letter to Robert Speer, BFM, April 8, 1902. This and previous letter in PCUSA, "Correspondence."

3. April 1, 1902. This and previous letter in PCUSA, "Correspondence." Unless otherwise noted, all descriptions below of young Emma's activities and feelings are from Emma Thomasina Alexander, *Personal Journal.*

CHAPTER 20

Papa Went to Heaven

He was surely, as everyone who saw him says, a lovely and saintly man.

Most days, Tom struggled to get out of bed. When he did manage to get on his feet, his pulse often raced unevenly, leaving him light-headed and breathless. Although overjoyed to have young Emma with him, he also wanted to be sure she saw something besides his sick room. So, when he felt up to it, he took her to Honolulu's museum and other interesting or scenic places, pushing himself more than he probably should have. About a week after young Emma's arrival, the two of them enjoyed a daylong excursion in town. When they returned to their rooms, Mrs. Cooke invited them to join her, her husband, and a few friends for a dinner party that evening at their summer residence in Manoa Valley, a few miles up in the hills above Waikiki Beach. A raw October wind had blown all day and soon brought in a driving rain, which soaked the picnickers before they could get into the shelter of the house. Afterwards, Tom caught cold, and young Emma was pressed into service as his nurse.

> He has been very sick—the effects of the cold are worse than the cold itself. It has prostrated him terribly. He is not able to dress and lies in bed most of the time and is almost helpless, he is so weak. And oh, how I have suffered with anxiety! . . .
>
> As soon as Papa took this cold, I made up my mind not to leave him. I told the Gulicks so and asked them to look out for something for me to do. Papa simply would not listen to such a thing, but as he grew worse he began to see that it was absolutely necessary for me to stay; and when Mr. Gulick came the other morning and proposed that I stay here and work among the Japanese and receive fifty dollars a month for my service, Papa slowly gave his consent and we accepted the proposition. Papa dictated a letter to Mr. Speer telling him of it.

These are dark days for me—Papa is so ill and we are so far from home; and Mama—I don't dare express all that troubles me.

October 19, Sunday

I am sitting at Papa's window overlooking the front yard. It is a beautiful morning outside. The sun is shining and the birds twittering, and the banana leaves are waving in the breeze. And it is warm, like a day in June in Tennessee. My heart is too heavy to be made glad by the outside world, no matter how beautiful.

Papa had a bad night. What little sleep he got was disturbed—his mind wandered and he talked of all kinds of things. I was with him till after ten and off and on until after two o'clock, trying to help him to endure the night. Only now and then did he seem to be fully conscious, tho' he would get up and sit in a chair part of the time.

He suffered dreadfully—he is so weak and unable to rest, and I suffered too. Mr. Kincaid called this morning, and by his sympathetic looks and words caused me to cry for the first time. I was weary from loss of sleep.

I must write to Mama today—but what on earth shall I tell her! God have pity on Mama, and help us all to bear it!

October 20

The doctor allowed Papa to have his sleeping medicine last night, so he had a much better night of it. He is dozing today and does not talk so much in his sleep as he did yesterday. His sleeping is uneasy; he can find no restful position; his breathing is hard and he groans a great deal. Tho' he has no acute pain, he suffers dreadfully. Such long, drawn-out, weary suffering.

Young Emma wrote to her mother, saying her father had a cold, but she didn't reveal how badly the cold had prostrated him. She poured out the whole story to one of her uncles in Maryville, though. She sat by her father's side, fanning him one moment to cool his fevered brow and applying hot compresses to his chest the next. She otherwise passed the days reading, writing letters, and occasionally leaving him long enough to go to church or on outings with friends. Letters for her father poured in from Japan. "How Papa's friends do adore and admire him! But it is not to be wondered at. His patience and cheerfulness is wonderful during these long days and nights."

Tom and Young Emma at 723 King Street, 1902. Tom's last photograph.

Tom, ever solicitous of his daughter, sent her out each day to buy an ice cream soda or some other treat for herself. Young Emma also embarked on her missionary duties by teaching English and the Bible to several Japanese women on the island, including the wife of Japan's official consul in Hawaii, Mrs. Okabe. When given a thirty dollar advance on her salary, she lamented, "It hurt my pride to take it. I know it is just the kindness of somebody that has given me the position, and now they give me thirty dollars in advance when I can do so little to earn it. . . . I have done nothing but receive kindness all my life. I will be glad when the day comes that I can be kind to somebody!"

Young Emma's spirits rose and fell with the state of her father's health. Some days and nights, he moaned in bed and mumbled incoherently; other days, he recovered enough to sit in a chair and read. One day, Tom even managed to write a letter to his wife, his first in a month. Young Emma hoped her mother would receive it with the same joy that her father had gotten from writing it. When he could, Tom also would talk to young Emma. "I am learning invaluable things from Papa. I am getting a view of Japan and missionaries and lots of things—and he has answered many a puzzling question. . . . I am surely blessed in having such a father and in having the privilege of being with him now."

Young Emma was determined to learn Japanese as well as possible. She vowed inwardly to follow her father's example of reading aloud in Japanese and writing the complicated kanji characters every morning, a custom that had helped him gain fluency in speaking and writing. On rainy days, when the oppressive atmosphere weighed down young Emma's mood, she learned it had the opposite effect on her father. "Papa says the sound of the rain is restful to him. He says it makes him feel he is not 'responsible for the universe.'" Even though Tom rallied every few days, the doctor warned young Emma that he was failing and could go anytime. "I suppose it is true, but I don't believe it." Tom himself seemed unwilling or unable to acknowledge the seriousness of his condition. In his last letter to his wife at home, penned on November 5, he wrote with a shaky hand:

My Dear Emma,

It is some time time [*sic*] since, I took up my pen, or laid it down either. I have had a serious illness in the way of a cold, which has caused me much discomfort and pain. But there there [*sic*] has been no time during the month past when I <u>could not</u> have written a little to you, and doubtless I <u>would</u> have written often, had E. [Emma] not been here to write for me, and to care for me.

I knew her presence here would be a constant assurance to you that I was being looked after. She is one in whom you can be at rest. She has taken care of me and done it easily, that is without undue strain on herself.

The Lord, "and other friends," as you know already, have arranged for her support here for an indefinite time, and God is at the helm. I am regaining strength. Last night brought me rest and strength. So I hope to be better and stronger daily. Everybody is good.

Your and the children's letters are a constant source of blessing and comfort. Be at peace, and do not worry. I been [*sic*] much better. I hope to write again <u>soon</u>.

Your own laddie.

Sadly, his doctor's prognosis was right. On November 14, 1902, Tom Alexander—missionary, husband, father, son—breathed his last, with daughter Emma at his bedside. The bereaved twenty-two-year-old waited two weeks to write the words her heart refused to accept.

November 28.

Two weeks ago today, Papa went to Heaven. It was about four o'clock in the afternoon, Friday, November 14. When I look at my grief and loss, I am awed at the greatness of it. I cannot realize nor comprehend it. Yet I am glad that he is free from his weak body and that he has no more pain; and O, how grateful and glad I am that I was here!

O! I am so glad that I was here, and could make his last days in some degree happy! I shall never forget his smile whenever I came into the room. His face was the most beautiful I have ever seen; he was surely, as everyone who saw him says, a lovely and saintly man.

I was sitting alone with him when he went away. He spoke of feeling unusually well in the morning, and right after break-fast, he helped me for about an hour with Mrs. Okabe's lesson. Then I left him and went to the consulate and did not get back until nearly lunchtime—and Papa spoke of being tired. After lunch, we talked awhile; then he lay down, saying he would rest awhile.

He rested quietly, I don't know how long . . . until I heard him breathe with difficulty. I got up and spoke to him, but he did not answer nor move. I was terrified and called to Mrs. Cooke. I came back to Papa and spoke to him again, but he drew a few breaths and was gone. Mrs. Cooke came and went to telephone for the doctor.

I remember now, walking about the room wringing my hands and sobbing without tears. . . . The doctor came before long, but nothing could be done. The doctor said his heart prob-ably stopped before I heard the difficult breathing. . . . After dinner—I could not eat—I went to take a last look at Papa, and I realized that he was really gone, and I cried as I have never cried before in my life.

Tom was just fifty-two years old when he died. The last thing Tom had talked about was what to give his wife for Christmas. He had decided to send felt slippers, a nice pair of shoes, and galoshes to protect them from the rain.

The funeral took place in the Cookes' living room on a Sunday afternoon. The Reverend Motokawa Gennosuke officiated, together with the Reverend Orramel Hinckley Gulick, brother of John Thomas Gulick, Tom's fellow Osaka missionary and naturalist colleague, who had taught Tom so much about evolution. Many of Tom's Japanese and American friends and col-leagues in Hawaii gathered for the service, filling the room to capacity. Piles

of colorful and fragrant flowers surrounded the urn, hiding it almost entirely from view. Although both ministers had led countless funeral services,
saying goodbye to their dear friend and fellow worker was hard, as young
Emma's account made clear.

> When Mr. Motokawa got up to address the Japanese, he could
> not speak at first and soon began to sob, and there was no sound
> in the room but crying. When he could speak, his words were
> of deep love and admiration. Mr. Gulick's words were very ap-
> preciative also. He said he had never known a man to become
> beloved of so great a number of people in so short a time.

A soprano's voice carried sweetly through the room, part of a quartet
singing one of Tom's favorite hymns, "O Gift of Gifts". The hymn's words
were fitting for a man whose humility and selflessness had led him to confess to a colleague shortly before leaving Japan that he felt unworthy of the
many blessings he had received during his life: "O gift of gifts, O grace of
faith, my God how can it be; that Thou who hast discerning love, shouldst
give that gift to me." Another verse surely had offered inspiration to a man
who had known his share of sorrow and disappointment: "The crowd of
cares, the weightiest cross, seem trifles less than light; earth looks so little
and so low, when faith shines full and bright."

Young Emma wrote home about her father's death and worried about
the effect the news would have on her mother, who was not only faring
poorly herself but also was caring for son Theron, who was sick once again.
"I am so afraid for her. I could bear the grief myself, but to think how she
must suffer is almost more than I can bear. Her letters are so brave. She said
it seemed almost too good to be true that I was going to stay. She had gotten
the photo of Papa and me, and she says she has it framed and hanging on the
wall, and I seem to say to her when she looks at it, 'Don't worry, I am here.'"

In the days after the service, Emma ventured into the dark, musty
basement of the old Kawaiahao Church, the first Christian church in
Hawaii, where Tom had stored his books and worshipped occasionally.
Locals considered the massive structure, whose chapel could seat nearly one
thousand people, an engineering wonder. Built in the 1830s, its outer walls
were made of massive coral blocks, each weighing more than a thousand
pounds. Stoneworkers had carved them from underwater reefs, and Hawaiian laborers had carried them on their shoulders to the construction site.
Young Emma didn't focus on the church's architecture, though, as she went
about her sad duty. She spent hours in the dark, dank basement, opening
and repacking her father's books. Most would be sent home to Maryville,
but he had wanted her to take some of them with her to Japan.

I had plenty of company as I worked—spiders, lizards, and various other varmints and the old native janitor who insisted on coming down to help (?) me. He packed one box, which I was obliged to do all over again. So I decided to do all the packing myself and let him wrap the books, which he did with much chewing of tobacco, spitting, and talking. His English was very funny. There were eight boxes—so it was quite a task.

When that job was done, young Emma steeled herself for the hardest task of all: sending her father's ashes home for burial. Somehow, that simple act made his death seem all too real and all too final. He would be buried next to other family members in Maryville's Magnolia Cemetery. As news of his death reached Tennessee, Maryville College flew its flags at half-mast and held a memorial service for its illustrious graduate.[1] His wife ordered a simple granite headstone and had it placed on his grave.

REV. THOMAS THERON
ALEXANDER

BORN OCT. 8, 1850
MOUNT HOREB, TENN.

DIED NOV. 14, 1902
HONOLULU, HAWAII

TWENTY-FIVE YEARS A
MISSIONARY TO JAPAN

Tom Alexander's headstone, Magnolia Cemetery, Maryville, TN

Left a widow at forty-seven with five headstrong children still at home, Emma faced a life of poverty, loneliness, and unaccustomed responsibility. She received a tiny pension from the Foreign Mission Board and a small allowance for each child until he or she turned eighteen, but she was not used to managing entirely on her own. She also was concerned about her eldest daughter. After Tom died, she wrote to Mr. Speer, begging him to allow young Emma to return home for rest after her sad and difficult experience. "After all," she wrote, "she is little more than a child."[2] Speer replied that the board would leave the decision to young Emma; and she, dedicated as she was, resolved to follow through on her commitment to go to Japan. Would her father have done anything different, she wondered? So just after Christmas Day, 1902, young Emma boarded the *Nippon Maru* bound for Japan.

Thirteen first-class passengers shared the best cabins and dining quarters on board the ship, playing shuffleboard, enjoying punch and other refreshments, and trading stories of their travels and adventures. They had a hard time believing that young Emma, with her youthful appearance and open, trusting nature, was a real missionary, journeying alone to her teaching post in Japan. She, in turn, found it hard to deal with the ship's captain.

> To my great amazement and bewilderment, he seems to have fallen in love with me. He is thirty six years old, and he has been married about two years. All the passengers say that he is the nicest captain they have ever known, and I thought so too, but I don't know what to make of him now. He sits beside me, walks up and down with me, and plays shuffleboard with me.
>
> Today the Russian sat by me talking for a long time, and when he got up the captain took the chair and said he was just about to get his revolver and shoot the Russian; and he looked as if he meant it too. Friday evening he kept wanting me to go off alone with him and I refused to go. He asked me if it was because I did not trust him, and I did not deny it. He said, "My dear girl, you could trust me with your very life, if you only knew it."
>
> So the next day he didn't come near me all day and did not go to his meals and we all thought that he must be sick. But yesterday he came and said that he had been staying away from me but that he could not do it any longer; and he stayed with me all day and all evening. He said that he wished to be counted among my very best friends, but he was not at liberty to say

all. He told me how pure and good he thought me and said he would not hurt a hair of my head for the world.

He said he had learned to know me well and had become very very fond of me and that if he had sinned he wanted me to think as well of him as I could. Sometimes he squeezes my hand and looks at me with a look that means love; at other times, he is a pleasant companion and likes to have a jolly time and teases me dreadfully. He really seems to be very much in love with me and looks very sad—and yet, I thought he seemed to be very fond of his sweet young wife.

All this is beyond me. I can't understand it. I am sure I did not do anything to make him fall in love with me. But to be frank, I feel flattered with his attentions—he does look so fine in his evening uniform.

As the steamer neared Japan, a hard rainstorm blew in, causing the ship to pitch and roll and sending passengers below to the shelter of their cabins. As soon as the rain stopped, young Emma went back on deck, even as the steamer plunged through the rough seas. "It was a beautiful sight to see the spray dashing over the bow. It was so exciting I forgot to be seasick."

On January 7, 1903, after the fastest ocean crossing young Emma had ever experienced—less than two weeks—the coastline of Japan appeared. Her heart beat so hard she thought it would break. She was glad to return to Japan, but oh, how she missed her papa. Despite her grief, she made up her mind to focus on her work and do the best job she possibly could. She looked forward to meeting teachers and students at Joshi Gakuin girls' school in Tokyo, which her father's mission had launched when she had been just a young girl. Joshi Gakuin already had earned the reputation as the best school for girls in Tokyo, if not all of Japan.

Her fellow teachers and the city's missionary community welcomed young Emma with open arms. Shortly after her arrival, they celebrated her twenty-third birthday with a surprise party, showering her with gifts, dinner, and a birthday cake. One Japanese teacher, Miss Mitani Tani, gave her a cute little purse with a rabbit on it, accompanied by a note that read, "A happy, happy birthday to Miss Alexander! 'As thy days, so shall thy strength be.'" Others gave her a silver breast pin, a lovely vase with pink azaleas in it, a brass and silver tray, and other thoughtful gifts. Her new friends' loving words, even more than their presents, made young Emma feel so welcome that she was able to forget her sorrow and homesickness for a few blissful hours. Letters soon arrived from her dear Reading and other friends, but not yet from the person she missed most: "I do want to hear from my Mama!" she lamented.

One fine day in January, young Emma joined several other American teachers on a call to her father's old colleagues at Meiji Gakuin. They hired a horse-drawn carriage for the occasion and traveled in style through the streets of "dear, old Tokyo". She and her friends felt grown-up and refined as they sipped tea and ate dainty cakes with the professors and their families. Young Emma had recovered completely from her bout of typhoid fever the previous year and looked forward to a healthy future, but illness always lurked in Tokyo's mosquito-filled waterways and foodstuffs contaminated with human waste. And as the year 1903 began, young Emma knew she would have to steel herself for an event that was rapidly approaching: the memorial service for her father, scheduled for January 31 in Joshi Gakuin's chapel. She hoped she would be able to contain her emotions.

Notes

1. Tom's record of service was honored for many years. In 1928, a full quarter century after Tom's death, Maryville College received a generous donation from James L. Getaz of Maryville and established the "T. T. Alexander Prize Fund." The prize aimed at promoting Christian education through an annual speech contest for young men and women to be run by the Department of Bible and Religious Education. Document establishing fund dated August 30, 1928. MC archives.

2. Mary Alexander, "Japan Notes."

CHAPTER 21

He Gave His Life for Japan

A year is a big step toward the time when I shall go home.

January 31, Saturday [1903]

Memorial services were held here in the Joshi Gakuin chapel for Papa this afternoon. The service was beautiful, but it brought my loss so vividly to me that it was hard to bear. It began to snow this morning, and by the time for the service there was a regular blizzard; and by the time the service was over, the ground was white. I don't remember seeing such a snow storm in Japan.

Of course, this kept many away; but still there were a great many present—and his dearest friends were there; and just the right ones were on the program: Mr. Ibuka, Mr. Uemura, Dr. Imbrie, Mr. Arima. I wish I could have understood all the Japanese, for they say the tributes were fine and that their words were beautiful indeed.

I wish I could always remember Dr. Imbrie's words and the way in which he spoke them. His friendship and love for Papa was very great, and his words showed the depths of his love and admiration.

During the memorial service, young Emma sat in a front pew, gazing up at a picture of her father on the pulpit, probably one taken in 1899, three years before his death. His hair, never thick on top, had been thinner than ever and prematurely white; his moustache and beard were fashionably short, with just a hint of a handlebar in his whiskers. He had worn his finest black wool suit, the one he used for preaching and funerals, contrasted with a white bow tie, which he donned for only the most formal occasions. His thin, almost gaunt face framed a pair of penetrating eyes, whose steady gaze reflected the inner strength that had propelled him forward in the face of hardship, pain, and loss. His erect bearing spoke of the quiet dignity that befitted him as a humble servant of the Lord.[1]

A mix of lilies, red winter berries, daffodils, chrysanthemums, and other colorful flowers surrounded Tom's picture, filling the chapel with their fragrance and offering a welcome taste of spring on the frosty winter day. Light filtering in through colorful stained glass windows added softness and warmth to the atmosphere inside. The tributes to Tom during the memorial service reflected the love and respect he had earned among his peers.

The Reverend Uemura Masahisa, the samurai son who had risen from poverty to the highest ranks of the Church of Christ in Japan—and who later would found Tokyo Union Theological Seminary, incorporating the theology department from Meiji Gakuin where Tom had taught—preached the sermon for his old friend. Uemura said that when we sorrow for those who have gone before us, we should consider carefully the path they have followed and try to emulate it. Uemura spoke of the ways in which Tom had faithfully followed Christ during his missionary service in Japan. *The Japan Evangelist* summarized Uemura's sermon in its pages. It read in part:

> First, in humility he was a disciple of Him who came not to be ministered unto but to minister.
> Second, in faithfulness he followed Him who was faithful unto death, even the death on the cross. He gave his life for Japan.
> Third, in love he learned from Him who having loved His own loved them unto the end. He loved the brethren and labored with them in the Gospel. We desire to be like such a man. The way we know: let us strive to follow him.

Dr. Ibuka Kajinosuke, President of Meiji Gakuin College who had wept at news of Tom's abrupt departure from Japan, gave a sketch of Tom's life and then offered personal observations about his friend and former colleague.

> He gave his whole life for mission work in Japan. To speak of my own impressions, I was struck first with his command of our language. Others were as proficient as public speakers, but he spoke like a scholar, in a way to which even we Japanese could not attain. Second, he was intimately acquainted with Japanese matters and this knowledge he obtained by close intercourse with the people. But the most striking characteristic was his sympathy with, and belief in the people, and on account of this he was greatly trusted.

The Reverend S. Arima spoke of Tom's influence in leading him into the ministry and in guiding him afterwards. His friend's humility had impressed him greatly. Speaking of one preaching session in Osaka, Arima recalled, "Dr. Alexander said, 'The people will gather to see a foreigner, so I am the sign-board to draw them to hear you preach the gospel.' And such a man," he continued, "called himself a sign-board for such as me!"

Tom's good friend and former colleague at Meiji Gakuin, Dr. William Imbrie, closed the memorial service, offering a long address filled with memories, love, and admiration for his friend of twenty years. He also spoke of Tom's dedication to the church in Japan.

> When I think of Dr. Alexander I think of him as a friend and as a servant of the Church of Christ in Japan; and those two thoughts are so closely joined together that I would not separate them if I could. . . . His love for the Church of Christ in Japan was a thing well known of all. There was no service that he was not ever ready to render it. And he loved it not merely as an organization; he loved it also in its members. "Remember me to Ibuka and Uemura and Ishiwara and all the others." That was one of his last messages; nor was it any mere piece of formal courtesy.
>
> But if one were asked, what one thing above all others was most characteristic of him, and should be especially an inspiration to all who knew him? I think the common answer would be, his deep feeling of personal responsibility. He was beyond most of us faithful in doing what he thought he ought to do. When about to sail for Hawaii and speaking of the work he hoped to do there, he said to a friend, "I do not know how soon I may fall; and I want every day to count." He was always redeeming the time. . . .
>
> When I look back over the five and twenty long years and what he did and was, my first thought is that his place cannot be filled. But that is not what he himself would have said. What he would have said I think I know. . . .
>
> It would be this: God has no necessary men. For whenever and wherever there is a need in the Church that there arise a burning and shining light, he has only to say, Let there be light. And the light will arise and shine.

More accolades flowed during memorial services held in Kyoto, Osaka, and other towns and villages where Tom had worked, preached, and brought new believers into the light. Kyoto's memorial service was held in February 1903 in the very church that Tom had helped finance just before leaving Japan. Members of Muromachi Church chose February 11 as the date for both the service and the dedication of the new church building. That date was the first anniversary of the gathering at which Tom had made the generous contribution that had inspired church members to raise the rest of the funds needed to build the sanctuary. It also was the date traditionally celebrated as the birthday of the Japanese nation.

More than two hundred mourners filled the new chapel, one of the most beautiful in Japan, according to missionaries who had seen many other churches throughout the country. Tom's friends offered touching tributes to the preacher and teacher from East Tennessee.[2] The Reverend Uemura Masahisa's words echoed the sermon he had offered during the memorial service in Tokyo. One Japanese church elder reflected the view of many mourners when he said of Dr. Alexander, "he was a man of rare gifts and attainments, but he lacked one thing: self." Tom's fellow missionary, Frederick Curtis, spoke of his friend's self-denying character and also of "his wonderfully deep sympathy for the Japanese, to which they had responded in a most remarkable degree." Tom's close friend and fellow seminarian, Thomas Winn—who, years before in New York City, had suggested that Tom consider the foreign field of labor—gave the main address.

Winn noted that shortly after Tom had committed himself to serving in Japan, he had received offers from several churches in America, "any one of which, if accepted, would have given him a more prominent position than the average young man just from his studies can aspire to. 'Well, how is it; are you sorry that you came to Japan as you now look back over the years spent here?'" was a question put to him just on the eve of his leaving Japan. Very promptly and emphatically came the reply: 'No. I am not sorry I came to Japan. . . . If I had a hundred lives I would be glad to give them all for Japan.' Yes, that was the feeling he had to the last, that he would be glad to do a great deal more for the spiritual and religious uplift of Japan."

Winn touched on other traits of his friend and fellow worker in Christ. Even though Tom was so widely respected and had been awarded the honorary degree of Doctor of Divinity by his alma mater, Maryville College, he had been too modest to make himself known or to bring his work to the attention even of churches at home in America. Tom's prodigious work and tireless efforts on behalf of Christianity in Japan, not to mention his fluency in Japanese, had earned him the respect and admiration of his Japanese and foreign colleagues, Winn noted.

He early began to get an unusually good use of the Japanese language, and continued to progress in this acquisition till he was one of the men recognized as the most fluent in using this difficult tongue. He once said in the presence of a few friends that when he got up to address a Japanese audience, the words for uttering his thoughts flowed out without an effort. He often stated that Japanese preaching was easier for him than preaching in English. Everywhere he went, he preached and spoke in response to invitations from the Japanese, who seemed to love to hear him. . . .

In the counsels of the Church of Christ in Japan, of which he was a regular member, he was prominent. His advice and opinions concerning the affairs of the church were always sought and valued. . . . He was able to so identify himself with the Japanese laborers that the difference between things foreign and Japanese was well-nigh obliterated. The heartiness of mutual cooperation was a joy to him and to the leaders in the church. . . .

It seems a very strange Providence which called this brother away from his activities at such a comparatively early age. But as one who knew him well has been heard to say; "He made good use of his short life."

Winn closed his remarks by noting Tom's devout belief in God and Christ, and also of his sense of unworthiness. "One day, when speaking of his being led to choose the ministry, his voice became choked and he said, 'My sense of unfitness and sinfulness have troubled me most.' When talking of his own future, he revealed how truly his soul was anchored to Jesus Christ in these words: 'I am more and more convinced that there is a life eternal beyond this world, and that outside of the teaching of Christ there is absolutely nothing to which to look for hope.' On the subject of death, he calmly expressed himself thus; 'I expect to receive grace for dying as I have received it for living.'"

Young Emma threw herself into her work and quickly made friends with fellow teachers at Joshi Gakuin, shopping with them, sharing meals, and venturing via streetcar to meetings at the Y.W.C.A. and other Christian societies.[3] She liked all of the Japanese teachers but was especially fond of Miss Mitani Tani, a cheerful companion, who watched out for her new American friend, even dragging her to the dentist one day for an abscessed tooth. One of her Sunday school students, Miss Uemura Tamaki, was the daughter of Tom's old friend, the Reverend Uemura Masahisa, who never did learn about Tom's strong defense of his character and faith when other missionaries attacked him for being too independent-minded and difficult. Miss Uemura found one of young Emma's lectures to be especially moving: the one on "truth". Emma's teachings were an early inspiration in Miss Uemura's ultimate decision to pursue a life and career in the church.[4]

Young Emma made a strong impression on her colleagues and students. Fair-skinned, tall, and slender like her father—standing 5 feet 6 and weighing 130 pounds—she wore a pince-nez carefully balanced on her nose. Her quiet, gracious manner and warm-hearted nature drew people to her. Students and colleagues often saw her walking on campus with a shawl draped over her shoulders in her favorite color, blue. One day, she plucked a leaf from one of the ornamental Ginkgo trees on campus and tucked it into her journal. When she wasn't teaching, young Emma spent hours writing letters to family and friends, rejoicing when she received their replies. One day, she got nine letters and three photos. How happy she was! One letter was from Reading, and one finally arrived from her mother. Young Emma also took the time to write to Robert Speer at the Board of Foreign Missions.

Joshi Gakuin, Tokyo
May 14, 1903

My dear Mr. Speer:

I have no business at all of which to write to you, but as I have not written since I reached Japan, I thought I would like to do so. I have not forgotten the kind letters that you wrote to me in Honolulu. I always think of you as a friend.

It is a little over four months since I arrived in Japan. School opened the day after I came and I began right away to teach and to study, and I enjoy doing both very much. I am glad that I can do something, even if it is only a little, while I am learning the language.

My life is very different from what I thought it would be when I first decided to come to Japan. I thought that I would be with my father. But I know that it is selfish to wish that he were here, and I try to be happy. And I really am happy in my surroundings and work. I find real pleasure and joy in it, and I am glad that I came.

I shall <u>try</u> to be a worthy daughter of my father, and hope that God may use me.

Sincerely yours,
Emma Alexander

As the summer of 1903 ended and autumn began, life was looking better and better. As she readied herself for the first day of a new school year, young Emma thought back to a special event in her life.

> Sept. 3. One year ago today, I wrote to Reading saying that I must yield to him. I took off the fetters with which I had bound my heart, and left it free to love. Now my heart is running over with love for Reading and for everyone else. My heart is filled with love instead of with the hard feelings with which I restrained my love. I was changed on that day—it has brought me happiness. I have had terrible sorrow since then, but there is a joy in me. I thank God for my love for Reading and for the great love he gives me.

A few days later, she noted another important milestone.

> Sept. 9. One year today since I performed the most heroic deed of my life—the most difficult feat I have ever done was to step off the porch at home one year ago today. What a <u>sad</u> child I was. But my heart strings were pulled toward Papa, too. The memory of it all has made me sad today. But I have not thought of the past only, I have thought of the pleasant today.
>
> The girls have been coming back all day, ready for the first day of school tomorrow. They are fat and rosy and so happy to get back and see their *sensei* [5] In between the times of saying *"Okairi na sai"* [welcome back], I have been looking over my work for the term and wrote part of a letter to Mama.
>
> This term I have the Junior Bible, the Science Reader, Junior Rhetoric, and drill in Essay work with the Juniors, besides music lessons. The last two classes are new institutions and are entrusted to me.
>
> This evening, Mrs. McCartee, Helena, and I went over to the Milikens to see Dr. and Mrs. "New York Observer" Devins. I met them several times in New York. Mrs. Devins remembered my speech, as she called it, at the closing exercise of the Training School and spoke very nicely of it indeed.

Typhoid fever develops when bacteria enter the digestive tract and then the bloodstream, causing severe inflammation of the intestines and sores that can perforate the intestine walls. The bacteria, passed in stool and urine, are spread by flies and mosquitoes, water and food contaminated by untreated sewage, and infected people who haven't washed their hands.

---

5. The word *sensei* is an honorific title that means "teacher." It is used to refer not only to teachers and professors, but also teachers of the message of the gospel.

Typhoid's first symptoms—headache, fever, loss of appetite, joint pain, sore throat, and diarrhea—often are mistaken for flu. That's what young Emma thought she had when she wrote to her mother in January 1904, saying she had the "grippe." The news gave her mother "more or less a feeling of anxiety," as her mother confessed in a letter to Mr. Speer.[6]

Young Emma recovered enough from her first attack to resume work, but a second and then a third attack felled her and sent her to bed in her second-floor room at the school. High fever kept her delirious much of the time, and bacteria released into her bloodstream ate through her organs, eventually finding their way to the lining of her brain. As fever consumed young Emma's body, fire destroyed the beautiful chapel on Joshi Gakuin's campus, site of her father's memorial service just one year before. The chapel's destruction led her mother to write, "Indeed, Japan is a sore country for calamities, as our Irish brethren would testify."

Meningitis inflames tissues surrounding the brain and spinal cord, causing severe headache, sensitivity to light, vomiting, confusion, extreme sleepiness, and even seizures. Young Emma lay in bed moaning and, when conscious, wishing for her mama and beloved Reading. No antibiotics existed to treat the disease ravaging her body, though, and she died on February 22, 1904, just fifteen months after her father's death. Miss Mitani Tani and her fellow teachers dressed young Emma in her favorite white dress, made in Western style from fine Japanese crepe. It was the same dress young Emma's father had sent to her in Maryville on her twenty-first birthday, to be worn for her college graduation. Little had she and her mother realized, as they had altered the dress to fit, that it would be her funeral shroud.

Her coffin was placed in the main room of the teachers' hall, where students filed past and took a last look at one of their favorite teachers. A strong scent of daffodils greeted them as they came in from the cold. One of young Emma's students later said she thought of her teacher every time she smelled the fragrant flowers. Deep purple violets scattered around her body looked beautiful against the pure white of her dress. Young Emma seemed to be sleeping peacefully and appeared to some students like an angel. Fourteen-year-old Uemura Tamaki was devastated by her teacher's death, but her loss only strengthened her faith. She was baptized into Christianity the following year.

Young Emma was buried in the foreigners' section of Tokyo's sprawling Aoyama Cemetery, where she became, like her sister, Ella, forever a part of Japan. The last words she had written in her journal were these: "Well, a year is a big step toward the time when I shall go home." Some people might say she did go "home," to a place where her father gathered her close in loving arms, showing her the way forward in heaven, just as he had on earth.

Notes

1. Description of memorial service from Emma Alexander, *Personal Journal*, and Akiyama, "The Humble Believer." Quotations below from *Japan Evangelist*, Vol. X, No. 2 (February 1903) 6–9.

2. This and other quotes from the Kyoto service, unless otherwise noted, are from Curtis, "Testimonial." Winn remarks in *Japan Evangelist*, Vol. X, No. 2 (February 1903) 1–4.

3. Young Emma and the other teachers, Misses Mitani, Kushibe, and Iseki, lived at the school at 33 Kami ni bancho in Tokyo. Emma Alexander, *Journal*, January 17, 1903.

4. Imawa Takeo, ed., *Uemura Tamaki*. Publisher, date unknown; copy of excerpt from MG archives. When young Emma's namesake and niece, Emma Shelton, visited Japan for the first time in the 1970s, the Reverend Uemura Tamaki made a special effort to visit Emma at her hotel. She told Emma how much she had admired Emma Alexander and had valued her guidance and kindness.

6. Emma Edwina Brown Alexander letter to Robert Speer, BFM, January 25, 1904. This and young Emma's letters in PCUSA, "Correspondence." Descriptions of young Emma, including the viewing of her coffin, are from Mary Alexander, "Japan Notes," and recollections by one of her students in "The Memorial, 1903," in Maeda Shinobu, *Fifty Years of Joshi Gakuin*. Publisher date unknown; copy of excerpt from MG archives.

EPILOGUE PART I

A Living Legacy

"Every little deed"—said Kim's lama—"sends out a wave of influence that never stops."

By the time the Reverend Thomas Theron Alexander died in 1902, Japan was a force to be reckoned with. As the only Asian country ranked among the world's great powers and with its own colonial possessions, Japan boasted an advanced economy, a democratic government, a rapidly developing industrial base, and a powerful army and navy. Japan entered into an alliance with Britain in 1902 and defeated Russia in war in 1905 (with China once again the battleground for war), marking the first and only time an Asian country ever vanquished a European power. President Theodore Roosevelt won the Nobel Peace Prize for brokering a peace settlement between the two warring nations.[1]

Japan's wartime successes and great-power status did not provide the degree of security and respect its leaders sought, however. Other world powers were still on the move, drawing ever closer to Japan through military and territorial expansion. Russia, France, and England continued their march into China and other parts of Asia, carving out territories they claimed for themselves. America had solidified its hold on possessions in the Pacific: not only Hawaii, but also the Philippines, Guam, and Wake Island acquired after Spain's defeat in 1898. Anti-Japanese sentiment in America grew as Japanese plantation laborers in Hawaii flooded into mainland states following Hawaii's annexation by America in 1898 and the islands' incorporation as a US territory in 1900. Responding to growing political pressure, President Roosevelt in 1907 banned Japanese immigrants from entering the mainland via Hawaii, Canada, and Mexico. The following year, the former Rough Rider of San Juan Hill negotiated a "Gentlemen's Agreement" with Japan, severely restricting immigration from that Asian country at a time when America placed no limits on immigrants from Europe or other countries.

Sadly, great-power jockeying for overseas possessions, foreign alliances, and political domination would culminate in two devastating world wars in the twentieth century.

By 1902, Christianity had gained a small, but firm foothold in Japan. Although the total number of Protestant and Catholic Christians was small—only about one in one thousand—about one in every hundred educated individuals was Christian. Japanese Christians held senior positions in government, industry, and the news media, giving them more influence than their numbers otherwise would suggest. By the turn of the century, one cabinet member, two supreme court justices, two speakers of the Lower House of the Diet, two of three members of the Liberal Party's executive committee, 4 to 9 percent of Diet members, vice ministers, appeals court judges, editors and owners of some of Japan's largest daily newspapers, and senior naval and army officers came from Christian ranks. "They fill these numerous positions of influence because, in spite of much prejudice, they have proved themselves worthy and have won the confidence of their countrymen," reported *The Japan Evangelist* in August 1900.[2]

The Meiji Regime, which ended upon the emperor's death in 1912, had recast Japan from a loosely knit country ruled by shoguns, lords, and samurai into a constitutional monarchy and parliamentary democracy, as well as a modern industrial powerhouse. Japan was the first country in Asia to undergo this transition and one of the only countries in history to make such a remarkable leap in the space of just one generation. Strong, visionary direction from Japan's own leaders fueled this transformation. However, foreign teachers, diplomats, and missionaries like the Reverend Thomas Theron Alexander and his colleagues also played an indispensable role in bringing Western knowledge, technology, culture, and religion to Japan, helping the county in its efforts to modernize and embrace the outside world.

If the work of Tom Alexander and the many other missionaries like him had died when they did, this story would end here as an interesting footnote in the long, shared history of the United States and Japan. But his legacy lives on in Japan and America today, offering proof that one person can change the world in more ways than he or she may realize. When she wrote her recollections of Japan, Tom's daughter, Mary, paraphrased lines from *Kim*, Rudyard Kipling's 1901 novel about India: "'Every little deed'—said Kim's lama—'sends out a wave of influence that never stops.'" The wave of influence set in motion by Tom Alexander continues to flow into many corners of the two countries he considered home—and even beyond. Churches, schools, charitable institutions, and individuals in the twenty-first century still enjoy the fruits of the teaching and traditions that the Reverend Alexander and his fellow missionaries introduced into Japan in the nineteenth century.

Organized today under two names, a legacy of World War II—the Church of Christ in Japan (CCJ) and the United Church of Christ in Japan (UCCJ)—churches founded by the Reverend Alexander and his fellow missionaries play a vital role in the life of Christians and non-Christians alike. Offering worship services and aid to disaster victims; speaking out on human rights, the separation of politics and religion, and other important secular matters; sponsoring missionaries in Korea, Hong Kong, Singapore, and other countries; and partnering with Presbyterian and Reformed churches in the United States, Taiwan, Korea, and elsewhere, these churches continue the tradition of teaching, seeking justice, and ministering to the needs of people in all walks of life. The National Federation of Kyodan [UCCJ] Women's Societies' programs for women and youth promote Bible study, offer home stays and youth missions for greater cross-cultural understanding, and support other theological missions. The joint and individual efforts of these churches and organizations truly reflect the spirit of Romans 12:5, "so we, who are many, are one body in Christ, and individually we are members one of another."

Most, if not all, of the churches founded by Tom Alexander in the 1880s and 1890s continue to serve Japanese believers today in Tokyo, Osaka, and other towns and cities throughout central and southern Japan. Japanese ministers and faithful adherents in those and other churches carry forward the work of early missionaries with steadfastness and devotion. And although less than 2 percent of Japan's highly secular population today is Christian, Christians have continued to figure prominently in leadership positions in business, government, and the media. Eight prime ministers have been Christian, including some in recent years; and Empress Michiko, while officially representing the Shinto religion, was raised in a Catholic household and attended Catholic schools.[3]

Churches founded by the Reverend Alexander carry on in ways both large and small the lesson of generosity that he taught and practiced. Osaka North Church offers hot meals and used clothing to Osaka's homeless population, whose numbers rose substantially after Japan fell into recession in the late twentieth century and many people lost their jobs and homes. This essential service for people in need stands out in a country in which private charity is not widely practiced—it even prompted one formerly homeless man to join the Osaka North Church, where he has found a new church family. Members of the Osaka Suita South Church tend Ella Alexander's grave in Kobe's foreign cemetery, keeping alive the memory and spirit of the young girl who had played the organ at their church just days before she died. In Yanagawa on southern Kyushu Island, an older woman who had been exposed to Christianity during her youth returned to the fold and joined the church after her husband died. And the Yokohama Kaigan Church, founded by Tom's fellow missionary, James H. Ballagh, stands today as the oldest Protestant church in Japan, offering religious services and support to the people of Yokohama. Many more examples like these can be found in cities and towns throughout Japan where churches and their congregations live out their faith on a daily basis.

The Presbyterian Church (USA)—created in 1983, when northern and southern Presbyterian churches that had split during America's Civil War finally reunited—continues to work both on its own and with partners in Japan on a variety of important missions. Tokyo Union Church, originally located next to Tom and Emma's first home in Tsukiji, offers worship services and delivers handmade rice balls each day to individuals unable to meet their daily nutritional needs without assistance. PC (USA) mission workers and their Japanese partners engage in evangelism, theological education, higher education, medical services, and programs for women and youth. Other Christian denominations carry on similar work with partners in Japan, carrying on missionary traditions begun in the mid-nineteenth century.[4]

Schools founded by missionaries also stand as a legacy of Christian workers in nineteenth-century Japan. Although only a small portion of Japan's population today is Christian, roughly 10 percent of the country's secondary and university-level students attend Christian schools offering high-quality education along with religious studies. Meiji Gakuin University, where Tom Alexander chaired Systemic and Biblical Studies, is a prime example. The university, which celebrated its 150th anniversary in 2013, offers a broad-based liberal arts curriculum to nearly thirteen thousand students. Although its department of religion was united early in the twentieth century with a seminary founded by Tom Alexander's friend and colleague, the Reverend Uemura Masahisa—which later became Tokyo Union Theological Seminary—Meiji Gakuin promotes Christian-based character and encourages students to live up to its founding philosophy of "Do for Others." Other examples of missionary educational facilities include Joshi Gakuin junior and high school for girls, where young Emma Alexander taught; and Tokyo Women's Christian University, where daughter Mary Alexander taught.

At Joshi Gakuin, young Emma made an impression on the people she worked with that was out of all proportion to the time she taught there. Her close friend and fellow teacher, Mitani Tani, eventually served as the school's principal. During World War II, when authorities banned everything American, Mitani kept Emma's picture in full view on her table. It also stood near her bedside many years later, where she could see it as she lay dying. Another young woman, Uemura Tamaki—daughter of the Reverend Uemura Masahisa—was a freshman in young Emma's Sunday school class at Joshi Gakuin. Like her father, Uemura Tamaki became a minister and only the second Protestant woman ordained in Japan, long before Presbyterians in the United States had accepted women into the ministry. She venerated Emma's memory until the day she died. She also became a close friend of Emma's younger sister, Mary, who later taught at Tokyo Women's Christian University.[5] To honor and remember their early teacher, Joshi Gakuin administrators, teachers, and students still tend Emma's grave in Aoyama Cemetery and lay flowers there each year on her birthday, always taking care to include some of Emma's favorites: fragrant yellow daffodils.

The fact that young Emma's grave still exists is a tribute to Joshi Gakuin and the citizens of Tokyo. In 2006, Tokyo's nationalist governor, Ishihara Shintaro, ordered the removal of all those gravesites whose cemetery fees had not been paid. The edict hit foreigners' graves hardest, because few descendants, scattered as they were around the globe, had known about or paid the fees. After an outcry from concerned Tokyo residents, who argued that Japan's history was bound up with the foreigners lying in the city's graveyards, Ishihara recanted. He even ordered that a bronze plaque be placed at the entrance to the foreign section of Aoyama Cemetery to commemorate the contributions made to Japan by deceased individuals of many nations. But it turned out that Emma's grave was never in danger of removal: Joshi Gakuin has faithfully paid her cemetery fees for more than a century.

Tom's fifth child, Mary Alexander, had hoped to pursue a career teaching in Japan and sought a position there as soon as she finished her studies at Maryville College. By then, Mary also had taken charge of her widowed and largely destitute mother. They both journeyed to Japan in 1919, where Mary joined the faculty of the year-old Tokyo Women's Christian College (now University) as one of its first English teachers. While there, she and her mother rekindled their friendship with old friends, including the Uemura family, especially daughter Tamaki. After graduating from Joshi Gakuin, Tamaki had studied at Wellesley College in Massachusetts and earned her undergraduate degree in 1915.

Mary also worked with TWCU's founders: Yasui Tetsu, Nitobe Inazo, and A. K. Reischauer. Dr. Yasui was one of Japan's foremost female educators at the time. Dr. Nitobe, later described as a "Bridge across the Pacific," eventually became Under Secretary-General of the League of Nations. Dr. A. K. Reischauer, an American Presbyterian missionary and educator, was the father of future US Ambassador Edwin O. Reischauer. Mary later wrote about her early experiences.

> The College had been started the year before in a big wooden building which originally had housed some other kind of work. It was in a large, walled-in yard full of trees and shrubs with a *yama* [mound] at one end. A Presbyterian mission church was next door and Mother and I were eventually installed in a small wooden house which was on church property. A most beautiful waxy-white camellia was at our front door and two fragrant pink daphne bushes were a little way out from the side porch.
>
> There all went well for two years. Mother even "commuted" down to Joshi Gakuin (Emma's school) for a few weeks to substitute for a teacher who was ill and enjoyed it enormously. Sugimori-san ([later] Mrs. Kitamura) and Mitani-san ([later] Mrs. Amatatsu) were my pupils. Mitani-san became very fond of Mother. When she came to visit she often brought a western doll with her for which she and Mother made clothes.
>
> But things began to go askew. At least one thing (of which I was ignorant at the time) made Mother unhappy and she became ill. The foreign doctor was out of Tokyo for an indefinite period. I took her to a doctor in Yokohama but she got no better. In desperation I asked the mission to let me take her back to the States and I was allowed to do so—by a narrow majority.

Mary at her home near Tokyo Women's Christian College, 1920

Emma and Mary's student, Sugimori Ko (later Mrs. Kitamura),
at home near TWCC, 1920

Mary with teachers at Tokyo Women's Christian University, ca. 1950

Though greatly disappointed by her forced departure from Japan after just two years, Mary sought and found work as an English teacher in New York City high schools. She passed the teacher examination with flying colors: the main essay asked prospective candidates about their qualifications for teaching English as a second language, something that came naturally to Mary after her experience teaching English in Japan. Mary's mother lived with her until her death in 1937. Then, as soon as she retired, Mary returned to Japan to teach English at Tokyo Women's Christian College. She described her emotional return just after World War II.

> In '49, thirty years and two months later, when I went back to teach at the College, I was met at the boat by Kitamura-san [Mary's former student and by then a teacher at TWCC] and three foreign teachers who had driven over to Yokohama in the College bench wagon. It was a dark, rainy day and our route back to Tokyo lay through miles of rubble with here and there stark, charred fragments of buildings still standing. Worst of all, American G.I.s were everywhere. I looked at Kitamura-san and wondered how she could be so spontaneously friendly to us.
>
> As we came into Tokyo city limits, the young teacher driving said, "Let's go 'round by Tsunohazu and see the place where the College used to be. I haven't seen it yet," and the others heartily agreed. The place was hard to find, but they finally located it by the reservoir nearby. That lovely garden was now a five acre mud hole, sodden with water, not a house on it nor a blade of green.[6]
>
> We went, then, to the new location, new buildings, lovely campus. I was shown into a cold, cheerless, bare-floored room containing an empty book-case, one straight chair and a cot— for my furniture would not arrive until the next day. But Fusako-san had put a beautiful spray of pink *sasanka* [anemone] on the book-case! After this dismal beginning the first year was an interesting one as I tried to learn to do what was expected of me.
>
> We "celebrated" my first Christmas by having twelve earthquakes of varying severity all before our one o'clock dinner. One shock sent us all scampering downstairs where we stayed the rest of the morning. A wry joke!

While at TWCU, Mary eventually moved into the Reischauer house on campus. Because of her Japanese language skills, Mary managed the household staff for three years, in addition to fulfilling her teaching duties. Her friendship with the Reverend Uemura Tamaki also deepened. Since 1934, Uemura-sensei had served as a minister in the Church of Christ in

Japan. Mary worshipped as often as she could at Kashiwagi Christ Church, founded and ministered to by the Reverend Uemura Tamaki.

One of Mary's students during this second stint at TWCU was a talented young woman, Minato Akiko, who arrived in 1951. Growing up in Sendai, a coastal city in northeastern Japan, she had spent World War II running from one bomb shelter to another, barely surviving the onslaught from American aircraft. Studying English was not only hard under those circumstances, but also greatly discouraged. As English teaching resumed after the war, her provincial teacher gave her and other students adequate preparation in English grammar but not in pronunciation. When Minato-san arrived at TWCU, her English enunciation had lagged far behind that of her fellow students, many of whom had studied at Joshi Gakuin, the best girls' school in Tokyo. Her test scores put her near the bottom of the class.

"I was so upset," she wrote later, "that Miss Alexander, a white-haired, pretty missionary teacher responsible for pronunciation, told me . . . 'Bring a mirror and come to me' in the foreign teachers' house. In the living room, one-on-one, I opened and shut my mouth while looking in the mirror, and she corrected everything thoroughly. That's why my pronunciation improved by leaps and bounds, so that on the next test I was promoted to a higher class." Dr. Minato later became president of Tokyo Women's Christian University.[7]

Reischauer House, TWCU

Mary with TWCU President Dr. Saito Takeshi at her farewell lunch, 1953

Churches, schools, and spiritual gifts are not the only legacy of the Reverend Tom Alexander and his fellow missionaries. Their involvement in the wider life of Japan also left a lasting mark. Itagaki Taisuke, Japan's nineteenth-century democracy activist, who invited missionaries to preach the gospel in his home region of Tosa on the island of Shikoku, is revered by the Japanese people today. They honor him as one of modern Japan's founding fathers, an elder statesman who helped establish constitutional democracy in that country. Itagaki's Liberal Party, many of whose followers were led into Christianity by the Reverend Alexander and his colleagues, was refashioned after World War II as the Liberal Democratic Party, which has ruled Japan almost continuously since the war. The democratic, egalitarian aspects of the constitution and practices of the Church of Christ in Japan surely influenced the thinking of Itagaki and his fellow statesmen as they worked to make Japan the first country in Asia to adopt a constitution ensuring popular elections, the separation of powers, and freedom of religion.

By weaving themselves into the fabric of Japan's daily life and work, Tom Alexander, his daughters, and other missionaries also influenced Japan in intangible ways that cannot be measured by the number of churches, schools, or institutions they founded or impacted. Tom's kindness, gentleness, and sincerity touched the lives of many individuals in Japan, whose own lives in turn have touched others. The wave continues to flow outward. Even today, according to the Reverend Inaba Hajime, members of the Yanagawa Church on Kyushu recall their founder as a gentle spirit, who never scolded or raised his voice in anger. Tom's light lives on in those believers and in countless other hearts as well, standing as an example of a man who preached the word with humility, grace, and tolerance.

Notes

1. See Iriye, "Japan's Drive," in Jansen, *Emergence of Meiji Japan*, 268–329; and Jansen, *Modern Japan*, "Imperial Japan," 414–55. Terms of Roosevelt's Portsmouth peace treaty, which did not provide for indemnification of wartime losses, led to destructive rioting in Japan and the imposition of martial law.

2. *Japan Evangelist*, Vol. VII, No. 8 (August 1900) 259–60. These Christians formed nearly six hundred churches. See also Brown, *One Hundred Years*, 724.

3. The Church of Christ in Japan, founded in 1877 by Presbyterian and Reformed missionaries as the Union Church of Christ in Japan (renamed as CCJ in 1890), was one of the largest Protestant churches in Japan before World War II, with about six hundred churches. Under pressure from Japan's wartime government, the CCJ merged in 1941 with other Protestant churches under the umbrella name United Church of Christ in Japan (UCCJ).

   After the war, most churches remained with the UCCJ, a reflection of members' desire for maintaining an ecumenical, unified church through their own choice. However, forty-nine churches left the umbrella group and reconstituted themselves in 1951 as the Church of Christ in Japan. Churches that chose to remain part of UCCJ identify themselves according to their founding Presbyterian and Reformed tradition. Information provided by ministers of CCJ and from "United Church of Christ in Japan: A Brief History," http://uccj-e.org/history. Information about the National Federation of Kyodan [UCCJ] Women's Societies' programs from http://uccj-e.org/knl/1173.html.

   Finding an accurate number of Christians is difficult, because many people who consider themselves Christian are not registered members of any church. Christian prime ministers were: Hara Takashi (1918–21, until assassinated); Viscount Takahashi Korekiyo (1921–22); Tetsu Katayama (1947–48); Shigeru Yoshida (1948–54); Ichirō Hatoyama (1954–56); Masayoshi Ohira (1978–80); Taro Aso (2008–09); Yukio Hatoyama (2009–10). Online: http://en.wikipedia.org/wiki/Christianity_in_Japan.

4. See "Presbyterian Mission Agency" at http://www.presbyterianmission.org/ministries/global/japan. Information about Union Church from *PC (USA) 2010 Mission Yearbook for Prayer & Study*, "Japan" (Louisville, KY: Witherspoon, 2010), 141. Information about Christian school student numbers and Meiji Gakuin from *Meiji Gakuin: A Century at a Glance, 1877–1977* (Tokyo: Meiji Gakuin, 1977), 47; author

conversation with Meiji Gakuin Chancellor Dr. Kuze Satoru in 2007; and "About Meiji Gakuin University, Founding Principles and History." Online: http://www. meijigakuin.ac.jp/en/.

5. Information about Mitani Tani's and Uemura Tamaki's friendship with young Emma and Mary is from Mary Alexander, "Japan Notes." Mitani's younger brother, Mitani Takanobu, served as Grand Chamberlain of the Imperial Court. Edwin O. Reischauer, *My Life*, 23.

6. Tsunohazu is Shinjuku ward today. The school's new location is in Suginami ward today.

7. Minato Akiko, "Liberal Arts: A Major Theme," in *Tokyo Women's Christian University 1918–1998*. [In Japanese. Translated by Robert Feldman.] Dr. Minato (née Onari), is the author of numerous books and received the Nitobe and Nambara Prizes in 2005. Mary Alexander had taught at TWCU when Mrs. A. K. Reischauer joined with Lois Kramer of the German Reformed Church and Japanese colleagues in forming Japan's first school for the deaf, the Japan Deaf Oral School (Nippon Rowa Gakko) in 1920. The school used the oral method of instruction. Perhaps that is where Mary learned about using a mirror to help students learn how to form English words. Edwin O. Reischauer, *My Life*, 20.

My Own Journey of Faith

Some people might say I'm my great-grandfather's latest convert.

The wave of influence set in motion by my great-grandfather, the Reverend Thomas Theron Alexander, has flowed far beyond Japan's shores, from the nineteenth to the twenty-first century, and reached back to America, where it has touched my own life. After long shunning organized religion, I have become an active member of the Presbyterian denomination he worked so hard to establish in Japan.

In many ways, I'm the most unlikely of converts to faith. I was raised in a household largely devoid of religion. Although my parents took me and my brother to church for a year or two as young children, I hated Sunday school and church day camp. We moved every two to three years, following my father's career as a chemical engineer with a large corporation; and my immediate family—not church—became my safe haven, the main constant in my life. My parents' love and support for me was unshakable, and they instilled in me values that I carry to this day: a love of learning and of hard work and persistence, self-reliance and independence, and the importance of treating everyone with kindness and compassion. My parents also were strong egalitarians and passed that belief on to me and my brother. "He puts his pants on one leg at a time, just like the rest of us," my father would say about a president, politician, or other "big wig," who seemed to feel superior to others. That egalitarian spirit applied to race and ethnic differences, too, even in the years before America's civil rights movement.

I have inherited a wanderlust and desire for adventure, a trait I certainly see in my great-grandfather. Maybe my footloose childhood also contributed to my willingness to pull up roots and cast myself far from home. After I entered high school, I longed to experience life in another country, so I applied my senior year to study abroad as an American Field Service exchange student. Even though I had studied French for many years and hoped to go to a French-speaking country, AFS sent me to live in Denmark for a year following graduation. As soon as I learned Denmark was my destination, I threw myself into learning as much about the country and language as I could, even borrowing a 33-rpm record from Wilmington, Delaware's public library so I could begin saying a few phrases in the notoriously difficult language. (The Danes humorously describe the guttural Danish language as more of a throat disease than a language.)

During my year in Denmark, I learned as much about myself and my own country—seeing it for the first time from another vantage point—as I did about my host country. From falling ill and landing in the hospital's isolation ward just three weeks after my arrival (due to mononucleosis, then a virtually unknown disease in Denmark) to changing host families several weeks after moving in with them, I fought feelings of profound loneliness and homesickness until I was able to speak the language well enough to join in conversations with my new Danish family and new-found friends. My experiences there—knowing no one when I arrived; not speaking the language; and living far from family and friends at a time before cell phones, email, and Skype—helped me understand the hopes, fears, and loneliness my great-grandparents experienced as they ventured to Japan. But my year in Denmark also strengthened me and built a greater sense of self-reliance; and I gained lifelong friends and fluency in a new language. I treasure my Danish friends to this day and consider them extended family.

Undergraduate studies followed at Duke University, with a junior year of study in Paris, France: another year of living on my own overseas and one of the hardest years of my life. My beloved father died three months before my departure after a long battle with lung cancer—he was fifty-four; I was twenty-one—and I struggled to adapt to the loss of my strongest anchor, while adjusting to living and studying in a new culture. To this day, I have a hard time thinking about that period of my life and the loss of my father without deep feelings of sadness.

My interest in international affairs and a summer internship on Capitol Hill with Delaware's lone congressman led me to graduate studies at the Johns Hopkins School of Advanced International Studies in Washington, DC. I thrived in the competitive atmosphere of the school and discovered a love of economics that shaped my career after graduation. Beginning at the US Treasury Department, I took part in global trade negotiations, jetting to Geneva, Switzerland, with fellow negotiators; served on the personal staff of Secretary Regan; and was the first woman selected as the "Japan desk officer"—advising the secretary, other senior Treasury officials, and the

White House on economic and financial developments in Japan at a time when trade tensions with Japan ran high. Then, nearly nine years on Capitol Hill followed. I wrote trade law, advised on trade negotiations; and briefed Members of Congress on trade and economic matters as a staff member of the House Ways and Means Committee.

I moved next to the US State Department as Deputy Assistant Secretary for Trade Policy, taking part in negotiations and public debates on the North American Free Trade Agreement and a host of other contentious trade negotiations and disputes with other countries. The capstone of my career was the post of Deputy Secretary General of the Organization for Economic Cooperation and Development (OECD) in Paris, France. I was the first woman and youngest person to serve as the number two official and most senior American in the (then) twenty-six country organization, which offers policy advice to member governments in a wide range of substantive areas.

During all these years of college, graduate school, and increasingly responsible career postings, I held religion firmly at arm's length. Oh, I respected it enough. But when I considered the impact of religion on human history and even on modern events, I felt it wasn't for me. Too many wars have been fought in the name of religion. The Crusades, the Inquisition, the practice of burning real or supposed heretics at the stake all flew in the face of the Bible's teachings (not to mention the teachings of other faiths). Devout worshippers, piously placing their offering in the plate each Sabbath and leaving faith behind in everyday life proved to me that hypocrisy flourished even among the so-called faithful. No, I decided, religion wasn't for me, even though I sometimes longed for an outlet for the spiritual feelings I harbored deep inside.

My life in Paris was great in many ways. I had a loving husband, a fantastic job, good health, and was living in a city that offered a wealth of interesting museums, historic neighborhoods, high-quality music and art, and world-famous cuisine. I traveled more often than I had in Washington, DC, to countries in Europe, Asia, North Africa, and Latin America, including more official visits to Japan. A prominent French businessman even sponsored my membership in an exclusive club, Polo de Paris, where I rode horses, played tennis, and enjoyed fine dining.

Yet something was missing. A feeling deep inside pushed closer and closer to the surface, nagging me with thoughts of a more "normal" life: a life of community and stability, of day-to-day rhythms focused more on family and friends than of international travel and high-level diplomacy. I found myself envying friends, who would talk of leaving their jobs and returning "home," wherever that was, maybe Wyoming, or Arizona, or some other place far removed from the pressure cooker of Washington, DC, or my job in Paris. During my college years, I had often dreamed of living for a year in the Rocky Mountains, of finding a cabin in the woods and spending my time working on the land and breathing in the fresh alpine air.

The opportunity to do just that came in 1999, when I traded chauffeured cars and dinners with ambassadors for cowboy boots and life on a 240-acre farm in the Rocky Mountain Northwest region of Montana—not far from my brother-in-law's farm and within reach of the University of Montana in Missoula. My husband and I reasoned that we could farm and teach part time; and I could pursue my lifelong passion for horses—which I did in competitive show jumping. And although I also thought about writing at long last a book about my great-grandfather's life and work in Japan—something I'd vowed inwardly to do during my first trip to Japan in 1980—some years would pass before I turned to that endeavor.

Just before my first official trip to Japan in 1980 as the US Treasury's new Japan economist, I read my great-grandfather's journal for the first time. I was overjoyed at the prospect of journeying to the land where he had spent so many years as a missionary. Flying from Washington by way of New York, the plane's descent paralleled Japan's west coast as we approached Narita Airport north of Tokyo. My eyes scanned fields and forests, straining to see farm houses, field workers, and small villages tucked in along hillsides or nestled along streams flowing from hills beyond. Tears welled in my eyes as I thought about my great-grandparents' anguish upon losing their firstborn daughter Ella at age fourteen. I also thought of my great-grandmother's grief on losing her beloved daughter Emma just fifteen months after her husband's death. And I thought about the fact that both girls, buried in Japan, would forever be a part of Japan's soil, forming an unbreakable link between my family and the land of my great-grandfather's labors.

My official schedule during that trip included meetings with government finance officials, bankers, economists, and the Treasury's two attachés at the US Embassy. The highlight was a private meeting with Finance Minister Watanabe, who gave me an autographed copy of a picture taken with me during his first meeting with Treasury Secretary Donald Regan a few months before. Tours of Japan's old imperial capital of Kyoto and nearby Nara, sites visited by my great-grandfather's family in the nineteenth century, introduced me to the beauty and splendor of Japan's culture and history.

Author with Finance Minister Watanabe Michio in his Tokyo office, 1980

Author with Mary Alexander's former student, Kitamura Ko, in Tokyo

On a weekend free of official meetings, I ventured alone on Tokyo's subway to visit one of my Great-Aunt Mary's first students at Tokyo Women's Christian University—Kitamura Ko—who, as a teacher at TWCU, had greeted Mary so cheerfully upon Mary's return to Japan after World

War II. A petite and gracious woman of nearly seventy, Kitamura-san took me to Aoyama Cemetery in Tokyo to visit young Emma's gravesite and to Meiji Gakuin, where she helped me retrieve documents about my great-grandfather from university archives. During this and subsequent visits to her home on later trips, she filled in details about my Great Aunt Mary, my Great-grandmother Emma, and their lives in Japan. She also gave me family photographs to take home. Inspired by these new connections with my great-grandfather's life and legacy, I vowed to myself during that first trip to Japan that I would write his story one day. Half a dozen years after moving to Montana, I finally embarked on the long-delayed project.

My path began to change in remarkable ways when I opened my email in January 2006. The message had been sent nearly four weeks earlier from Tokyo, tracing the path of my career from Washington, DC, to Paris, and finally to my new home in Montana. "I have been able to ascertain, with a high degree of certainty, that Joanna Shelton is the great-granddaughter of Reverend Alexander," it read. The writer had asked recipients to forward it to me. Fortunately, no one along the way had broken the link. I was amazed by the coincidence. An American Presbyterian missionary in Tokyo, the Reverend Thomas John Hastings, had sent it at about the same time I had started rereading my great-grandfather's diary and begun to write the story of his life in Japan, a country I knew well from my long involvement in US-Japan relations and many official trips there.

I was thrilled to read on. One of my great-grandfather's churches in Osaka—the Osaka Suita South Church—was planning its 120th anniversary celebration in February, and I was invited to join the festivities. The church's minister, the Reverend Akiyama Hideaki, had found my great-grandfather's name on the Internet, and my name had appeared along with a speech I had given in Tokyo in 1999. The fact that I had traveled to Tokyo that year was itself a bit of a coincidence.

A few weeks after my move from Paris in September 1999, I had been surrounded by moving boxes and struggling to bring order out of chaos when the phone rang. On the other end was the director of the Maureen and Mike Mansfield Foundation in Washington, DC, a foundation established in honor of Montana's long-serving senator and America's highly respected ambassador to Japan. "Our scheduled speaker for the annual Mansfield American-Pacific Lecture in Tokyo has just told us he can't make it, and we're wondering if you'd be available to give the US lecture this year?" The director explained that each year, the Mansfield Foundation asked one distinguished Japanese to speak in Washington, DC, and one American to speak in Tokyo, both on the same subject. The topic for 1999 was "National Identity and International Pressures: Are They Compatible?" Honored to be asked, and already scheduled to chair an international conference in Korea, I agreed to travel to Tokyo in December after my trip to Seoul.

I had given hundreds of speeches during my career and never mentioned my great-grandfather. But I did just that in Tokyo in December 1999 while talking about the challenge of maintaining our cultural identity in the face of a rapidly shrinking world, a topic my great-grandfather and the people of late nineteenth-century Japan surely would have understood. The Mansfield Foundation put my speech on the Internet, forever linking my name with my great-grandfather's in cyberspace. That one speech would change my life.

Many people believe there is no such thing as coincidence; that there was a reason I mentioned my great-grandfather in that speech. I had never been among those people. Like many other people in our modern secular society, I considered myself spiritual but shunned many of the practices and beliefs that go along with everything from organized religion to so-called New Age teachings. But when I read that email from Japan in 2006, I felt that something was pulling me toward Japan and the story of my great-grandfather's struggles and triumphs there. After more trips to Japan tracing his footsteps and opening myself to a new way of thinking and believing, I finally joined him on my own journey of faith.

It would take another book to describe how five trips to Japan in six years—visiting many of my great-grandfather's churches; getting to know their ministers and congregations; and exploring places where he lived or traveled—not only revealed a great deal about my great-grandfather's life and legacy, but also began to reshape my own spiritual beliefs. Instead, I offer snippets of my experiences that I hope will convey some sense of the deep emotions and surprise discoveries I encountered while on these trips.

After flying from Montana to Osaka, I took part in Sunday worship and an afternoon anniversary celebration at the Osaka Suita South Church in February 2006, meeting the Reverend Akiyama and elders and members of the church, as well as the Reverend Tom Hastings, the Presbyterian missionary who had sent the surprise email several months before.

Hastings explained that the service the Reverend Akiyama led that day was just as it was in my great-grandfather's day; Japanese Protestants have changed very few of the rituals and practices missionaries taught in the nineteenth century. As I listened to Akiyama's preaching, with Tom whispering a translation in my ear, my gaze fell on the organist. She focused intently on her music as the organ's pedals creaked and squeaked in time with the hymn being sung. I thought about my great-grandfather's struggles to control his emotions during Sunday services following young Ella's death, when the empty organist's chair and silent organ sat as mute reminders of his loss.

The day before the church's anniversary celebration, I'd had the opportunity to visit young Ella's grave in Kobe's foreign cemetery, guided by the Reverend Akiyama, a church elder, and the elder's husband: Ito Fumiko and Takabumi. I hadn't known whether the grave had survived the many earthquakes and floods that had hit the area or repeated raids by American bombers during World War II. It had. Kobe City authorities had moved the foreign cemetery in 1952 from the seashore to a lushly wooded mountaintop overlooking Kobe harbor. Mrs. Ito and her husband, a retired newspaperman, had located the grave after I'd told them about my desire to visit. As the four of us drove to Kobe with Akiyama-*sensei* at the wheel, my new friends told me about their first visit to young Ella's gravesite a month earlier.

They said as they had driven up the steep, winding road to the cemetery one blustery January day, snow had pounded their car, making driving very difficult. They thought about turning back, but pushed on, finally finding young Ella's grave among those of nearly eight hundred other foreigners. Standing before her tomb, they had offered a simple prayer. Suddenly, the sun had broken through the dark winter storm clouds, spreading light and warmth on the small party of mourners. Ella had been found again. From that moment on, she would be cared for by members of the Osaka Suita South Church, where she had played organ one last time before her final walk home.

We retraced the path they had taken, driving by hundreds of well-tended graves from the eighteenth, nineteenth, and early twentieth centuries. France, Spain, Russia, England, America, and other countries were represented, poignant evidence of the many sojourners who had died so far from home. Then on foot, as we approached the area where Ella lay, I somberly reflected on my great-grandparents' grief as they had borne their fourteen-year-old daughter to her final resting place.

Our route ended at a promontory overlooking countless graves, all of them bordered by neatly trimmed azalea hedges. Barren trees, interspersed with dark green pines, blended in with the natural surroundings of the cemetery. We picked our way carefully down narrow stone steps to a terrace below and followed a walkway to Ella's grave, located at the base of a high granite wall that towered above like a turret protecting its wards. I laid a bouquet at the foot of her headstone. Pale pink and white lilies folded into flame-like spires recalled Ella's middle name, Lillian. Bright pink tissue paper enveloping the flowers and a pale pink bow tied around their stems complemented the soft red granite of Ella's headstone, whose gracefully arched top stood as high as my shoulders. I read the inscription.

ELLA LILLIAN

ELDEST DAUGHTER
OF
Rev. T. T. & Mrs. E. E. Alexander

Born, October 18th, 1878
Died, May 23rd, 1892

The epitaph my great-grandparents had chosen for her headstone, from "The Reaper and the Flowers" by Henry Wadsworth Longfellow, conveyed the depth of their sorrow.

And the mother gave, in tears and pain,
The flowers she most did love;
She knew she should find them all again
In the fields of light above.

The heart-rending words my great-grandfather had written in his journal after Ella's death played in my mind: "In the Foreign Cemetery at Kobe, near the seashore where the restless sea surges back and forth we laid her to rest. There her fair young form will molder back to dust again while numerous pines keep solemn vigil over her grave." I listened while Akiyama-*sensei* offered a prayer in Japanese, his deep, resonant voice reflecting the solemnity of the occasion. We recited the Lord's Prayer and sang "Amazing Grace" as a final tribute. After our impromptu service, we washed the headstone in Japanese tradition, carefully scrubbing moss and dirt from the crevices of Ella's name and epitaph. I fought to hold back tears.

Author at Ella Alexander's gravesite, Kobe Foreign Cemetery, 2006

More visits to Japan followed, bringing more discoveries and new friends into my life. In May 2007, I spoke at the 122nd anniversary celebration of my great-grandfather's Osaka North Church at the invitation of the Reverend Morita Yukio. I had met Morita-*sensei* the previous year, along with another Presbyterian minister, the Reverend Mochida Katsumi, who had acted as our constant companion and interpreter. The three of us had toured Osaka, visiting sites of importance to my great-grandfather and his family—Osaka castle, the hospital nearby where the family had fled a devastating flood, and the low-lying area that once had served as the city's foreign settlement. This second trip gave me a welcome opportunity to strengthen bonds of friend-ship with members of Osaka North Church and Osaka Suita South Church. During my visit, the Reverends Morita and Mochida took me to visit Kyoto's Muromachi Church, to which my great-grandfather had donated most of his life's savings on the eve of his departure from Japan, helping the city's Christians build one of the country's most beautiful sanctuaries.

Author with L–R: Rev. Akiyama Hideaki; Rev. Mochida Katsumi; Rev. Morita Yukio, saying goodbye at Osaka train station, 2009

From Osaka, I journeyed north to Tokyo, where I delved deeper into my great-grandfather's world there. The morning after I arrived, I took a taxi to Meiji Gakuin University, where he had chaired Systemic and Biblical Studies and taught countless theological students. The cab dropped me at the entrance where the oldest buildings still stood, including ones central to my great-grandfather's life at Meiji Gakuin: Memorial Hall, which formerly housed the theology department and now is home to the university's museum and archives; and a two-story beige clapboard house built by William Imbrie, my great-grandfather's fellow missionary and close friend. When I had visited the campus many years before with my Great Aunt Mary's friend, Kitamura-san, we had not made it to this old part of campus, making my find all the more exciting to me.

I entered the Imbrie house and explored inside, admiring the highly polished, dark wooden staircase and curved banister, with matching wainscoting on the walls. When I explained the reason for my visit, a young university employee passing through the entry hall kindly gave me a tour of the house and then guided me next door to Memorial Hall, with its museum and archives. She had called ahead to alert the staff to my arrival. Soon the chief archivist arrived and began searching for documents and photos from my great-grandfather's time at the university. Many of the items he found were so old and fragile that I was surprised, but pleased, he would photocopy them. I lingered for about an hour and a half, surveying the museum's contents as the archivist and his colleague scoured their files. Pictures of the school's founders and its original buildings, an early handwritten version of the first Japanese-English dictionary by J. C. Hepburn, and other mementos traced the history of Meiji Gakuin through the years.

One picture, taken in 1895, captured my attention: an outdoor photo of thirty-five male theological school graduates, clad in kimonos, and standing on several rows of risers. Palm trees fanned out behind them, framing the picture. My great-grandfather sat in the front row, flanked by fellow faculty members and Meiji Gakuin President Ibuka Kajinosuke. Unlike other posed photos I had seen of my great-grandfather, this one seemed to reveal more of his personality. Arms folded across his chest, loosely creased fedora balanced on his knee, and eyes focused slightly to the right of the camera, his face wore a look of steely determination. The photo helped me picture the inner strength that had sustained him through the many challenges he had faced during his quarter century in Japan.

Tom with Meiji Gakuin seminarians and faculty. Front row L–R: Rev. Uemura Masahisa; Rev. Henry Landis; Rev. Tom Alexander; President Rev. Ibuka Kajinosuke; Martin Wyckoff; Rev. Guido Verbeck; Rev. Ishihara Yasutaro; unknown student

The melodious, high-pitched sound of a hand bell echoed up the staircase, interrupting my reverie. A church service was about to begin in the small chapel below, which had housed my great-grandfather's office years before. Venturing downstairs, I entered the chapel, sitting in a dark wooden pew toward the back. As the only Westerner in the room, I attracted subtle, but noticeable attention from the Japanese minister and assembled students. I did not understand the words but did capture the meaning of this twenty-first-century service, with students of Meiji Gakuin University being guided in their prayers and Gospel readings much as their nineteenth-century predecessors had been led in their devotionals by my great-grandfather.

I finally departed Memorial Hall, armed with many useful documents and pictures. A light rain fell, but I found a bench sheltered by an aging ginkgo tree near the Imbrie house and sat down. I wanted to absorb the atmosphere and try to visualize my great-grandfather walking these same grounds and being received into the warm embrace of his good friend as he strode up the walkway to his front porch.

Eventually, I decided I should make my way back to my temporary home in Tokyo. First, though, I needed to refresh myself and went back inside Memorial Hall. I stepped outside again and remembered I had wanted to take a picture of the main chapel across from the hall. I spent a few minutes moving from one spot to another, snapping photographs. Then I realized I needed to refill my water bottle, my constant companion on longer outings. So I entered Memorial Hall a third time. A young man striding ahead held the door open for me. He bounded upstairs to the archives, as I walked to the back of the building. I emerged from the back and was just about to exit, when the archivist rushed downstairs in a frenzy, pointing urgently to his watch and asking, "You have time? You have time?"

I was starving by then. I hadn't eaten lunch, even though the hour was approaching four o'clock; but, of course, I said I had time. It turns out the young man who had headed upstairs had come to fetch me to a meeting with the college president, who by then had heard I was on campus. I had a delightful meeting with Chancellor Kuze Satoru; and his being a fellow economist gave us even more to talk about. As I told him about my work on my great-grandfather's life story, he gave me many insights into the world in which he had lived and worked. He described Itagaki Taisuke's fight against the increasingly dictatorial powers of the Meiji government and his belief in the link between Christian values and Western democracy. Kuze also told me about the formation of Meiji Gakuin University from several early missionary schools founded by my great-grandfather's colleagues. Later, I recounted this surprising sequence of events to the Reverend Tom Hastings, the Presbyterian missionary who had sent me the unexpected email the previous year, saying, "The meeting was wonderful, and it was completely unplanned."

"By you," he replied.

Rev. Dr. Thomas John Hastings in his Tokyo Union Theological Seminary office, 2007

Rounding out my visit in 2007, I spoke to students at Joshi Gakuin Junior and High School Girls' School about my Great Aunt Emma, who had taught there until her death at age twenty-four. Standing in an auditorium packed with eight hundred fifty high school girls, I felt as Emma must have when she had taught an earlier generation. The girls' high-pitched voices repeated after me in sing-song fashion the English words to a hymn we were about to sing. I smiled inwardly and reveled in the moment. Later that morning, as I toured the grounds with the school principal, Dr. Tanaka Hiroshi, some of the girls saw me from their homeroom balcony. They waved and screamed at me, as if I were a rock star. That definitely was not the sort of greeting American high school students would give the descendant of one of the school's early teachers. It confirmed for me the important place held by ancestors in the lives of the Japanese. Dr. Tanaka also took me to visit Emma's gravesite in Aoyama Cemetery, accompanied by my long-time friend and Tokyo host, Robert Feldman.

The next day, I traveled to Tokyo Women's Christian University, where my Great Aunt Mary had taught on two separate occasions: in 1918–19 and after World War II. As soon as I arrived on campus, my guide ushered me to the president's office for an unexpected meeting. Despite her heavy schedule, President Minato Akiko had summoned me after learning about my visit from Dr. Tanaka at Joshi Gakuin, a sister school of TWCU. When I entered her spacious, light-filled office with expansive views of campus, Dr. Minato greeted me warmly and told me how much I reminded her of Mary. (I do resemble Mary in height and build.) During our meeting, Minato-*sensei* recalled how Mary had spent many hours showing her how to form English words by looking in a mirror. Her perfect English was living proof of the helping hand she had received from her dedicated teacher.

Author at Emma Alexander gravesite in Aoyama Cemetery with Joshi Gakuin Chancellor Tanaka Hiroshi and friend Robert Feldman, another East Tennessean who made a life in Japan, 2007

Author with TWCU President Dr. Minato Akiko, 2007

A final surprise in my journeys came as I was thinking ahead to the day when I would have a book about my great-grandfather ready for publication. I had made it a point to ask knowledgeable people about publishing options. A great-granddaughter of the Reverend Uemura Masahisa—Dr. Nakai Ayako, professor of literature at Aoyama Gakuin Women's Junior College—offered to put me in touch with the president of one of Japan's Christian publishing houses. She and I arranged to meet at her college; from there, we would travel to the publisher's office. When I met her, she looked at me with wide eyes and a broad smile, unable to conceal her excitement: "You'll never believe it. When I called the president this morning to ask for an appointment, he was reading an article by your great-grandfather on the history of Christian literature in Japan. Isn't that amazing? And he's only available for the next hour, so let's hurry."

We hopped on the subway and made it to the president's office in time to meet him. He said my great-grandfather's article, written in 1900 for the Conference of Protestant Missionaries' meeting in Tokyo, was the best he had read on the subject, because it covered several centuries of Christian literature in Japan. He was using it to prepare for a speech he had been asked to give. We all marveled at this unexpected fluke.

I have had a successful career, working to forge closer ties and bridge differences between countries through negotiation and compromise. I speak a number of languages fluently; have lived in Europe six years; and have traveled to thirty countries around the world on countless trade and economic missions from my bases in Washington, DC, and Paris. I never would have expected religion to appeal to me after a lifetime of skepticism. But following the path my great-grandfather carved so many years ago and researching his life's story set my own life on a new path.

As I studied books about Christianity and Buddhism, began reading the Bible for the first time under the guidance of my devout brother- and sister-in-law, deepened my relationships with ministers and congregations of my great-grandfather's churches, and witnessed the continuing impact my great-grandfather and his daughters have had on lives in Japan, my attitude began to change. And as I reflected on the many "coincidences" that had accompanied my journey, I opened myself to a new way of thinking and believing. The spiritual yearning I had felt much of my life gained a new focus. My great-grandfather's hand, still for over one hundred years, seemed to have beckoned, and I followed. Some people might say I'm my great-grandfather's latest convert.

In 2007, my husband and I attended Easter services at a Presbyterian church in a little town nearly an hour's drive from our home. The church, built in 1917, resembles a vision from a Norman Rockwell painting. Covered in white clapboard siding and shaded by mature maples and oaks, the chapel is topped by a steep, cedar shake roof and a small bell tower, whose deep, resonant tones announce the start of services each week. Unsurprisingly, the pews were full on Easter Sunday. Pastor Dave Anson's extemporaneous preaching style and the warm welcome from parishioners during fellowship hour after the service appealed to both of us. We returned week after week.

My husband and I joined the church in August 2007, a true milestone for me after holding religion at arm's length all my life. In 2011, I was ordained as a ruling elder in the Presbyterian Church (USA), taking largely the same vows my great-grandfather took in 1877 when he was ordained as a minister. Our small congregation contributes funds to support the homeless mission work of the Osaka North Church, deepening the ties that extend across time and continents. As a delightful surprise, the Reverend Morita Yukio of the Osaka North Church visited our church in June 2008, along with the Reverend Mochida Katsumi, then of the Osaka West Church. They came to thank our congregation for its generosity in helping people in need halfway around the world.

In 2009, I returned to Japan to address hundreds of leaders in the Church of Christ in Japan, who were celebrating the 150th anniversary of the first Presbyterian missionary's arrival in Yokohama. I also visited nineteenth-century democracy activist Itagaki Taisuke's home town of Kochi and the church near which newly baptized ex-samurai warriors once demonstrated their swordsmanship skills to my great-grandfather and his fellow missionaries. In 2011, I spoke at one of my great-grandfather's churches in Tokyo, Omori Church, and rekindled ties with the Reverend Uemura Masahisa's descendants, whom I had met on a previous visit. In 2012, I journeyed to southern Kyushu Island, visiting churches in Fukuoka and Yanagawa and walking the battlefields where "the last samurai," Saigo Takamori, had fought and died in Japan's 1877 civil war that ended just before my great-grandfather's arrival.

These back-and-forth visits remind me of an old gospel song, which begins, "Will the circle be unbroken, by and by, Lord, by and by?" Numerous circles, carved between Japan and America, and between the nineteenth and twenty-first centuries, are in play. As one has closed, another has opened, bringing with it endless possibilities for binding people and continents closer together.

The Reverend Sawa Masayuki of Fukuoka Johnan Church wrote to me just after Easter 2013, saying: "Whenever we read the passage from John 12:24, we think of the work and life of the missionaries like Dr. Alexander. We believe we Christians in Japan are the grains which are brought forth through the one grain which fell into the earth." That passage of John's Gospel contains the words Jesus spoke when explaining to his disciples why he had to die:

> Very truly, I tell you, unless a grain of wheat
> falls into the earth and dies,
> it remains just a single grain;
> but if it dies, it bears much fruit.

Whatever Happened To . . . ?

Emma Edwina Brown Alexander (1855–1937)

Very few of Emma's writings remain, but those documents that do exist give some insight into her life and personality, as does information shared by one of her granddaughters—my aunt, Emma Shelton—who knew her.

Emma Brown Alexander was born June 10, 1855, in Spring Place, Murray County, Georgia, to the Reverend William Beard Brown (known as "Parson Brown") and Mary Elizabeth Bicknell Brown. During the Civil War, her family fled north to Cleveland, East Tennessee to escape a climate that had become increasingly dangerous for pro-Union sympathizers. When her father learned of efforts to revive his alma mater, Maryville College, which had closed during the Civil War, he moved his family to Maryville in January 1867. Emma first attended a school held in Maryville's old Methodist church and then a small girls' school run by the widow of Civil War General William H. L. Wallace, who had died in 1862 after being wounded at the Battle of Shiloh.

Emma graduated from Maryville College in 1875 as part of the first graduating class for women (five in all, along with four young men). Nearly twenty years later, Emma was asked by a Professor Wilson to share her recollections for the college's 75th anniversary celebration. Writing from Tokyo on May 3, 1894, Emma begged off writing a long treatise, noting: "I am just now engaged in preparing a boy and five girls to become graduates of Maryville College, and this being a very busy time, I don't feel I have time to write an essay worthy of the occasion nor of a graduate of Maryville College." But Emma did offer a short and poignant memory of her graduation.

The "First Girl Graduates" brings to my mind the picture of a row of girls dressed in white Swiss muslin, all puffs, ruffles and lace with overskirts—short and round in front and long and round at the back. (How funny that would look now, although they have frizzled bangs.) But they were as pretty on the whole as "sweet-girl graduates" usually are, because they were young, full of hope and flushed with pride and bright anticipations for the future, and joy at having finished school—not realizing that they had finished perhaps the brightest days of life.

The people of Maryville greatly admired Emma for journeying to Japan in 1877 with her new husband, the Reverend Thomas Theron Alexander. They were the first missionaries from New Providence Presbyterian Church and Maryville College to serve abroad. Their daughter Mary later recounted what her mother had told her about those times.

Those [first] years in Tokyo were, I think, very happy ones, perhaps the happiest of all. The family lived in Tsukiji, the section of the city allotted to foreigners by the Japanese Government, where American, British, and other nationalities lived in pretty close association, and Mother and Father made lifelong friends.

Two baby girls were born, Ella (October 18, 1878) and Emma (January 18, 1880) and Mother, many years later—in the last year of her life—said sadly one day, "It is hard for me to realize that I am the only one left of that little family"—as if the remaining family were not quite so precious.

Father and Mother were young, full of ideals and enthusiasm, devoted to the little girls and to each other. Father, however, kept his eye on the goal of doing evangelistic work out in the provinces, away from the city.

Emma had hoped that Lois—her fourth child—would be the last baby. She already had her hands full with her children, her duties as a missionary's wife, and Tom's frequent absences and failing health. But she loved each of the three new babies that came.

In 1897, twenty years after journeying to Japan with her husband, Emma returned to Maryville with their six surviving children. Not only had her doctor advised her to leave Tokyo for her health, but the oldest children were close to college age. Daughter Mary wrote about the years leading up to her family's return from Tokyo, beginning in 1893:

Christine was born on November 10 of that year. One of the servants, knowing of Mother's grief over Ella's death, said to Mother that it might be that Ella was reincarnated in Christine.

In contrast to their first years in Tokyo, these years were very difficult ones for both Father and Mother. Father's health was failing. Mother was in a very nervous condition; and coping with six children and an ailing husband put her in such a state that the doctor ordered her to go home. Accordingly, we landed in San Francisco in time for Eve to celebrate her eighth birthday (1897) in the hotel. But Father remained in Japan for one more year to finish out his second ten years of service. . . .

Father came home on furlough, thin almost to emaciation and very pale. In spite of Mother's efforts to get him to rest, he was very restless and uneasy. He bought a house next door to Mother's brother, established his family in it, and went back to Japan as soon as his year was up. Mother wanted to go back with him but Lois was not yet ready to enter college, and it was agreed to be best that Mother should stay until Lois was old enough to be left. Then she would take "the three little girls" [Mary, Eva, and Christine] and join father.

The house where Emma and the children lived was on High Street, next to her Brother Tom's home. Mary later reflected on how difficult the transition to single motherhood had been for her mother.

Father himself was a man of very strong affections and so—starved for affection in his own boyhood—he poured out his love on his wife and children. Mother was first in his heart, however, and all of us children were taught to consider her. His eyes could look as sharp as gimlets, and when he spoke, we hopped to obey. He was sometimes irritable, and his quick temper (gone almost as soon as it came) made him sometimes say sharp words which, Mother said, he regretted bitterly afterwards. He often delighted us with his sense of humor, which was very strong; and we loved to see him laugh. He read to us, walked with us, humored us in some ways, and gave us many, many good times. We trusted him and loved him.

Mother, for the first forty years of her life, was accustomed to being appreciated and considered. But from the time that she came back to America at the age of forty-one with six very individualistic children on her hands, she had to face a difficult situation. Left a widow at forty-seven with only a tiny pension from the Board of Ministerial Relief and a small allowance for each child until it was eighteen, when the pension ceased, she faced poverty, loneliness and unaccustomed responsibility.

[Young] Emma was her stand-by as long as she was at home. But Emma soon left to go to be with Father—and died about a year after Father did. Mother rallied bravely from each blow and for years worked almost slavishly, sewing, cooking and cleaning, though we tried to help her as much as we could.

We loved her and considered her, but we missed Father's stabilizing influence. She bore a great deal from us headstrong and individualistic children, but she tried her best to understand us and loved every one of us to the end.

In 1919, nearly penniless and unable to afford the large home in Maryville, Emma returned to Japan with her unmarried daughter, Mary, who had been assigned by the Presbyterian Church's Board of Foreign Missions to teach at Tokyo Women's Christian College (later University). Emma, who was sixty-four, occasionally helped teachers at Joshi Gakuin girls' school, where young Emma had taught and died. After two years, though, Mary took her unhappy and ailing mother back to the United States—via Canada—regretfully breaking her contract with TWCC. While Mary traveled to New York City to find a job as a high school English teacher, Emma stayed several months with Daughter Eva Shelton's family—including my Father John and Aunt Emma—in Saskatoon, Saskatchewan, where my grandfather taught ceramic chemistry at the university.

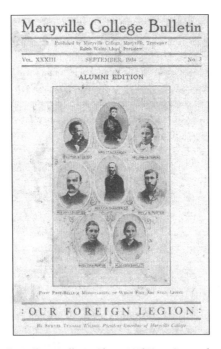

Maryville College Bulletin Alumni Edition, September 1934.
Emma: top center; Tom: center

Emma moved to New York City in 1921 and lived with Mary. For some years, she was the oldest surviving graduate of Maryville College, which honored her service and that of Tom and other post-Civil War foreign missionaries in its 1934 college bulletin. She died at age eighty-one and was buried next to Tom in Maryville's Magnolia Cemetery. Her simple epitaph— Emma Edwina Brown; Wife of Thomas Theron Alexander; Born June 10, 1855; Died March 20, 1937—is engraved on the back of Tom's headstone. On the side of the grave marker is a simple memorial to a young girl whose death at age fourteen had broken both their hearts:

Ella Lillian

Born
Oct. 18, 1878
Tokyo, Japan

Died
May 23, 1893
Osaka, Japan

Buried in Kobe

Our eldest born

After Emma's death on March 20, 1937, Maryville College held a memorial service for her. Although Emma had not lived in Maryville for nearly twenty years, the April 15, 1937 edition of the local newspaper, *The Maryville Enterprise*, reprinted in its entirety the eulogy given by college president Dr. Ralph Waldo Lloyd.

Although the townspeople of Maryville never forgot her, Emma died a rather tragic figure. None of her many grandchildren liked her. They found her cold, harsh, and bitter, with rarely a kind word to say or a smile to brighten her face. Encouraged by her daughter, Mary, to record memories of her life, Emma wrote a rather rambling ten-page account a few years before she died. It describes the earliest years of her life, first in Civil War Georgia and then in Maryville, Tennessee, and closes with these lines about her years at Maryville College.

> I had numerous "affairs" with boys till in my Senior year when I became engaged to Tom Alexander. He tutored one year in the college before going to Union Seminary in New York. I graduated in 1875 at the age of twenty. The next year the . . . .

Her account ends there. Emma says nothing about the twenty years she spent in Japan with Tom, the deaths of her two firstborn daughters, nor other memories that must have been too painful to recall. Emma evidently never lost her feelings of guilt over leaving her husband alone in Japan for the last five years of his life, nor over the fact that she had not been able to be by his side in Hawaii in the months and weeks before his death.

Heartache, loss, poverty, and separation from loved ones had transformed a young woman—whose "girlish face, form and manner . . . round cheeks, short hair and keen black eyes" had captured the heart of Tom Alexander—into a lonely, unhappy, embittered woman. What a sad ending to a rich life. But she and Tom left a strong legacy, not only through their own work but also through the accomplishments of their children, five of whom survived and lived long, productive lives. As Maryville College President Lloyd said in the closing words of his eulogy when speaking about Emma's life:

> It is the story of a Christian's life which we tell. It is a Christian burial for which we have come today. It is a Christian's influence which we celebrate, an influence which helped to inspire four daughters to take part in the foreign missions enterprise and a son to become a Christian minister. To live usefully to be more than four score, to keep faith in life, in mankind, in God, in the Good News of Christ—this is to live triumphantly.

Quoting from Paul's second letter to Timothy (4:7–8), in which the apostle speaks about himself when drawing near to the end of his life, Lloyd concluded Emma's eulogy with these words:

> I have fought the good fight,
> I have finished the course,
> I have kept the faith;
> henceforth there is laid up for
> me the crown of righteousness,
> which the Lord, the righteous judge,
> shall give to me at that day;
> and not to me only, but also to all
> them that have loved his appearing.

Sources: Letter of Emma Alexander to Professor Wilson, May 3, 1894; MC archives. Alexander, "Japan Notes." Oral account by Emma Shelton. McTeer, *History*.

Alexander Children

Despite the sad circumstances surrounding their deaths, Tom and Emma Alexander left a strong legacy of education and service. All five surviving Alexander children graduated from Maryville College and some continued with graduate studies. Clearly inspired and guided by their parents, three daughters served in foreign mission fields; one daughter performed mission and education work in Tennessee; and son Theron became a Presbyterian minister.

> General sources for Alexander children: Shelton, "Descendants." McTeer, *History*. Other sources noted where appropriate.

Ella Lillian Alexander (1878–92)

Ella was born in Tokyo, the first of seven children. She died in Osaka of a burst appendix at age fourteen. She was buried in the Ono Foreign Cemetery of Kobe near the foreign settlement of Kobe. All graves were relocated in 1952 to the mountains behind Futatabi, known as Shuhogahara.

> Harold S. Williams, *The Foreign Cemeteries of Kobe and Osaka*. Kobe: The International Committee of Kansai, 1978, 18.

Emma Thomasina Alexander (1880–1904)

Emma was born in Tokyo, the second of seven children. She returned with her family to America in 1897 and graduated from Maryville College in 1901. She prepared for missionary service in Japan with a year of study at the Training School for Christian Workers at 128 East 10th Street, New York City. The Presbyterian Church's Board of Foreign Missions assigned Emma to work in the East Japan Mission, where she expected to join her father in Kobe. With his sudden departure from Japan to Hawaii due to failing health, Emma received Board permission to travel to Japan by way of Hawaii. Emma was with her father when he died. After his death, she traveled to Tokyo, where she was a teacher at Joshi Gakuin girls' school. She taught there from January 1903 until her death from typhoid-related meningitis, just fifteen months after her father's death. Emma was engaged to Reading Karns Beatty of Pennsylvania when she died.

Theron Ralph Alexander (1882–1968)

Theron was born in Osaka, the third of seven children. He returned with his family to America in 1897 and graduated from Maryville College with a BA in 1903 and then an MA. He graduated from McCormick Theological Seminary in Chicago in 1908 and was ordained as a Presbyterian minister, serving in Tennessee, Florida, and other states. Theron married Mary Helen Jones. He was survived by two sons. Maryville College awarded Theron an honorary Doctor of Divinity degree—as it had his father years before—in 1935. The samurai sword given to Tom Alexander passed down to Theron.

Lois Alexander (1884–1958)

Lois was born in Osaka, the fourth of seven children. She returned with her family to America in 1897 and graduated from Maryville College in 1905. From 1906 until 1909, Lois served as a teacher in Puerto Rico. She married Ernest George Ritzman in Maryville, Tennessee, in about 1912. Lois died in Concord, New Hampshire at age seventy-four and was buried in Durham Cemetery, Durham, NH. She was survived by a son and a daughter.

Mary Victoria Alexander (1887–1973)

Mary was born in Osaka, the fifth of seven children. She returned with her family to America in 1897 and graduated from Maryville College in 1908. The Presbyterian Board of Foreign Missions assigned Mary to teach in Japan at the new Tokyo Women's Christian College (later University). Taking her mother with her to Japan in 1919, Mary was forced by her mother's health problems to break her contract and return to America after just two years at the school. Her mother, Emma, lived with her on 122nd Street near Columbia University until her death in 1937. After a career teaching English in New York City public high schools, Mary returned to Japan just after retirement, teaching once again at TWCU from 1949 until 1953. Prior to her departure, TWCU President Saito Takeshi presented her with a bound copy of the Proceedings of the Conference of Protestant Missionaries in Japan in 1900, in which an article by her father on the history of Christian literature in Japan appeared.

After leaving Japan, Mary lived in a Presbyterian retirement village in Claremont, California, joining the children of other missionaries to Japan. One of her closest friends there was Annie Hail (Hoekje), daughter of A. D. Hail, a missionary from the Cumberland Presbyterian Church, who, with his brother J. P. Hail, opened the church's mission station in Osaka while the Alexander family lived there. Mary welcomed periodic visits from old Japanese friends and colleagues at her home in Claremont. Mary became a Quaker and is buried in an unmarked grave in a Quaker cemetery in Claremont.

Eva Alexander (1889–1980)

My grandmother, Eva ("Evie"), was born in Oakland, California, during her father's first sabbatical from mission service in Japan. The sixth of seven children, she was three months old when she traveled by steamer to Japan. She lived in Osaka and Tokyo, returning to America with her family in 1897 when she was eight years old. Evie graduated from Maryville College in 1910 and taught English at Maryville Preparatory School. She served as Maryville High School's first principal beginning in 1918. Evie married George Reed Shelton in Maryville, Tennessee, July 14, 1915; both had been officers of the class of 1910. The couple taught "Big" Will Walker's children in the Great Smoky Mountains of East Tennessee for one or two summers. Walker was a legend in the area. With one legal wife and several common-law wives, he fathered as many as twenty-seven offspring. He valued education, though, and welcomed Evie and Reed as some of the teachers who came over the years to the valley bearing his name.

Evie and Reed ("Pappy" to his children and grandchildren) moved frequently, following Reed's doctoral studies and subsequent career as a ceramic chemist. Their final move was to Chevy Chase, Maryland, a suburb of Washington, DC, where Reed worked at the National Bureau of Standards. They were members of Chevy Chase Presbyterian Church, where Reed served as an elder. Evie eventually withdrew from church membership in the face of what she considered hypocritical attitudes on the part of some members toward people of other races. Evie died in Chevy Chase and is buried next to Reed in Congressional Cemetery, Washington, DC. They had two children: my father, John Alexander Shelton (1917–72) and Emma Shelton (1920–).

Lula Christine Alexander (1893–1975)

Christine was born in Tokyo, the last of seven children. She returned with her family to America in 1897 and graduated from Maryville College in 1914. From 1916 until at least 1921, Christine taught in a mission school in Egypt. From there, she relocated to New York City, where her mother and sister Mary lived. She became Curator for Classical Art (particularly Greek and Roman) at the Metropolitan Museum of Art in New York City. Christine never married.

Reading Karns Beatty (1877–1914)

According to Princeton Theological Seminary alumni records on young Emma's fiancé:

> Reading Karns Beatty was born in Doylestown, Pennsylvania, the son of Joseph Henry and Olive McConly (Karns) Beatty. His preparatory studies were done at Doylestown High School, followed by studies at Maryville College in Tennessee. He took his first two years of theological studies at Western (now Pittsburgh) Theological Seminary from 1905 to 1907. His final year was at Princeton Theological Seminary, from which he graduated in 1908. He was licensed on April 14, 1909, by the Presbytery of Aberdeen in South Dakota and ordained on June 15, 1909, by the same presbytery. [He was at one time moderator of the Presbytery of Aberdeen.]
>
> He served congregations at Mellette and Mansfield, South Dakota, until October 10, 1910. Following his time in South Dakota, he accepted a call to Kansas, where he served as stated supply to the Harmony and Linwood churches from 1910 until 1912. He then became the pastor of the Nickleville, Richland and Rockland churches in Venango County, PA, on October 3, 1912.
>
> He was married on August 31, 1910, in Mellette, South Dakota, to Minnie Nora Braun, and died at the home of his parents in Germantown, Philadelphia, on December 5, 1914. He is buried at West Laurel Hill Cemetery in Philadelphia. He had no children, but was survived by his wife, his parents, four sisters and two brothers.

Like his first fiancée, Emma, Reading died young from a particularly painful disease. His death at age thirty-eight was due to lipoma of the mediastinum, a rare tumor of the chest whose symptoms include difficulty swallowing and breathing, dry cough, jugular distention, and irregular heartbeat. If not removed—an unlikely procedure in 1914—the tumor slowly compresses the heart until the heart fails.

> Princeton Theological Seminary Special Collections. C. S. Robinson, "Necrological Report of Princeton Theological Seminary." Princeton: 1930, 373. Online: https://archive.org/details/necrologicalrepoo6prin.

Hosokawa Gisho (1849–1923)

Baptized during Tom Alexander's visit to Kochi in 1885, Hosokawa was a leader of the *iaijutsu* school of swordsmanship, a complex method of drawing a sword with controlled movements and intense mental concentration. At some point, Hosokawa also opened and ran a *kendo* martial arts studio located at the base of the hill where Kochi castle was located. He devoted his life to purposes that he considered ideal, including both the samurai warrior credo of Bushido and Christianity. Hosokawa taught many young men the art of swordsmanship before his death in 1923.

> Kochi Church, *History.* "Biographies of Important Members of the Church," 432.

Ibuka Kajinosuke (1854–1940)

Ibuka was a leading Japanese Presbyterian minister and educator who had fought in the 1867–68 war to unseat the shogun and install young Emperor Meiji as Japan's sole ruler. Son of a samurai, Ibuka was among the earliest Japanese Christians baptized by missionaries serving in Yokohama and became pastor of Kojimachi Church in Tokyo in the late 1870s. Along with Uemura Masahisa and other Christian leaders, Ibuka was instrumental in the establishment of the YMCA in Japan. In 1891, he was appointed as the first Japanese president of Meiji Gakuin. Ibuka remained active in theological life even after stepping down as president. As Moderator of the United Church of Christ in Japan, he participated in the path-breaking World Missionary Conference in Edinburgh, Scotland, in 1910, and was the only non-Western member of the conference's business committee.

> *The World Missionary Conference, Edinburgh, 1910* (Grand Rapids: Eerdmans, 2009), 94, 232. Hamish Ion, *American Missionaries, Christian Oyatoi, and Japan, 1859–73.* (Vancouver, BC: University of British Columbia Press, 2010), 219, 230.

Itagaki Taisuke (1837–1919)

Itagaki Taisuke, Japan's best known leader in the movement for people's rights and constitutional government, studied Christianity and invited missionaries to his home base of Tosa to preach the gospel. Although he supported the missionaries' work, he was never baptized. Itagaki founded

Japan's first political party, Jiyuto (Liberal Party), predecessor of today's Liberal Democratic Party. Itagaki also had served as a top councilor to Emperor Meiji but resigned in disagreement over regime policy toward Korea and other issues. Having fought to eliminate the Tokugawa-era system of class rankings and led a movement for equality and human rights, Itagaki reluctantly accepted the title of "count" in 1887 under a new peerage system, but insisted that it not be hereditary.

With the adoption of the constitution in 1889, Itagaki ran for the Diet (Japan's parliament) and served from 1890 until 1900, striving to make parliamentary government work well. He served as Home Minister (responsible for managing internal affairs of the empire) in the cabinets of Ito Hirobumi and Okuma Shigenobu and retired from active political life in 1900. Although he made an occasional speech and launched several small-circulation magazines after his retirement, he largely disappeared from public view. He never lost his interest in social reform and democratic rights of the people, however.

Cody, "Itagaki Taisuke."

Kataoka Kenkichi (1843–1903)

A prominent Christian politician, Kataoka Kenkichi of the Tosa region was one of the "men of influence" baptized during Tom Alexander's visit to Kochi in 1885. Son of a samurai, he had fought alongside Itagaki Taisuke to overthrow the shogun's regime and restore the emperor as Japan's sole ruler. He collaborated closely with Itagaki in the push for constitutional government and in Jiyuto (Liberal Party). While an elder of Kochi Church, he was elected to the Diet in 1890 along with Itagaki and served first as vice president and then president of the Lower House of that body for nearly a decade. When advised as a candidate during his first election that his Christian faith might be a disadvantage and that he should consider resigning as elder, he was quoted as saying, "If I am to choose between them, I would rather be an Elder in the Church than elected to the House." He later told his friend and fellow collaborator in the people's rights movement, Sakamoto Naohira, that he regretted his decision to pursue politics rather than Christian work, where he felt he might have done more for his country. In March 1902, Kataoka was appointed by the board as President of Doshisha, the Christian university where Tom Alexander had taught theology from January 1900 until his departure from Japan in late February 1902.

Cary, *History of Christianity*, 282. Cody, "Itagaki Taisuke." *The Reformed Church Review* (Philadelphia: Reformed Church Publication Board, 1905), 267.

Sakamoto Naohiro (1853–1911)

Sakamoto Naohira was another of the "men of influence" baptized during Tom Alexander's visit to Kochi in 1885. He had devoted himself to the liberal civil rights movement and also served in the Diet, ultimately resigning out of disgust with what he viewed as a corrupt, authoritarian Meiji government. After resigning from the Diet, Sakamoto devoted himself to Christianity. In 1896, he moved to Japan's northern island of Hokkaido—then considered remote frontier territory—where he joined a Christian community, started a farm, and pursued missionary work. He also became a successful editor and politician in the island's main city of Sapporo.

> Kochi Church, *History*, "Biographies of Important Members of the Church," 432. *Reformed Church Review*, 267.

Uemura Masahisa (1858–1925)

The *Historical Dictionary of the Reformed Churches* describes Uemura Masahisa as a

> Japanese Presbyterian minister, evangelist, and president of Tokyo Theological Seminary (Tokyo Shingakusha). Uemura was born into a samurai family in Edo. Following the Meiji Restoration, his family lost its wealth and standing. Uemura left home and traveled to Yokohama, where he became a Christian. He was baptized in 1873 and entered into S. R. Brown's theological training school, which later became the theological department of Meiji Gakuin.
>
> He was ordained in 1880 and began a small church in Tokyo, now Fujimicho Church, which grew to 1,600 members during the 1920s. In 1890, he organized a monthly journal, *Nippon Hyoron* (Japan Review), which discussed the political and social questions of the time, but like his *Fukuin Shinpo* (Gospel News), also stressed evangelism, Uemura's greatest concern.
>
> Uemura reorganized the evangelistic work of the Church of Christ in Japan (Nihon Kirisuto Kyokai), which became independent and self-supporting. In 1904, he organized Tokyo

Theological Seminary. He was a critic of modern currents in theology that tried to reduce Christian faith to a cultural or social expression.

Benedetto, McKim, *Historical Dictionary*, 488.

Uemura Tamaki (1890–1982)

Third daughter of Uemura Masahisa, Uemura Tamaki graduated from Joshi Gakuin girls' school in Tokyo and Wellesley College in Massachusetts. Uemura may have been inclined to become a minister on her own volition, but after her father's death in 1925, her mother told her, "The family has lost one minister, so you should become one." That year, she traveled to Scotland to study theology at New College, Edinburgh. She founded Kashiwagi Church in Tokyo and became only the second woman ordained into the ministry by the United Church of Christ in Japan (1934), long before women were so eligible in America's northern Presbyterian Church (1956). Uemura was very active in the YWCA in Japan, serving as its president and board chair, and worked diligently for world peace after World War II. She served as pastor of Kashiwagi Church until 1973.

In 1946, Uemura was invited to the United States by the National Council of Presbyterian Women's Organizations (of the northern Presbyterian Church) to speak at their 1946 national meeting. She was the first civilian allowed by U.S. occupation authorities to leave Japan and travel to the United States after the war. Planning to use her trip to apologize to Americans for Japan's role in the war, Uemura met with the emperor and empress before her trip and brought with her a gift from the empress to the Presbyterian Women. The Presbyterian Women, in turn, presented a Bible to the Reverend Uemura as their gift to the empress. The trip was a very difficult personal journey for Uemura, because of the heavy burden it placed on her shoulders.

During her trip, Uemura visited Mary Alexander in New York City before traveling to Washington, DC, for an audience with President Harry Truman at the White House. Mary listened in awe as Uemura repeated the words she had spoken to the emperor and empress during her meeting with them, including the apology she would convey to the president. Mary later told a niece she had never heard Japanese spoken in such a refined and sophisticated way.

Uemura's visit to the United States brought about a lasting change in the Presbyterian Church in America. The refusal by northern Presbyterian

Church authorities to allow Uemura, an ordained minister in the United Church of Christ of Japan, to assist in serving communion during her visit sparked heated debate and bolstered support for the eventual decision in 1956 to allow women to be ordained to the ministry and other official church positions.

Benedetto, McKim, *Historical Dictionary*, 488–98. Bradley J. Longfield, *Presbyterians and American Culture: A History* (Louisville: Westminster John Knox Press, 2013), 182–83. Uemura family members Saba Shoichi, Nakamura Taeko, and Nakai (Nakamura) Ayoko. Emma Shelton.

T. T. Alexander Letter Defending Uemura Masahisa

Tom Alexander wrote this letter[1] in defense of one of Japan's leading Christians, the Reverend Uemura Masahisa, and the journal he edited, *Fukuin Shimpo* (Gospel News). Other missionaries had criticized the strong-willed Uemura, who had long fought to free the Church of Christ in Japan from missionary control.

Tokyo, Japan
Feb. 22, 1894

My Dear Dr. Gillespie [secretary of Board of Foreign Missions, New York City]:

In a recent letter to the Mission, you expressed surprise that the Missions had voted to continue aid to "The Fukuin Shimpo," and gave it as your opinion that the Board would hardly consent to grant funds for this purpose another year, unless it should appear that there had been a marked improvement in the paper.

As I must write in haste, allow me to begin at once without further preamble and without apology. I have known Mr. Uemura, the editor of the periodical referred to, for sixteen years—and though for the greater part of this time, my home was in Osaka, still I had occasion to meet Mr. Uemura very often—and did not lose much from my acquaintance with him. My judgment of him is based, therefore, I think upon a better knowledge of the man than that of any other man in the Mission—excepting Drs. Imbrie and Knox, now at home.

1. PCUSA, "Correspondence."

My testimony in regard to him is that there has been a marked improvement in his character during these years—in two particulars.

1. In his theological belief. When I first knew him, his theological views were very unsettled. If he was anything, he was probably Arminian—certainly, he had no idea of accepting the Westminster Confession as the substance of his doctrine. It was some years later that he visited me at my house in Osaka and saw upon some of my bookshelves H. B. Smith's "Christian Theology," which I had just gotten out from America. He begged me to sell it to him, which I finally did. He took the book home and the next time I saw him he told me that he had read the book and regarded it as the best book on theology he has ever seen. This book had much to do, I think, in settling his views.

Within the last six months, he has read Dr. L. F. Stearns' "Present Day Theology," and A. M. Fairbaim's "Place of Christ in Modern Theology." Dr. Stearns' book is little more than a repeat of Dr. H. B. Smith's Theology—and it is this book, rather than Fairbaim's, that led to an improvement in the doctrinal views of Mr. Uemura.

2. In his spiritual life. Here there has been growth that ought to be gratifying to all Mr. Uemura's friends. He is of the intellectual, rather than the sentimental, type. His piety does not trickle down his cheeks, but it is real. His prayers are fervent. He takes a deep interest in spiritual matters and regards the great lack of the church in Japan at present as a want of spiritual life. So far as the man is concerned, therefore, I regard him as a safe leader, and one who is determined to exert a still wider influence for good.

Now a word in reference to the paper. I have taken the paper ever since it started and have been accustomed to read more or less in it almost every week. I cannot regard it as otherwise than as an excellent paper of the kind. It generally contains good articles of practical interest, which I know are helpful to its readers. There is but one other Christian weekly that can compare favorably with it, and that is the Congregational organ, called "The Christian."

Mr. Uemura has certain personal characteristics which have rendered him obnoxious to many of the missionaries. He is independent, self-reliant, and sometimes disagreeably so. He does not often consult with missionaries and there are very few whom he ever invites to preach in his church. His personal

traits of an unpleasant sort, together with a long train of circumstances which I cannot explain, have led to a dislike of him on
the part of some of the missionaries, so strong as to prevent their
being able to do him justice.

I cannot but feel that this fact has led to an over-sensi-
tiveness in the attitude of Drs. Thompson and McCartee, for
example, toward the "Fukuin Shimpo". Both of these brethren
are my personal friends, and I do not intend to reflect upon
them in the least, by using their names in this connection. At
the same time, it is evident to me that they are unable to see the
good points of the paper, which in my judgment are far more
than the bad ones.

It is for the reason just indicated that I am persuaded you
have been treated to a very one-sided view of the paper, to say
the least of it. Dr. Hepburn is also of a like mind with the brethren above named in his personal attitude toward Mr. Uemura,
and his estimate of "The Fukuin Shimpo" is accordingly much
the same as this, no doubt.

Considering the general state of religious ferment and the
reaction against foreign influence which have prevailed in Japan
for several years past, Mr. Uemura's paper has been remarkably
free from objectionable features. Its attitude toward Unitarian-
ism, and extreme liberalism, as represented by the Universalists
and the German missionaries, has been straightforward and so-
ber. Its influence has been always strongly in favor of evangelical
Christianity.

In none of the articles translated and sent home to you, I
venture to say, have you found heretical views advocated. Mr.
Uemura has for some time past been writing a series of articles
for the paper in the way of Outlines of Systematic Theology.
So far as I know, these articles have not been objected to, with
one exception, and that, not for Mr. Uemura's own views, but
because he gave the views of certain unorthodox writers, from
which he dissented. It was thought that he ought not to have
mentioned the erroneous views even.

I have not time to write longer. I will only add that I am far
from being alone in the opinion that if the Board decides not
to continue aid to the "Fukuin Shimpo," it will thereby cripple
one of the most influential agencies now at work in favor of the

evangelical faith in Japan. Great injury will be done to the cause which we all have at heart, and that, in more ways than one.

I may further add that within the last few weeks, Mr. Uemura's paper has been under discussion again on account of an extract which he reproduced from the "Outlook" about Dr. Briggs' case.[2] Doubtless the objectionable (?) article has been duly translated and forwarded to you. But Mr. Uemura has made an explanation, which, I think, will be thought satisfactory.

If you wish me to do so, I will engage to translate and forward to you one or two articles every month from the paper, showing its better features, as well as those which might be regarded as objectionable, if any such appear.

This letter is solely on my own responsibility.

Yours sincerely,

T. T. Alexander

2. Dr. Charles Augustus Briggs was a noted biblical scholar at New York's Union Theological Seminary, Tom Alexander's alma mater. Briggs was tried and convicted for heresy in 1893, because he challenged prevailing conservative views of biblical inerrancy and Darwin's theory of evolution.

T. T. Alexander Publications (partial list)

Books in Japanese

A Great Miracle of Christianity. Tokyo: Christian Documents Co., 1896. Reprinted 1897.

Discourse on the Personalities in the Old Testament. Translation assistance by Tanaka Tatsushi. Tokyo: Choshunkan, 1894.

Lectures on the Book of Amos. Translation assistance by Tatsuji Hotta. Tokyo: Kyobunkan, 1900.

Lectures on the Book of Philippians, with Tatsuji Hotta. Tokyo: Kyobunkan, 1897.

Journals and Magazines

"The Preparation and Spread of Christian Literature: Past Work and Present Needs." *Proceedings of the General Conference of Protestant Missionaries in Japan.* Tokyo: Methodist Publishing House, 1901, 439–57.

Biblical Expositor, founder (ca. 1898) and contributor, with E. R. Woodman

Fukuin Shimpo (*Gospel News,* sometimes also referred to as *The Evangelist*)

These articles, listed in chronological order, appeared in the *Fukuin Shimpo* between 1893 and 1901. Volume and edition numbers not available. The number following each title refers to the number of editions in which the topic was continued. Translated by Dr. Masato Nishimura.

Lecture on Book of Philip
Jesus as a Prophet (2)
Origin and Development of the Foreign Missionary Works in the U.S.A.
Can God Be Known? (2)
The Existence of God (2)
The Origin and the Development of the Notion of God (2)

On Monotheism (2)
God Has Heart (2)
The Evidence for God's Existence (4)
Critique on Dr. Gordon's "The Reasons to Observe the Sabbath"
Nature of God (2)
The Christian Notion of God (4)
God as the Father of All (2)
God as the Father of Believers (2)
On Trinity (3)
Lord, To Whom Do We Go? (3)
On Baptism
The Meaning of Baptism
Baptism of Children
God's Will for Managing the World (6)
The Creation of the Universe (2)
On Providence (5)
Miracles (3)
On Human Nature (2)
On Theology (critique on Dr. Clark's Doctrine of Christian Theology, 1899)
Trip to Palestine
    Jerusalem
    Calvary
    Jericho, the Dead Sea and the Jordan River (2)
    On the Dead Sea Again
    Hebron
    Bethlehem
    Judea (4)
    Samaria (3)
    Important Places in Samaria (3)
The Unity of Christians (4)
On Missionary Works (letter to the editor)

Fukuin Shimpo articles about T. T. Alexander (1894–1915)

Church activities news
News on Meiji Gakuin
On Dr. Alexander's activities in Yamaguchi
Report on the Conference of Japan Christian Church. (Synopsis of speech by Dr. Alexander and his liberal interpretation of Kepler, Galileo, Copernicus, and Darwin.)
On Alexander's speech
News on Dr. Alexander's return to the U.S.A
News on Dr. Alexander's arrival to Kyoto
Dr. Alexander's departure from Tokyo to Kyoto
News on Dr. Alexander's illness
The departure of Dr. Alexander to Hawaii
The activities of the church in Kyoto after Dr. Alexander's departure
Death of Dr. Alexander

The memorial service for Dr. Alexander

Remembrance of Dr. Alexander by friends

News from Hawaii on church activities after Dr. Alexander's passing

On the 30th anniversary of the establishment of North Christian Church of Japan in Osaka that was started by Dr. Alexander in Meiji 17th [1885].

Acknowledgements

I am indebted to many people who have helped me during the long journey of researching and writing this book. Friends and family members too numerous to name offered useful comments on drafts and provided much needed support and encouragement along the way. I know who you are, and I thank each and every one of you.

Dr. M. William Steele, Professor of Japanese History at International Christian University in Tokyo, and Dr. Naotaka Matsukata, Professorial Lecturer of Modern Japanese History at my alma mater, the Johns Hopkins School of Advanced International Studies in Washington, DC, read the manuscript and offered many helpful comments and suggestions that pushed the final product to a much higher level.

My aunt, Emma Shelton, gave me my great-grandfather's journal to read before my first trip to Japan as a young US Treasury economist and provided many helpful insights into Alexander family members and their history. She also helped shape this book by saying, "I want to know what everyday life was like." I have tried to add some of the flavor of daily living into the story. My grandmother, Eva Alexander Shelton, sparked my interest in family history through her stories, not only about her life in Japan but also about other family members who live on only in memory.

In Japan, I treasure the friendship and invaluable assistance offered by so many individuals. The late Kitamura Ko, one of my Great Aunt Mary Alexander's first students at Tokyo Women's Christian University and a lifelong family friend, opened her home to me over the years. Kitamura-san spoke to me about Mary and my great-grandmother, and, sometimes in the company of her daughter and son-in-law, Takatsuki Miyoko and Akiji, took me to places in or near Tokyo that figured prominently in the Alexander family's life, including Meiji Gakuin University, Lake Hakone, and young Emma's grave in Aoyama Cemetery.

Words cannot adequately convey my gratitude to ministers and members of my great-grandfather's churches and of other churches in Japan who

281

continue to play such an important role in my life. The Reverend Akiyama Hideaki of the United Church of Christ in Japan identified me as the great-granddaughter of the Reverend Alexander through the marvels of the Internet. Akiyama-sensei, Elder Ito Fumiko, and her husband, Ito Takafumi, offered me my first glimpse into Christian life in Japan beginning in 2006 and helped me discover more of my family's history in Japan through their research and investigation. They located Ella Alexander's grave in Kobe and drove me to Shikoku Island, where we met Minister Nomura of Kochi Church and toured the castle that towers above the city. It was during our visit in Kochi that I learned the probable identity of the recently baptized samurai who gave his sword to my great-grandfather.

The Reverends Morita Yukio and Mochida Katsumi of the Church of Christ in Japan also have provided invaluable assistance, taking me to places relevant to my great-grandfather's work in Osaka and Kyoto, locating documents in the archives of Doshisha University, and introducing me to the homeless feeding program of Osaka North Church. I was delighted to welcome them to northwestern Montana during their visit to my church in 2008. To each of these ministers and to members of their churches, I extend sincere thanks for all they have done and for the warm friendships we share after many hours spent together.

The Reverend Dr. Thomas John Hastings, a Presbyterian missionary who served twenty-three years in Japan, including as Professor of Practical Theology at Tokyo Union Theological Seminary, played an important role in connecting me with my great-grandfather's Osaka churches and in educating me about the Protestant Reformed church in Japan. Although now working with Japan from the United States, his long service and fluency in the language are a testament to the continuing commitment of American missionaries and theologians to Christian life in Japan. I thank him and my Japanese Christian friends for their role in my faith journey.

Special thanks are due to Dr. Robert Alan Feldman of Tokyo, a fellow economist and longtime friend, whose in-depth knowledge of Japan, fluency in the language, and interest in history contributed greatly to the success of my periodic visits and to my research for this book. He and my great-grandfather are two "boys" from East Tennessee who made their way to successful lives in Japan. I also thank Uchikoga Maki in Tokyo for her helpful research and kind assistance.

Dr. Nakajima Koji of Meiji Gakuin University guided me on a fascinating tour of the Tsukiji area of Tokyo, showing me the location of my great-grandparents' first home and other landmarks in the old foreign settlement. He also provided pictures, documents, and helpful insights into the life of early missionaries in Tokyo.

Other individuals in Japan whom I thank for insights and friendship include descendants of my great-grandfather's colleague and friend, the Reverend Uemura Masahisa: Nakamura Taeko, Professor Nakai Ayako, and the late Saba Shoichi. I value the continuing ties between the Uemura family and my own. Thanks also are due to the Reverends Sawa Masayuki and Inaba Hajime of the Church of Christ in Japan for assistance and support during my visit to Fukuoka and Yanagawa on Kyushu Island. Generous assistance also has been provided by Sakaguchi Mako in Kumamoto and Tamura Yasufumi at Kobe's Municipal Foreign Cemetery. Many thanks also to Hayashi Mika, librarian of the Church of Christ of Japan, who generously located and copied all of the Reverend Alexander's articles in the *Fukuin Shimpo* journal; and to the librarian of the International House of Japan, who found helpful articles during my stay in 2009.

Administrators and staff at schools and universities in Japan welcomed me and expanded my knowledge and understanding of my family's life in Japan. My appreciation goes to Dr. Kuze Satoru, then-chancellor of Meiji Gakuin University, and Hara Yutaka, university archivist; also to Tanaka Hiroshi, then-chancellor of Joshi Gakuin Junior and Senior High School for girls and Nagamine Yuzo, the school's administrative officer; as well as other staff members who aided me during my visits. Then-President Minato Akiko of Tokyo Women's Christian University fit me into her busy schedule for an unexpected meeting and told me how my Great Aunt Mary Alexander had taught her how to form English words by using a mirror.

In the United States, I have benefited greatly from the tireless long-distance translating skills and helpful insights of Dr. Masato Nishimura, now-retired Professor of Japanese at the University of California at San Diego. It was a pleasure to meet him and his wife, Linda, during my visit to San Diego in 2014. I thank the staff of the Presbyterian Historical Society for their able assistance during my two weeks of research in 2006. Eileen Meyer Sklar, Bridget Clancy, and Quincina Jackson went out of their way to help me and make my visit both productive and enjoyable.

My second cousin once removed, Dr. Sarah Brown McNiell, Professor Emerita of History and then-historian for Maryville College and the city of Maryville, welcomed me into her home with her late husband, Stuart. She gave generously of her time and knowledge to guide me through Maryville College archives and to places of importance in my great-grandfather's life, including his boyhood home and church near Mount Horeb, Tennessee. Dr. McNiell also contacted Albert Blackburn, unofficial historian of the Hebron Presbyterian Church, who showed me church records of the Alexander family and explained the central role Tom's father, Elias, had played in the Hebron Church. Mr. Blackburn also located the Alexander farm where Tom grew up and showed me the original church of Mount Horeb, still standing across the road from the family homestead.

My second cousin, Mary Alexander, graciously welcomed me to her home and showed me the samurai sword given to our great-grandfather, as well as the original books comprising his personal journal. She also provided family photos and letters to help round out the story. My brother-in-law and his wife, the Reverend David and Glenna Erb, introduced me to the Bible at a time when I was just beginning to explore a new interest in Christianity. I thoroughly enjoyed the many hours we shared on our front porch delving into spiritual questions and the mysteries of faith. I also thank the Reverend David R. Anson of the First Presbyterian Church of Polson, Montana, for helping to draw me into my new faith and for expanding my knowledge of Scripture and biblical times; and Marsha Anson, General Presbyter of Glacier Presbytery, for her unwavering and enthusiastic support. I thank Susan Lake for her masterful photographic skills. And I greatly appreciate the support from Cascade Books of Wipf and Stock Publishers and my editor, Dr. Robin A. Parry.

Others whose support, friendship, and/or comments I deeply appreciate include Sharon Barrett, the late Mary Box, Mary Ellen Campbell, Karli Clift, Carol Cummings, Dr. Victoria Burkhart Faherty, Robert Fauver, Paul Fugleberg, Rich Gebhardt, Cathe Carruthers Hartung, Coreen Kelly, Michael Punke, the Rev. Dr. Christian Scharen, Dr. Judith Trunzo, Steve and Carol Woodruff, and Robert Zoellick.

Finally, I thank my husband, Richard Erb, my partner and best friend in life, who has inspired and supported me in numerous ways and patiently endured many years of hearing me recount my great-grandfather's story to friends and family members. I can't imagine life without him.

Picture Credits

Unless otherwise noted, all photos are family possessions or were taken by the author.

Maryville in the 1870s. Reproduction by Blount County Historic Trust, courtesy of Friends Historical Collection, Guilford College, Greensboro, NC.

The City of Tokyo steamer. Courtesy of Project Gutenberg. Photo appeared originally in *Lippincott's Magazine of Popular Literature and Science*, February, 1876, Vol. XVII, No. 98.

Yokohama photos courtesy of Yokohama Archives of History.

Tsukiji foreign concession. In "The Spirit of Missions," March 1894. Board of Missions of the Protestant Episcopal Church in the USA. MG archives.

Tsukiji home, No. 6B. In "Foreign Missionary," vol. 34, 1875. MG archives.

Tsukiji home and Union Church. In *The Far East*, date and edition unknown. Photo ca. 1875. MG archives.

Osaka South Church from *Fifty Year History of South Church*, copy given to author.

Osaka North Church from *One Hundred-Year History of Osaka Kitakyokai*, 1990.

Samurai sword courtesy of Mary Alexander.

Map of Nineteenth Century Japan. Source uncertain; see link to map in "Historical Maps of Japan" in "Maps on Other Sites" section of http://www.edmaps.com.

Maryville scene and campus, 1895. Courtesy of Blount County Genealogical and Historical Society, Lorene B. Smith, Elgin P. Kintner, eds. *Blount County Remembered: The 1890's Photography of W.O. Garner*, 1991.

Itagaki Taisuke, courtesy of National Diet Library, "Portraits of Modern Japanese Historical Figures."

Uemura Masahisa. Ibid.

Ibuka Kajinosuke. Courtesy MG. http://www.mg150th-whoswho.jp/images/atc10/atc10_img01.jpg

Cloisonné vases courtesy of Emma Shelton.

Robert E. Speer. Courtesy of Presbyterian Historical Society. Presbyterian Church (U.S.A.), Philadelphia.

Selected Bibliography

Note: Sources that are cited only once in the text appear with a full citation in notes.

Abbreviations

MG   Meiji Gakuin University, Tokyo, Japan
PHS   Presbyterian Historical Society, Philadelphia, PA

Akiyama, Shigeo. "The Humble Believer: Dr. T. T. Alexander." In *Tales of the Great from the Meiji Era: The Family Tree of Christianity* [in Japanese], translated by Robert Feldman, chapter 10. Shinkyo Shuppan, Tokyo, 1982. First published in Meiji Gakuin University magazine, *Shirokane Tsushin*, August 1, 1973.

Alexander, Emma Edwina Brown. "Recollections." Personal account of her early life written ca. 1935–36 in New York City. Copy in author's possession.

Alexander, Emma Thomasina. *Personal Journal* of daughter Emma written from January 1, 1901, through September 3, 1903. All five volumes are in author's possession.

Alexander, Mary. "Japan Notes." Unpublished account of the family's life in Japan, 1965.

Alexander, Thomas Theron. *Personal Journal* written from 1877 to 1901. A copy of this family document is in author's possession. Also available in the "Thomas T. Alexander Papers." RG 373. Philadelphia: PHS.

———. "The Preparation and Spread of Christian Literature: Past Work and Present Needs." In "Christian Literature in Japan," *Proceedings of the General Conference of Protestant Missionaries in Japan*, held in Tokyo October 24–31, 1900, 435–57. Tokyo: Methodist Publishing House, 1901.

Baxter, James C. *The Meiji Unification through the Lens of Ishikawa Prefecture.* Cambridge: Council on East Asian Studies, Harvard University, 1994.

Benedetto, Robert, and Donald K. McKim. *Historical Dictionary of the Reformed Churches.* 2nd ed. Lanham, MD: Scarecrow, 2010.

Benfey, Christopher. *The Great Wave: Gilded Age Misfits, Japanese Eccentrics, and the Opening of Old Japan.* New York, Random House Trade Paperbacks, 2004.

Bird, Isabella L. *Unbeaten Tracks in Japan: Travels on Horseback in the Interior.* 2 vols. New York: Putnam's Sons, 1881.

Brown, Arthur Judson. *One Hundred Years: A History of the Foreign Missionary Work of the Presbyterian Church in the U.S.A., With Some Accounts of Countries, Peoples and the Policies and Problems of Modern Missions.* New York: Revell, 1936.

Burkman, Thomas W. "The Urakami Incidents and the Struggle for Religious Toleration." *Japanese Journal of Religious Studies* 1.2–3 (1974) 143–216. Nagoya, Japan: Nanzan Institute for Religion and Culture, Nanzan University. Open Access Journal. Online: http://nirc.nanzan-u.ac.jp/nfile/2741.

Carrothers, Julia D. *The Sunrise Kingdom, or Life and Scenes in Japan*. London: Ganesha, 1879.

Cary, Frank. *History of Christianity in Japan, 1859–1908*. Tokyo: Kyo Bun Kwan, 1959.

Church of Christ in Japan. [Nippon Kirisuto Kyokai.] Online: http://www.reformiert-online.net/adressen/detail.php?id=1381&lg=eng.

Cody, Cecil Earl. "A Study of the Career of Itagaki Taisuke (1837–1919): A Leader of the Democratic Movement in Meiji Japan." PhD diss., University of Washington, 1955. ProQuest.

Cosenza, Mario E., ed. *The Complete Journal of Townsend Harris, First American Consul and Minister to Japan*. Rutland, VT: Tuttle, 1930.

Crawford, Earle W. *One of Those Tall Tennesseans: The Life of G. S. W. Crawford 1849–1891*. Maryville, TN: Maryville College Press, 1986.

Curtis, Frederick S. Unpublished "Testimonial" read during memorial service for Alexander, February 18, 1903, in Kyoto, Japan. Tokyo: MG archives.

Dohi, Akio. "The First Generation: Christian Leaders in the First Period." In *A History of Japanese Theology*, edited by Yasuo Furuya, 11–42. Grand Rapids: Eerdmans, 1997.

Doshisha Church. *Christianity in Kyoto, A Century of Doshisha Church* [in Japanese]. Translated by Masato Nishimura. Kyoto: Doshisha Church, 1998.

Encyclopedia Britannica. *Britannica Encyclopedia of World Religions*. Chicago: Encyclopedia Britannica, 2006.

Endo, Shusaku. *Silence*. 1969. Translated by William Johnston. New York: Taplinger, 1980.

Hane, Mikiso. *Peasants, Rebels, Women, and Outcastes: The Underside of Modern Japan*. 2nd ed. Lanham, MD: Rowman & Littlefield, 2003.

Hidetaka, Yamamoto. *One Hundred Year History of the Christian Church in Japan* [in Japanese]. Translated by Masato Nishimura. Publisher, date unknown. Copy of excerpt given to author from MG archives.

Higuchi, Susumu. *One Hundred Year History of Muromachi Church* [in Japanese]. Translated by Masato Nishimura. Kyoto: Muromachi Church, [2003?].

Hiroshima Church. *One Hundred Twenty-Year History of Hiroshima Church* [in Japanese]. Hiroshima: Hiroshima Church, [2006?].

Imbrie, Charles. "Into the Sunset, personal recollections of Tsukiji by the son of missionary William Imbrie." Montauk, NY, February 4, 1949. MG archives. Imbrie's account covers the years he lived with his family in Tsukiji, 1881 to 1893.

Imbrie, William M. *Church of Christ in Japan: A Course of Lectures*. Philadelphia: Westminster, 1909.

———. Eulogy at TTA memorial service, Tokyo, January 31, 1903. *Japan Evangelist* X.2 (February 1903) 6–9.

International Christian University. *Comparative Chronology of Protestantism in Asia, 1792–1945*. Tokyo: Institute of Asian Cultural Studies, International Christian University, 1984.

Iriye, Akira. "Japan's Drive to Great-Power Status." In *The Emergence of Meiji Japan*, edited by Marius B. Jansen, 268–329. Cambridge: Cambridge University Press, 1995.

Jansen, Marius B. *The Making of Modern Japan*. Cambridge: Belknap Press of Harvard University, 2000.

———. "The Meiji Restoration." In *The Emergence of Meiji Japan*, edited by Marius B. Jansen, 144–202. Cambridge: Cambridge University Press, 1995.

The Japan Evangelist. Yokohama: Seishi Bunsha, August 1893–March 1903.

Keene, Donald. *Emperor of Japan: Meiji and His World, 1852–1912*. New York: Columbia University Press, 2002.

Kimura, Yukiko. *Issei, Japanese Immigrants in Hawaii*. Honolulu: University of Hawaii Press, 1988.

Kochi Church. *One Hundred Year History of Kochi Church* [in Japanese]. Translated by Masato Nishimura. Kochi: Kochi Church, 1985.

Kujinosuke, Sasaki. "Recollections." In *One Hundred Twenty-Year History of Hiroshima Church*. Publisher, date unknown. Copy of excerpt given to author from Doshisha University archives.

Lone, Stewart. *Japan's First Modern War*. New York: St. Martin's, 1994.

Longfield, Bradley J. *The Presbyterian Controversy, Fundamentalists, Modernists, and Moderates*. New York: Oxford University Press, 1991.

Mason, R. H. P., and J. G. Caiger. *A History of Japan*. Boston: Tuttle, 1997.

McTeer, Will A. *History of New Providence Presbyterian Church Maryville, Tennessee, 1786–1921*. Maryville, TN: New Providence Church, 1921.

Morse, Edward S. *Japan Day by Day*. 2 vols. Boston: Houghton Mifflin, 1917.

Nakazawa, Shoshichi. *Thomas Clay Winn: The Life of an American Missionary in Early Modern Japan*. Translated by Komei Go. Japan: Kohro-sha, 1932.

National Diet Library. *Portraits of Japanese Historical Figures*. Tokyo: National Diet Library. Online: http://www.ndl.go.jp/portrait/e/contents.

Omori Church. *Omori Church History* [in Japanese]. Translated by Masato Nishimura. Tokyo: Omori Church, 1994.

Osaka North Church, Church of Christ of Japan. *One Hundred-Year History of Osaka Kitakyokai* [in Japanese]. Translated by Masato Nishimura. Osaka: Osaka Kitakyokai, 1990.

Osaka South Church, United Church of Christ of Japan. *Fifty Years of Osaka Minami Kyokai* [in Japanese]. Translated by Masato Nishimura. Osaka: Osaka Minami Suita Kyokai, 1935.

Presbyterian Church in the U.S.A., "Church of Christ in Japan, Annual Report of the Council of the Three Missions, 1886." United Presbyterian Church in the U.S.A., Commission on Ecumenical Mission and Relations. Japan Mission, 1879–1972. PHS.

Presbyterian Church in the U.S.A., The Board of Foreign Missions Correspondence and Reports, 1833–1911; Japan Mission 1859–1911: Incoming Letters. PHS.

Presbyterian Historical Society (PHS). Online: http://history.pcusa.org.

Proceedings of the General Conference of Protestant Missionaries in Japan, held in Tokyo October 24-31, 1900. Tokyo: Methodist, 1901.

Ravina, Mark. *The Last Samurai: The Life and Battles of Saigō Takamori*. Hoboken, NJ: Wiley & Sons, 2004.

Reischauer, Edwin O. *My Life between Japan and America*. New York: Harper & Row, 1986.

Reischauer, Haru Matsukata. *Samurai and Silk*. Cambridge: Belknap Press of Harvard University, 1986.

Scheiner, Irwin. *Christian Converts and Social Protest in Meiji Japan*. Berkeley: University of California Press, 1970.

Scidmore, Elizabeth Ruhamah. *Jinrikisha Days in Japan*. New York: Harper & Brothers, 1891.

Shelton, Emma. "The Descendants of T. T. Alexander." Unpublished genealogy. Bethesda, MD: n.p., 1999.

Smith, Thomas C. *Political Change and Industrial Development in Japan: Government Enterprise, 1868–1880*. Stanford: Stanford University Press, 1955.

Smylie, James H. *A Brief History of the Presbyterians*. Louisville: Geneva, 1996.

Thomas, Winburn T. *Protestant Beginnings in Japan: The First Three Decades 1859–1889*. Tokyo: Tuttle, 1959.

Uemura, Masahisa, ed. *Fukuin Shimpo* (*Gospel News*, also sometimes called *The Evangelist*). Tokyo: Fukuin Shimpo-sha, 1893–1901.

Union Theological Seminary. "History and Mission." Online: https://utsnyc.edu.

United Church of Christ of Japan. Online: http://uccj-e.org.

Vlastos, Stephen. "Opposition Movements in Early Meiji, 1868–1885." In *The Emergence of Meiji Japan*, edited by Marius B. Jansen, 203–67. Cambridge: Cambridge University Press, 1995.

Walworth, Arthur. *Black Ships Off Japan: The Story of Commodore Perry's Expedition*. New York: Knopf, 1946.

Whitney, Clara A. N. M. *Clara's Diary: An American Girl in Meiji Japan*. Edited by William Steele and Tamiko Ichimata. Tokyo: Kondansha International, 1979.

Wilson, Samuel Tyndale. *Chronicles of Maryville College: A Story of Altruism; Book I: A Century of Maryville College, 1819–1919*. Maryville, TN: Maryville College, 1935.

Yamamoto, Yuji. *History of Ozu Church* [in Japanese]. Translated by Masato Nishimura. Publisher, date unknown. Excerpt given to author from copy in Doshisha University archives.

Yanagawa, Chitoshi. *Japan Since Perry*. New York: McGraw-Hill, 1949.

Yanagawa Church, Church of Christ of Japan. *Acts of the Chinzei [Kyushu] Presbytery* [in Japanese]. Translated by Masato Nishimura. Tokyo: Yanagawa Church, 1980.

Yokohama Kaigan Church. "Brief History of Yokohama Kaigan Church." Online: http://www.kaiganchurch.or.jp/history-of-yokohama-kaigan-church.